FANTASTIC ANIMALS

FANTASTIC ANIMALS

FOG CITY PRESS

Published by Fog City Press
814 Montgomery Street
San Francisco, CA 94133 USA

CEO: John Owen
President: Terry Newell
Publisher: Sheena Coupe
Project Coordinator: Vanessa Finney
Picture Editor: Jenny Mills
Captions: Terence Lindsey
Design: Di Quick
Maps: Stan Lamond
Life Cycle Illustrations: Alistair Barnard, Frank Knight
Illustrations and Diagrams: Tony Pyrzakowski
Production Manager: Helen Creeke
Production Assistant: Kylie Lawson
Business Manager: Emily Jahn
Vice President, International Sales: Stuart Laurence

Copyright © 1991 Weldon Owen Pty Limited
Reprinted 2000

ISBN 1 875137 89 0

Printed by Toppan Printing
Printed in China

A WELDON OWEN PRODUCTION

Page 1: Poison-arrow frogs, Guyana (*Michael Fogden/Oxford Scientific Films*)
Pages 2–3: Emperor penguins gather at Auster rookery, Antarctica (*Jonathan Chester/Extreme Images*)
Pages 4–5: Black swan, a native of Australia (*Scott Camazine/Oxford Scientific Films*)
Pages 6–7: The orang-utan is a native of Southeast Asia (*Tom McHugh/Horizon*)
Pages 8–9: (left to right) Spotted pufferfish, Hawaii (*Doug Perrine/Planet Earth Pictures*); A dragonfly
caught in a spider's web (*John Shaw/NHPA*); tropical fruit bat (*Hans and Judy Beste/Ardea*); emperor
penguins and chicks (*Doug Allen/Oxford Scientific Films*); stonemarten (*Horizon/IFA*); silkmoth
caterpillars (*Carol Hughes/Bruce Coleman Limited*)
Pages 10–11: Mating cuttlefish, Maldive Islands (*Herwarth Voigtmann/Planet Earth Pictures*)
Pages 12–13: A bubble-raft snail feeds on a bluebottle (*Kathie Atkinson/Oxford Scientific Films*)
Pages 56–57: Egg-eating snake (*John Visser/Bruce Coleman Limited*)
Pages 100–101: Black-necked grebes mating (*Hellio and Van Ingen/NHPA*)
Pages 144–145: A wolf spider at its nest (*Geoff du Feu/Planet Earth Pictures*)

CONTRIBUTORS

Dr. Tim Guilford
Royal Society University Research Fellow,
Zoology Department,
Oxford University, U.K.

Professor Timothy Halliday
Professor of Biology,
Open University,
Milton Keynes, U.K.

Dr. Michael Hansell
Department of Zoology,
University of Glasgow, Scotland, U.K.

Terence Lindsey
Wildlife writer and ornithologist,
Sydney, Australia

Dr. Michael H. Robinson
Director of the National Zoological Park,
Smithsonian Institution,
Washington D.C., U.S.A.

CONTENTS

CONTENTS

INTRODUCTION

Terence Lindsey

Living organisms inhabit every corner of the surface of planet Earth. It is almost impossible to find any region so inhospitable that it cannot support any life at all. The deep ocean abyss and the eternally frozen wastes around the center of Antarctica come closest, yet even here there is life. A rich and diverse aerial "plankton" of tiny insects, spiders and other life forms inhabits even the atmosphere itself, extending to several kilometers above the ground. It is not in any trivial sense that the surface of our planet has been labeled the biosphere.

Some estimates place the total number of different living organisms on Earth at perhaps as high as 30 million. Of these, only about 1.4 million species have been formally described and named. Even within this small fraction, only a few have been any more than christened: biologists know little more than the names and brief identity of most.

We have barely scratched the surface in our exploration of the biosphere. Only very recently, for example, have we begun to survey the canopy of tropical rainforests, that ocean of leaves that functions as the global air-conditioner and where, perhaps, live the vast majority of all animals and plants. Something like six percent of the Earth's total surface is home to more than half of the total number of different kinds of living things. What we know of the rainforest environment is almost all on the ground, but biologists now guess that the ground level contains only half the richness and diversity of the canopy. Yet this diversity is being destroyed at the rate of about 142,000 square kilometers (55,000 square miles) each year, cut down just as biologists are finally discovering effective techniques to explore it. As one prominent rainforest specialist has recently said, "It is as though the stars began to vanish the moment astronomers focused their telescopes".

Animals vàry enormously in size and appearance. The very largest exceed the size of the very smallest by a factor of about 100 million. Most, of course, are very small: it has been estimated that one in every three animal species is a beetle, on average about a centimeter in body length. Since speciation is a dynamic, apparently endless process, it follows that there are newly evolved forms so similar to their relatives that it is difficult to be certain they are truly distinct. Others are so distantly related to their nearest kin that the vast gulf that separates ourselves from our own nearest relative, the chimpanzee, seems narrow by comparison. Some closely related animals differ wildly in appearance, jostling others so similar that we must X-ray their teeth, or wait until they lay an

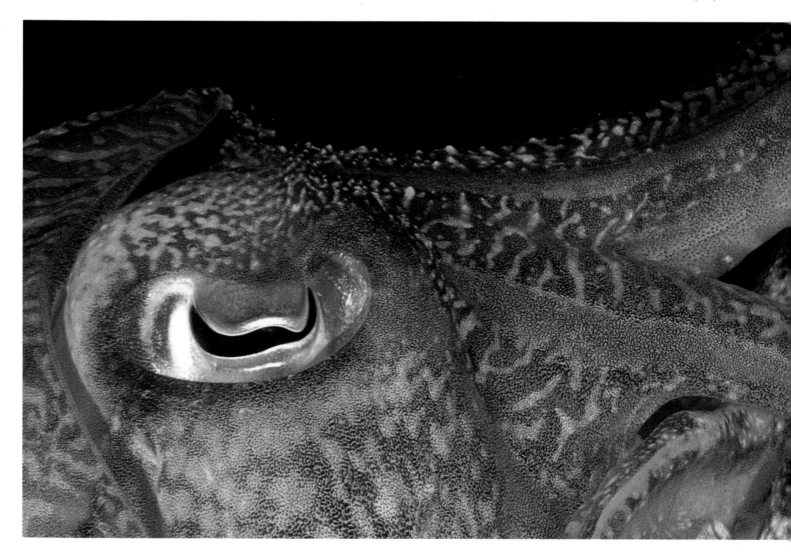

egg, or perform some equally preposterous exercise, in order to be certain which species we are dealing with. Obviously, the animals themselves can tell each other apart, but the means they use to accomplish this are not necessarily directly accessible to us.

Many animals live their entire adult lives in one spot, while others use a bewildering range of different means of moving about, guiding their movements and responding to their environments by means of sensory systems often so subtle and sophisticated that it is only within the twentieth century that human technology has evolved the tools with which to study them effectively. On land, cheetahs bolt after their prey, exploiting accelerations that would not disgrace a modern racing car. Some fish cruise the open ocean with such freedom that zoologists studying them are thwarted merely by the difficulty of finding transport fast enough to keep up with them. Riding thermals with breathtaking mastery, eagles and vultures scan the ground far below with a visual acuity matched only by the finest precision optics. Bees can see in ultraviolet light, snakes in infrared, and birds in polarized light.

But far more amazing than the range of appearance, sensibilities and movements in animals is the variety of ways in which they organize their daily lives—their strategies for survival. The notion of an "unconscious strategist" is useful here: a computer performs a series of actions that can, in sum, be viewed as a strategy for accomplishing the task at hand, but it does not plan those actions. Similarly, any animal's tendencies to do one thing rather than another are often themselves genetically based, and will be passed on to any surviving offspring. The forces of evolution can therefore program an animal's behavior in much the same way that they mold its anatomy and morphology. Some strategies turn out to be more successful than others when put to the test in the endless game of life; "successful" strategies tend to proliferate in the population at the expense of "unsuccessful" strategies.

Over the last few decades, much insight has been gained into the complexities of animal behavior by use of developments in an entirely different field: pure mathematics, in particular that branch known as game theory, the science of strategies. This has introduced into zoology such arcane but fascinating abstract concepts as "zerosum games", "non-zerosum games" and the "prisoner's dilemma", but zoology has profited enormously in making sense of the often bizarre and fantastic ways in which animals solve the ordinary everyday problems of life—finding food, choosing mates, and so on.

This book is an exploration and a celebration of the bewildering range and variety of the animal world, the subtlety and sophistication of the senses with which animals relate to their environment and with each other, and the incredible strategies they use to order and organize their lives.

Herwarth Voigtmann/Planet Earth Pictures

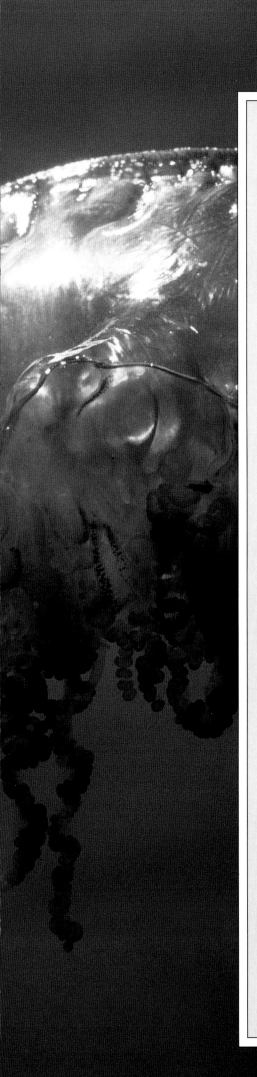

Chapter 1

SHAPE, SIZE AND SYMMETRY

Terence Lindsey

As a result of the long processes of evolution through the Earth's history, today's world includes a diversity of animal species. Within this extraordinary range, animals differ enormously in their shape, size and structure.

THE NATURE OF THE BEAST
Of course, it is impossible to know each one of the millions of animal species on Earth, but there are some avenues of understanding open to us. One way is by looking at the marvel of their forms.

THE IMPORTANCE OF CELLS
The essence of all life is the single cell. It determines the shape, size and structure of every living thing. From this simple beginning all diversity of animal life springs forth.

THE ANIMAL KINGDOM
Out of a need to place the vast range of animal species into some kind of order, experts have devised a general classification which is known as the animal kingdom.

SKINS, SHELLS AND OTHER OUTER LAYERS
Animals need a skin to protect themselves from the hazards of their environment. As a result of this, evolution has created an amazing and unusual array of protective covering.

. . . AND APPENDAGES
External additions and elaborations may also be diverse and at times bizarre. Such features include the extraordinary "antlers" of stag beetles, the incredibly elaborate antennae of beetles and moths and the sensitive and dexterous trunks of elephants.

ON THE MOVE
On land, animals display their fantastic footwork—wolves lope, while small animals crawl, scuttle and slither. In the sea, spider crabs mince along on spindly legs, while in the air, animals, perhaps in their most graceful form, take flight.

THE FIVE SENSES AND OTHERS
To help them survive, animals rely on ingenious senses, to see, hear, touch, taste and smell the many facets of their environment.

SHAPE, SIZE AND SYMMETRY

Terence Lindsey

Throughout the ages, evolution has created an extraordinary range of animal species. The human race is just one group amidst a spectrum of marvelous forms—from the ingenious, to the spectacular and the unusual. Somehow we must try to grapple with this awesome phenomenon.

▲ The axolotls (*Ambystoma mexicanus*) of Central America exist as larvae until raised iodine levels in water activate adulthood.

Stephen Dalton/NHPA

THE NATURE OF THE BEAST

Nobody knows how many different kinds of animals there are on Earth. There is no central register of any kind, and their names and formal descriptions lie for the most part scattered in the technical literature, almost impossible to compile into a single source.

Many animals are known but uncataloged, and in many groups new species are being discovered faster than they can be formally named and described.

Even in such conspicuous animal groups as birds, new forms are being found once or twice per decade. Many parts of the world, including

some tropical rainforests and the deep seas, remain essentially unexplored from a zoological point of view. But if a grand, overall catalog were prepared, it would show the total number of species on Earth as certainly in seven figures, and very probably eight. Some estimate a final tally of about 30 million.

How does this diversity arise? The key to comprehending it lies in the living things themselves. A tree can obviously provide homes for many more different kinds of animals than could the naked patch of land on which it stands: aphids graze on its leaves, grubs burrow into its bark, birds forage in its branches, and so on. All would not be there if the tree were not. The tree can even support other plants, such as orchids, ferns and mistletoes—each providing further micro-habitats into which some small animals may evolve. So the evolution of a species opens up the potential

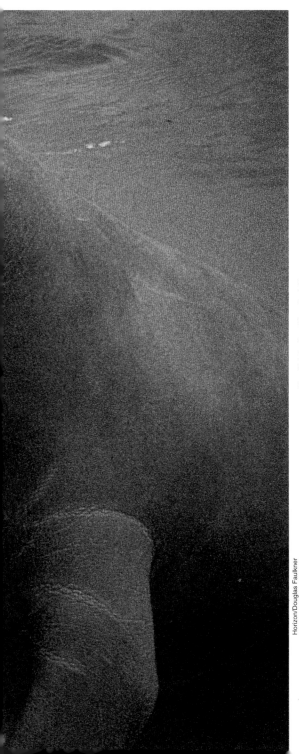

Horizon/Douglas Faulkner

Hans Christian Heap/Planet Earth Pictures

for other species to develop in an apparently endless process.

Animals may themselves provide the environments, or niches, for other animals. These we usually call parasites. Lice, fleas and mites may live on an animal's skin, while nematodes and other parasitic worms inhabit its gut and tissues. Although at first sight this might seem an easy way to earn a living, in fact a parasite is confronted with a variety of special difficulties. An internal parasite must take care, for example, not to trigger the host's immune system. A parasite that is sufficiently specialized to defeat such systems is not likely to be very successful in some other species of host, with

▲ The key to understanding the extraordinary structure of the flamingo's unique bill is to note that it is used upside down. Long-legged and long-necked, the flamingo wades in shallow water with its head down, bill pointing backwards. Water flows into the half-open bill, and the piston-like tongue forces it out again through the fringes along the sides, trapping inside the brine-shrimps and similar animals on which the bird feeds.

◄ Placid, slow-moving and long-lived, manatees are among the very few completely aquatic herbivores among mammals, eating about 10 percent of their body weight in sea-grasses per day. They inhabit sheltered inshore waters and estuaries in tropical America and Africa.

BIRDS, NICHES AND SPECIES DIVERSITY

Temperature and rainfall are traditionally known as dominant influences on plant and animal diversity. Daily and annual extremes in weather will naturally affect the survival of a variety of species in any one area. But there is also diversity geographically. In general, as one travels from the equator towards the poles, the quantity of sunlight falling on the surface declines, average temperatures decline, and temperature fluctuations between summer and winter widen.

Of course, these are by no means the only factors influencing the variety of climates and therefore the variety of flora and fauna. Diversity amongst animal species has often emerged as a result of their very special needs. Birds in different locations, for example, have evolved different techniques for acquiring food by refining their biological equipment. For example, a slender, pointed, slightly curved bill is almost essential to probe effectively in the crannies of bark for food, but the same bill would be clumsy and ineffective in capturing flying insects. For these, a short, very broad bill is far more effective, especially with a network of bristles around the gape, so that even a near miss stands a better chance of capturing the flying insect.

Evolution has witnessed the arrival of entire guilds of birds to live in woodlands, which have adapted to foraging insects on the ground, in the bark, in flight and so on. As these groups have gravitated towards their specialized niches, they have even created subdivisions within their species. In Australian woodlands, for example, thornbills of the genus *Acanthiza* feed in broadly similar ways, but do so at different levels in the forest: one on the forest floor, another in the undergrowth, and another in the canopy; and one in the middle levels focuses its activities on the bark while another searches the leaves. Under certain circumstances, it is possible to encounter flocks of these birds moving through the woods together.

The fact that some tropical areas possess high mountains offers another range of environments for birds. Some New Guinea mountain ranges tower well above 3,300 meters (10,800 feet), and whistlers of the genus *Pachycephala* tend to sort themselves out in altitudinal bands: the grey whistler (*P. griseiceps*) from sea level to about 1,370 meters (4,500 feet), the rusty whistler (*P. hyperythra*) from 460 to 1,280 meters (1,500–4,200 feet), Sclater's whistler (*P. soror*) from 1,066 to 1,830 meters (3,500–6,000 feet), the regent whistler (*P. schlegelii*) from 1,520 to 3,050 meters (5,000––10,000 feet), and the brown-backed whistler (*P. modesta*) from 1,830 to 3,050 meters (6,000–10,000 feet).

▼ Closely related animals occupying the same geographic area are usually adapted to different niches, exampled by these thornbills, a group of small, common, Australian songbirds (genus *Acanthiza*). All feed on small insects, but differ in where and how they catch them.

THORNBILL NICHES

striated thornbill

feeds in woodland canopy

brown thornbill

feeds in lower branches and understory

yellow-rumped thornbill

feeds on the ground

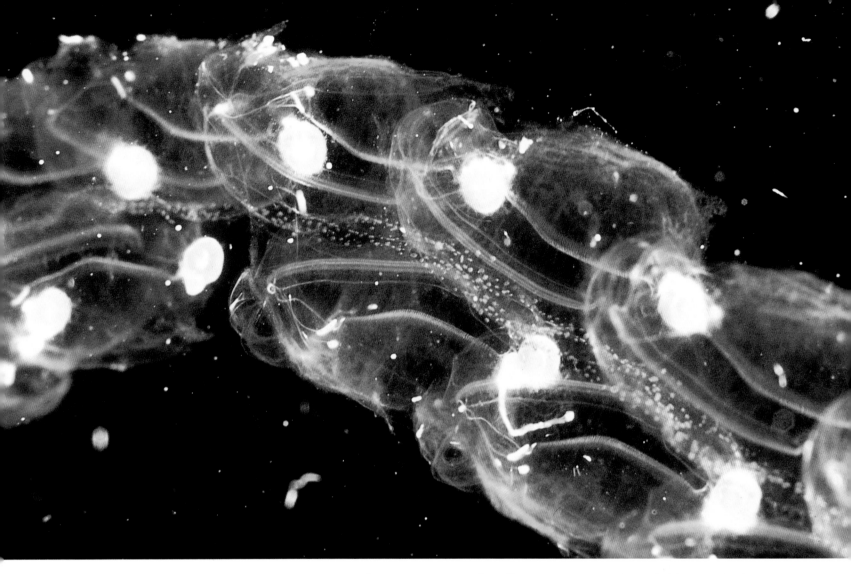

differing immune systems, and parasites are accordingly often very strongly host-specific. In other words, the common situation is that parasite species A is found only in cats, for example, while parasite species B may be found only in dogs.

There are about 250,000 species of beetles. Suppose every one had its own species of parasitic nematode. Suppose each had its own mite species on its surface as well as the nematode in its gut. Sometimes the parasites themselves have parasites. The insect order Hymenoptera, for example, contains a group of species of wasps that parasitize beetles. The adult wasp hunts a grub, paralyzes it with her sting, then lays an egg on its surface. A little later the egg hatches, the grub burrows into its helpless host, and proceeds to eat it alive. But some parasitic wasps of this kind themselves have other parasitic wasps that lay their eggs on the wasp egg. This phenomenon, known as hyperparasitism, may have several links—in fact chains are known that have four links.

Suppose every species of beetle not only had a particular nematode in its gut and mite on its surface, but also its own particular chain of hyperparasitic wasps four links long! If there are one quarter of a million species of beetles, then that comes to a grand total of 1.5 million species of animals involving beetles alone.

Suppose this situation is true also of bees, cockroaches and spiders!

All this is of course merely speculation for the sheer fun of it. Obviously we cannot know what parasites a beetle (or any other animal) might have until the beetle itself is studied. And most beetles remain unnamed, let alone studied. The real point is that the variety of

▲ A colonial salp (*Thea punctata*). Salps are small, little-known, obscure animals that vaguely resemble small tadpoles and belong to the group Tunicata. Together with a wide variety of other small animals they make up plankton, as numerous in the ocean as insects in the air.

▼ Weighing only about 2 grams (0.07 ounce), the pygmy-shrew (*Sorex minutus*) is one of the smallest of all mammals.

Tony Tilford/Oxford Scientific Films

animals is such that the body of facts known about them is an insignificant part of the whole. Our knowledge of most animals is only just beginning. Even in the case of such conspicuous animals as mammals and birds there remain many species that are still known

The shape and structure of animals vary too greatly even to summarize. They encompass everything from the ultimate streamlining of the tuna and other ocean fish to the absurd long-leggedness of some spiders, harvestmen and crabs. Some animals, like clams, lie on the

▲ A killer fungus (*Cordyceps*) growing on (and in) a grasshopper on the rainforest floor, Costa Rica. In tropical forests, much of the breakdown of fallen branches, leaves, dead animals and other litter is performed by fungi.

only from a handful of carefully preserved museum specimens.

Animals differ enormously in their shape, size and structure. The largest animal alive today is a mammal, the blue whale, which weighs around 100 tonnes (220,400 pounds). This makes it about 50 million times bigger than the smallest mammal, a pygmy-shrew weighing in at about 2 grams (0.07 ounce), and a good deal bigger still than the smallest of all animals. Some animals are very small indeed. The feather-winged beetle (*Nanocella*), for example, is about 0.25 millimeter (0.01 inch) long and weighs about 0.4 microgram (0.04 grain—440 grains equal 1 ounce). This is a good deal smaller than some single-celled organisms like the Paramecium, for example, which may grow to about 0.33 millimeter (0.01 inch) in length.

sea floor for years, showing little more in the way of movement than the periodic opening and closing of their two shells. Some are plant-like, and others, such as corals, live in huge dense communities.

While animals do vary in appearance, they also vary just as widely—if not more so—in their behavior, environments and ways of organizing their lives. Being highly visual animals ourselves, we tend to expect that different animals "look" different. Every animal must have some way of discriminating individuals of its own kind from the vast range of other animals, but these means are not necessarily visual. Even among such highly visual animals as birds, there are many species that recognize each other by such non-visual means as calls, behavior, and their habitats.

THE IMPORTANCE OF CELLS

With the exception of viruses, all life is made up of cells, some of which are quite large. The alga, *Acetabularia,* for example, consists of a single cell shaped very much like a slender-stalked toadstool that may be nearly 2 centimeters (0.8 inch) high. Eggs (even chicken eggs) normally consist of only a single cell, and specialized cells known as neurons (the "wiring" of an animal's central nervous system), may have thread-like extensions many meters in length. However, all of these are very special exceptions to the generalization that cells are extremely small, normally ranging in size from about 1 to 1,000 cubic micrometers—literally microscopic.

Cells are of two kinds: prokaryotic and eukaryotic. There are a number of technical differences between the two, but in essence eukaryotic cells are very much more complex in structure than prokaryotic cells. In fact, there is some reason to suspect eukaryotic cells may have originated from a symbiotic or parasitic relationship between two prokaryotic organisms. In any event, prokaryotic organisms were the first life forms to appear on Earth, some 3.5 billion years ago. For almost 2 billion years they had the planet entirely to themselves, and reached considerable diversity in structure and mode of life. They are still very much with us (there are more of them in your mouth than the total number of human beings who ever lived). We call many of these organisms bacteria, and biologists usually group all such organisms in a kingdom (Monera) distinct from other life forms.

Eukaryotic organisms are believed to have made their appearance about 1.4 billion years ago. Though different from the prokaryotes in many ways, they too were single-celled, and nearly a billion years went by before the first multicelled animals evolved a mere 600 million years ago. Eukaryotic cells still form the basis of all life forms on Earth today (other than the Monera). The single-celled forms are grouped in the kingdom Protista; those with certain additional characteristics are placed in the two kingdoms Fungi and Plantae; and the rest belong to the kingdom Animalia, the animals, the main subject of this book.

We do not know how or why the first multicellular animals arose, but there are several ways in which it might profit an organism to move from a unicellular to a multicellular mode of life. The most obvious edge a large animal has over a small one is that if you are a great deal bigger than your neighbors, you don't need to run away from them. If you are hungry you can even eat them! However, there are purely mechanical limits to how big a single cell can be, so any increase in

Ian Beames/Ardea London

size thereafter must involve groups of cells. Also, no matter how complex a single cell might be, it remains possible to build even more complex things by using them as building blocks to construct bigger units, so that the complexity of the construct is itself an addition and extension of its own complexity.

Presumably, there gradually arose a pattern of increasing specialization in the function of various cells in the organism. In humans, some of our cells are "liver" cells, others are "brain" cells, and yet others are "skin" cells. Each type is so specialized that it is unable to serve any function other than its own, but this is not true of all animals. The individual cells in a sponge are so unspecialized that the animal may be broken up into pieces, each of which will develop into a new sponge. In some ways, it is not easy to decide whether a sponge is a "genuine" multicellular animal or merely a well-organized colony of individual cells.

▲ Enough of a good thing: a giraffe (*Giraffa camelopardalis*) stoops to drink. Its long neck gives the giraffe a unique advantage over other animals when it comes to reaching high into trees to munch their foliage, but the same length of neck enforces an ungainly effort to reach the surface when it comes time to take a drink.

THE DIVERSITY OF ANIMAL FORMS

Animals can be arranged into some 33 distinct groups, called phyla (singular, phyllum), each with profoundly different body architectures. Three phyla dominate the environment in terms of our everyday perceptions: mollusks, arthropods and chordates (especially vertebrates). Most mollusks have soft bodies protected by shells, like snails, although the group also includes the octopus and squid; arthropods have jointed legs and external skeletons; while vertebrates have an internal skeleton, and can therefore increase in body size in a gradual, uninterrupted fashion. In numbers of species, the arthropods (in particular the insects) vastly outnumber all other animal species put together. Starfish, worms and jellyfish are examples of other phyla that are, in the main, less conspicuous in life style, smaller in size and fewer in numbers of species. Each band roughly represents a phyllum, and its width is intended to convey the relative number of species within the phyllum.

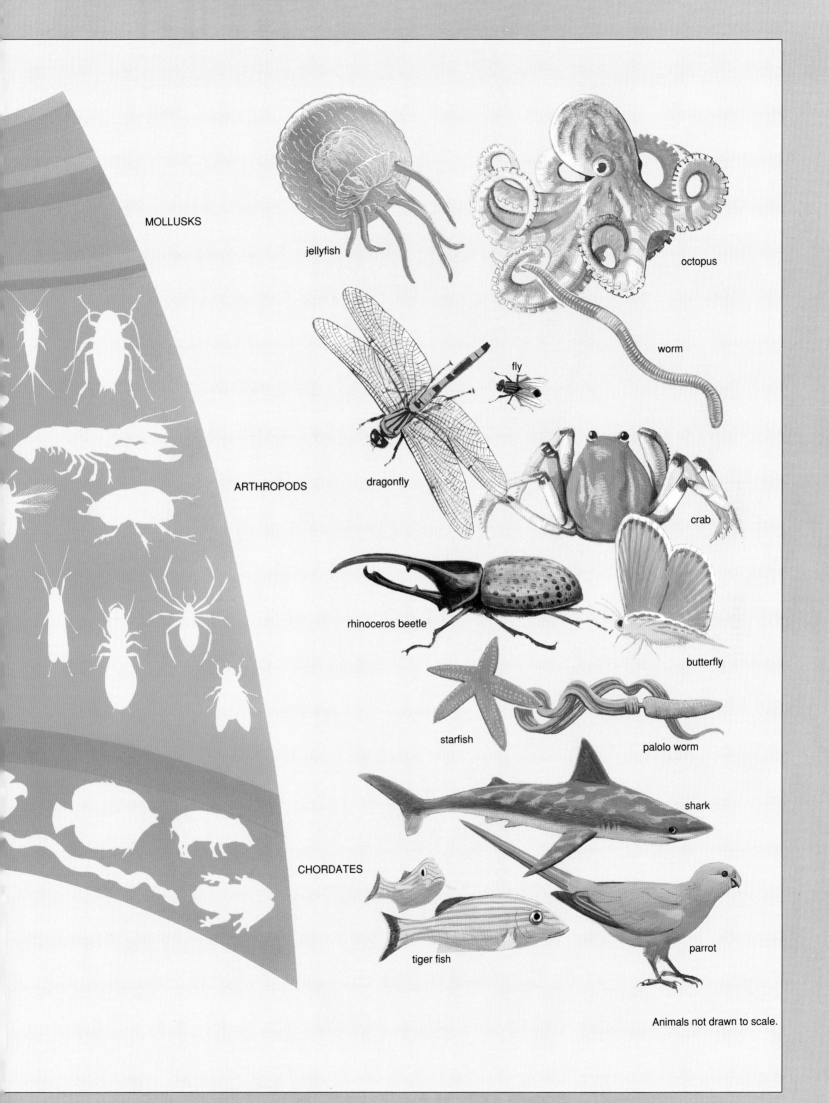

MOLLUSKS

jellyfish

octopus

worm

ARTHROPODS

dragonfly

fly

crab

rhinoceros beetle

butterfly

starfish

palolo worm

shark

CHORDATES

tiger fish

parrot

Animals not drawn to scale.

▼ The animals most familiar to us tend to show bilateral symmetry, with a definite head and tail and near-identical right and left halves. But many animals conform to an entirely different architecture, like the seastars, or starfish (class Asteroidea), which show radial symmetry. This is the common sunstar (*Crossaster papposus*), which grows to about 90 millimeters (3.5 inches) in diameter, lives mainly in warm shallow seas, and feeds largely on mollusks.

Roger Tidman/NHPA

THE ANIMAL KINGDOM

The kingdom Animalia can be divided into about 33 major groups, called phyla (the exact number depends on which zoologist is writing the book). Some of these are small groups of very obscure animals that are unlikely to be encountered by anyone but the zoologists who choose to study them. Others are common, widespread and familiar, and three (the arthropods, mollusks and vertebrates) shape our everyday impressions of what an animal is.

Three features dominate the decisions that zoologists make in distinguishing one animal group from another—the number and structure of body cavities, the details of early embryology, and symmetry. The first two need not concern us here, but the question of symmetry ultimately determines the shape and general appearance of the animal.

The term "bilateral symmetry" applies to those animals that could be divided into two more or less equal halves by an imaginary cut from tail to snout. This is true of, for example, a lobster, a spider and a parrot. But it is not true of a starfish, which exhibits radial symmetry, having a top and bottom but no front or rear. Some animals, such as sponges, often show no particular symmetry or shape.

Mollusks are often popularly known as shellfish and include the bivalves, of which the familiar oyster is a reasonably typical example, and the gastropods, a group which might be represented by the ordinary garden snail. Some organisms, such as the slugs, have abandoned their shells. Another group, the cephalopods, has an internal rather than an external shell, well-developed eyes, and eight or ten tentacles—these are the octopi and squids.

Arthropod means "jointed leg", and these are all bilaterally symmetrical animals with six, eight or more pairs of appendages serving as legs with several articulated joints. This group encompasses the crabs, scorpions, spiders, insects and millipedes. It includes more species than all the other groups of animals.

The chordates are characterized by the possession of a structure known as a noto-chord, in which a stiffened rod extends down the length of the animal. The major group is the vertebrates, the group to which we human beings belong, along with other mammals, fish, frogs and birds.

Some other phyla, such as the water bears, are very small, obscure and perhaps relatively unimportant in the general scheme of things. But other groups have an importance far out of proportion to their obscurity for most people. The nematode worms, for example, swarm in the upper levels of the soil in numbers that defy description. There is in fact a range of animals, which we encounter so seldom in our everyday lives that they lack even common names, that still dominate their environments. Minute shrimp-like animals called copepods teem in the oceans of the world in such numbers that they may be the most numerous of all animals. Similarly, leaf litter on the floor of all forests contains staggering numbers of tiny primitive insects known as Collembola.

SKINS, SHELLS AND OTHER OUTER LAYERS

All animals require a skin or its equivalent to separate and protect the animal from its environment. In humans this boundary layer is by no means as clear-cut as might appear at first sight. Most of us have had the uncomfortable experience of being crowded by some overly aggressive individual who comes too close, though not actually touching. We say of such an incident that our "personal space" has been invaded. So there is some sense, however intangible, in which the function of our skin is being extended to some extent beyond its physical structure.

It seems that this is also true of other animals. We might have noticed, for example, that members of a flock of migrating swallows, pausing to rest on roadside telephone wires, tend to space themselves out along the wire at intervals of a few centimeters. In contrast, one of the most distinctive characteristics of Australasian woodswallows (Artamidae) is their persistent habit of cuddling up together on a branch or limb. In fact, in some fundamental, restricted sense, this concept of a boundary layer or interface, detectable to the organism and subject to whatever "awareness" it might have, must be true of all animals. The skin is one of the most vital of organs.

The skin, or whatever we might choose to call it, varies widely in structure in the animal kingdom. In some, it dictates the basic architecture of the animal. The skin of an arthropod, for example, serves also (to a large extent) as its skeleton. Since it is rigid and unelastic, this means that the animal cannot grow within it. It must therefore be periodically shed and replaced, leaving the animal extremely vulnerable while this process is going on.

The chief function of the outer layer is to control the internal environment of the animal by selectively influencing the exchange of such factors as heat, water and chemicals across it. Perhaps the most vital of all these factors is water, especially in land animals.

This factor is so critical that some animals have evolved special behaviors to augment their physiological mechanisms for water conservation. In the Namibian desert in southern Africa, for example, where

▲ A banded anole (*Anolis insignis*), an inhabitant of the rainforests of Central America. Reptiles such as this one are characterized by a covering of tough, horny, close-fitting scales, precursors of the feathers of birds. Unlike birds and mammals, reptiles have only limited control of their own internal temperature. While this puts them at a disadvantage in cold climates, the fact that they do not need to invest large amounts of energy in maintaining a high metabolism means that they can get by on much less food than that required by a similarly-sized bird or mammal. This gives them a distinct edge in warm but otherwise inhospitable environments such as deserts.

temperature extremes join with the nearby ocean to produce frequent fogs, a small tenebrionid beetle absorbs water by facing into the breeze and standing almost on its head; the fog condenses on the beetle's back and trickles down special grooves leading into its mouth.

Most multicellular animals have special organ systems to deal with the gaseous exchange of carbon dioxide and oxygen—fish have gills, spiders have book-lungs, insects use a system of trachea ramifying through the body, while most vertebrates breathe by means of lungs. Single-celled animals, of course, absorb

▼ An African crested porcupine (*Hystrix* sp.). Porcupines are equipped with a formidable defense in the form of long, sharp-pointed quills that, loosely attached, easily become embedded in the face and paws of any attacker.

Ken Lucas/Planet Earth Pictures

Anthony Bannister/NHPA

oxygen directly through their outer membranes. But so also do many multicellular animals, even including some vertebrates. Many salamanders, for example, lack either gills or lungs as adults, and breathe entirely through their skins. Some frogs have extremely baggy skins, or have hair-like extensions of the skin, which increase the surface area exposed to water and enable improved oxygen transfer.

Frogs also excel in the art of exuding unpleasant substances from their skins. Skin secretions of all species are at least mildly toxic or irritating, but some take chemical warfare to further extremes. The marine or cane toad (*Bufo marinus*) can squirt a toxic brew from special parotoid glands behind the eyes, with a range of up to a meter (more than 3 feet). The batrachotoxin secreted by the Kokoi poison-

arrow frog (*Phyllobates bicolor*) of South America is one of the most deadly substances known: a lethal dose for a human being.

In many animals, especially birds and mammals, the skin also has an important role to play in controlling heat loss. Many zoologists believe, for example, that feathers in birds may originally have had nothing to do with flight. Instead, they suggest, feathers were first evolved as a temperature-control device. In mammals, a thick pelt of fur serves essentially the same purpose. Both feathers and fur work by trapping a layer of air against the skin. The thickness and other characteristics of this layer can be manipulated by movement of the fur or feathers. A good example of this mechanism is a sparrow with its feathers all fluffed out on a frosty morning.

As well as serving as a skeleton, the cuticle of many arthropods, especially crustaceans and many beetles and bugs, serves double duty as armor plating, protecting the animal from predators. However, this function is by no means restricted to arthropods, and the skin of some animals as diverse as crocodiles, fishes and mammals is highly modified to serve as armor. Turtles and tortoises have taken this device to its extreme, at least among vertebrates, but some mammals, notably the armadillos and pangolins, are also heavily armored. One species, the nine-banded armadillo, is even able to roll into a tight ball that leaves nothing for a predator to take hold of. Hedgehogs and porcupines take this defense concept one step further and are what might be called aggressively armored. Porcupines are

▲ The nine-banded armadillo (*Dasypus novemcinctus*) is relatively common in arid and semi-arid regions from southern Texas to Argentina. Armadillos differ from other armored mammals in that their protection consists of plates of bone rather than toughened skin, but most species augment this defense by spending most of their time in subterranean burrows.

▲ A Parson's chameleon (*Chamaeleo parsoni*). Chameleons are arboreal inhabitants of Africa, India and Madagascar. They stalk insects along branches with almost imperceptible movements, anchoring themselves with prehensile tails, surveying their surroundings with independently rotating turreted eyes, and capturing their prey with lightning flicks of their extremely long, sticky tongues.

covered with quills which are long, stiffened, sharp-pointed and with highly modified hairs. If attacked, Eurasian porcupines of the genus *Hystrix* raise and rattle their quills in warning, then charge backwards or sideways, attempting to drive the sharp quills into the attacker.

The skins of a number of animals play an active role in camouflage; such animals include squids, flounders and chameleons. Special cells known as chromatophores lie within their skins or close beneath. Granules of pigment can be moved about within the cell under the animal's hormonal or nervous control (or both): when clumped the cell is pale, but when the pigment is dispersed throughout the cell it appears dark. Some animals have several layers of such cells, each a different color and each under independent control. These animals can often mimic their surroundings with extraordinary fidelity, and adapt to changed surroundings quickly.

But an animal's skin can also serve as a canvas or banner, on which to paint all manner of signals and announcements. Sometimes color and pattern serve defensive or aggressive purposes, as in the bright warning colors of wasps and other dangerous animals, or in various kinds of camouflage and mimicry. But the maximum extension of color and pattern tends to arise where many different but related species live in close communities, as in the case of fish on coral reefs or birds in the canopy of a tropical rainforest, not to mention a host of butterflies. In such crowded environments, each animal needs to know promptly whether an interloper is a potential mate to be attracted, or a rival to be ejected, or another species entirely which might safely be ignored. Bold patterns and bright colors tend to shorten the recognition time, so that each animal wastes less time in inappropriate interactions with others that may prove costly.

. . . AND APPENDAGES

The function of the skin is augmented and supported by a range of supplementary structures, which are often diagnostic of the animal. Feathers, for example, instantly identify a bird because only birds have them.

In insects, in particular, external additions and elaborations are so diverse and so bizarre that a brief paragraph or two cannot even begin to summarize them. Such features range from the extraordinary "antlers" of stag beetles, to the incredibly elaborate antennae of some beetles and moths. Sometimes it is as though some element of the body itself becomes an appendage. For extreme deviation in head shape, for instance, it would be hard to better

the leaf-curling weevils (*Trachelophorus*) of Madagascar. Sometimes the entire form and structure of the body is modified for some defensive purpose, as in the lichen weevils and the stick insects. The proboscis, the mouth parts and ovipositors are also subject to extreme variation. The genitalia of many male insects are designed to interlock securely with those of the female, and the incredible range of structures would require a book in itself.

But insects are not alone in the possession of bizarre and exaggerated appendages. Fiddler crabs of the genus *Uca,* for example, have one claw enormously enlarged relative to the other. This fearsome weapon is used in fights with other males, and is waved to attract the

▼ A cockchafer (*Melolontha melolontha*) displays the extraordinary complexity of its multi-forked antennae. Cockchafers are related to the insects widely known in North America as "junebugs". They are nocturnal, feed on foliage and flowers, and often congregate around street-lights.

Stephen Dalton/NHPA

▶ (facing page) A red-faced batfish (*Platax pinnatus*) photographed in the Red Sea. The batfish (family Ephippidae) are remarkable for the pronounced change in body shape they undergo between the juvenile form and full adulthood. Young batfish have a markedly sickle-shaped outline resulting from enormously elongated dorsal, ventral and anal fins. These gradually shrink as the fish grows, and adults have a much more conventional fish silhouette.

▲ Toucans, like this red-billed toucan (*Ramphastos tucanus*), are characteristic of tropical American rainforests, and notable for their enormous, brightly colored bills. They live in the canopy and feed on fruit, swallowed whole. The bill is thin-walled and honeycombed within, so it weighs far less than its outward appearance would suggest, but its function is uncertain.

attention of passing females in the visual analog of the wolf-whistle in humans. Nor is the possession of extreme appendages restricted to the invertebrate world. The hummingbird *Ensifera,* for example, has a bill longer than the rest of its head, body and tail combined, while some long-tongued bats, family Phyllostomatidae, have tongues the same relative length. Both structures are used for extracting nectar from flowers.

Often we have no idea of what the function and purpose of such remarkable additions might be, as in the aptly named hammerhead sharks, family Sphyrnidae, in which the head is uniquely flattened and extended out to the sides, with the eyes at the ends like outriggers. Similarly, the proportionately enormous and brightly colored bills of toucans constitute the most striking feature of these birds, but their function remains uncertain. Male narwhals (*Monodon monoceros*) have a single tooth (usually the left, occasionally the right, and very rarely both together) that extends, spiraled, straight and spear-like, up to nearly 3 meters (10 feet) in length. Presumably this structure, which has given the narwhal a mythological quality, is used in battles with other males, but nobody really knows.

Sometimes the function is obvious, but no less extraordinary for that. The elephant's four pillar-like legs are almost fully occupied in bearing the animal's enormous weight, and these limbs are far from ideally suited to such purposes as, for instance, scratching that elusive itch behind the ear. Instead, the elephant relies on its trunk for almost everything that requires careful manipulation. Anatomically an extension and fusion of the nose and upper lip, this extraordinary organ contains an estimated 100,000 muscle units. It is extremely sensitive, and capable of remarkable dexterity.

Very often such specialized features are obvious only while being used, as in display, and kept more or less hidden—or at least relatively inconspicuous—at other times. The hooded seal (*Cystophora cristata*) is named for the extreme enlargement of the male's nasal cavity, which forms a visible hump on the top of the head while at rest. However, by closing one nostril and blowing, the male can evert the septum membrane out through the other nostril to form a conspicuous red "balloon." The function of this extraordinary display is still uncertain. Similarly, in one of the most striking courtship displays among birds, the male frigate bird (genus *Fregata*) takes up a position on the breeding island, spreads and waves his enormous black wings, wails and claps his mandibles, and inflates a naked pouch on his throat to form a large red balloon.

Apart from their function in flight and temperature control, the feathers of birds offer enormous potential for secondary use as displays of various kinds. The gorgeous train of the male peacock, erected fan-like in display, has made it a valued ornamental bird for centuries, but even it only barely eclipses the displays of such birds as the crested argus (*Rheinartia ocellata*) for sheer extravagance. Among the birds of paradise of New Guinea, the genus *Astrapia* are notable for the extremely long tail streamers, white or satin-black, of the males, while the King of Saxony bird of paradise (*Pteridophora alberti*) has long, mobile plumes on the head, and members of the genus *Paradisaea* have long, filmy flank plumes. Many South American hummingbirds have equally spectacular adornments, and some are veritable jewels of vibrant, metallic color. Less brightly colored but equally striking, two species of African nightjar have greatly elongated wing feathers, forming streamers 50 centimeters (20 inches) or more in length. In the standard-winged nightjar (*Macrodipteryx longipennis*) it is the ninth primary that is elongated, while in the pennant-winged nightjar (*Semeiophorus vexillarius*) the innermost flight feathers are elongated.

Stephen Dalton/NHPA

► A cheetah (*Acinonyx jubatus*) at full gallop in the Masai Mara Reserve, Kenya. Cheetahs catch their prey by running it down in sudden high-speed sprints from cover. Chases seldom last more than 10-20 seconds, but in that time the animal may reach speeds of almost 110 kilometers per hour (70 miles per hour), the fastest of all animals on land.

ON THE MOVE

Fantastic footwork

On land, animals use a variety of methods for locomotion. In larger beasts, these methods range from the well-known bounding of kangaroos, to the magnificent gallop of horses, the tireless amble of camels, and the unique bipedal gait of humans. Wolves lope and tortoises plod.

▲ The underside of a Costa Rican flying frog (*Agalychnis spurrelli*), photographed on a sheet of glass, reveals the webbing between fingers and toes. Originally an adaptation for swimming, in a few arboreal species this feature is so pronounced that the animal can use the webs as gliding surfaces to extend jumps, slow the rate of fall, and increase maneuvrability in mid-air.

The fastest animal on land is the cheetah. This magnificent cat typically stalks to within 100 meters (330 feet) or so of its prey, then relies on acceleration and agility to overwhelm it in a sudden all-out sprint. The chase seldom lasts more than 10 or 20 seconds, but in that time the cheetah may reach 110 kilometers per hour (70 miles per hour). (See Chapter Two)

But not all animals are built for sheer speed, and there are many undramatic means of getting from one place to another.

Underground, worms literally chew their way along, using bristles (setae) on each of their body segments in turn to dig in and hitch the hinder segments along. Moles use spade-like hands to tunnel almost like rotary machines.

Above ground, slugs glide on a carpet of mucus laid down by the animal itself. Millipedes and centipedes scurry along on sinuous segmented bodies equipped with hundreds of pairs of legs, leading one to marvel how they can keep them all under control and, at the same time, move in step. Birds such as flamingos wade in water on almost absurdly long slender legs.

Some animals are adapted to jumping, and many can make prodigious leaps. A flea, for example, can jump about 150 times its own body length, and about 80 times as high. Ignoring other aspects of scale, a human with equivalent performance could easily clear a multistorey building. However, much of this spectacular performance derives from the fact that the power of a muscle varies with the area of its cross-section, while the mass it works against is proportional to volume. In short, small muscles in small bodies are more effective than large muscles in large bodies, and—gram for gram—there is little to choose between insect or vertebrate muscles.

Gunter Ziesler/Bruce Coleman Limited

Heather Angel/Biofotos

THE CONSTRUCTION OF A MOLE TUNNEL

▼ Like other moles, the common European mole spends most of its life underground, constructing systems of tunnels just below the surface. These are cylindrical in cross-section (center) and periodically emerge above the surface in the form of small heaps of excess soil. The mole feeds largely on earthworms, usually biting the head off to immobilize them, and often storing them in subterranean chambers.

The mole stores earthworms in the tunnel chambers.

constructing the tunnel

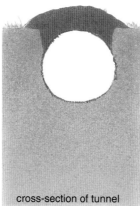

cross-section of tunnel

completing the tunnel

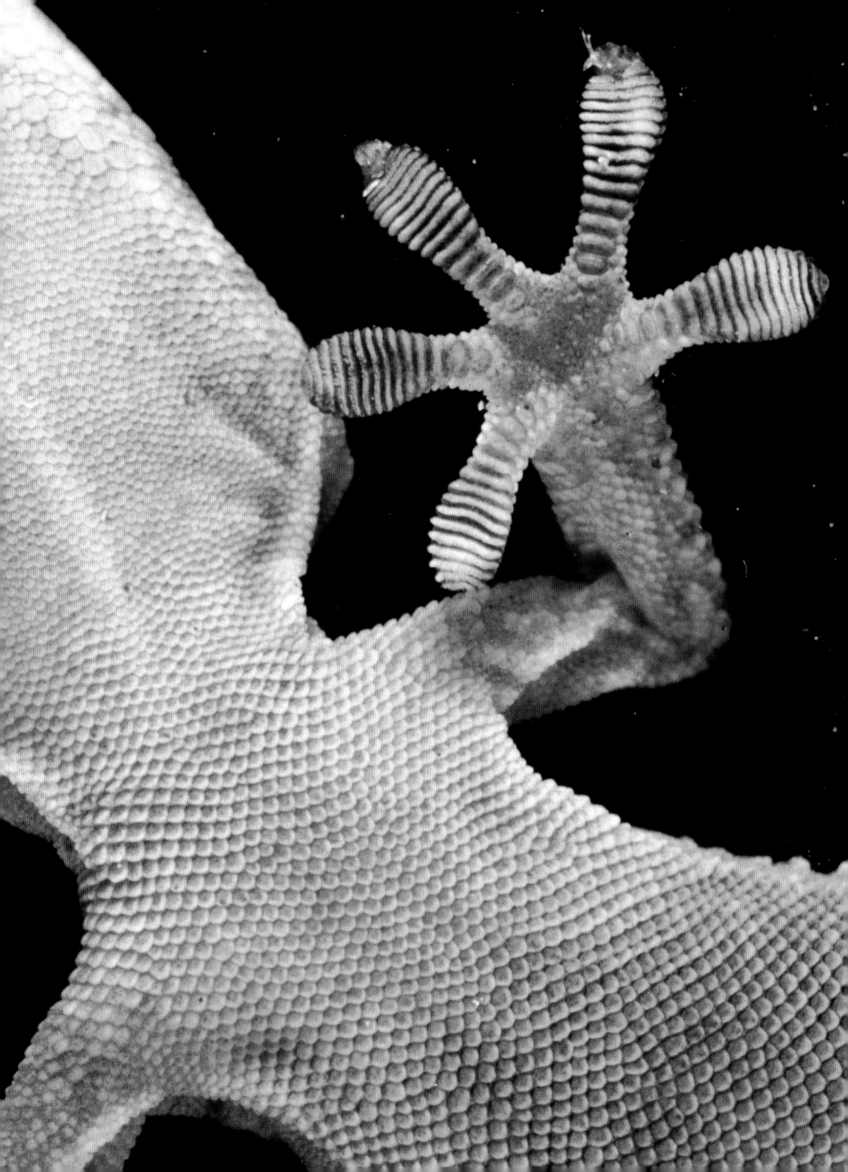

◀ (*previous pages*) A gecko (*Tarentula* sp.) on a window-pane. Like glorified fingerprints, the intricate pattern of ridges and whorls on the gecko's digits enables it to cling even to glass, and even upside down. *Stephen Dalton/NHPA*

Other animals are designed to move about in complex environments of three dimensions, such as forests, and are aided by devices as varied as the prehensile tail of a monkey and the velcro "suction" caps on the toes of such animals as geckos and tarsiers. These aids are so effective that a gecko, for example, can quite easily climb the smooth walls of a room, and even dash about upside-down on the ceiling. There are some animals that do quite well lacking limbs altogether. Snakes, for instance, can move easily on the ground or in trees, and many are very fast and agile.

In the sea

The sea is where locomotion originated, and its inhabitants have developed some bizarre means of getting about. Squid propel themselves by what can only be described as jet propulsion, while spider crabs mince along the sea floor on spindly legs that may span 2 meters (over 6 feet) or more. Nudibranchs ripple along, while jellyfish pulse rhythmically, often with hypnotic and unearthly beauty. Many take the easy option, and hitch rides on other animals, while fish may take to swimming.

A fish can travel through the water either by moving its body or moving its fins. From the bioengineering point of view, there are three significant factors involved in swimming: accelerating, cruising and maneuvering. These are related in what has been called the principle of mutual exclusion of optimum designs. In other words, improvement in one aspect of locomotion can only be achieved by some sacrifice in the other two.

Because thrust is applied by unit area against mass, acceleration specialists need to minimize their non-muscle "dead" weight and maximize their relative depth along the body in order to get the most out of a sudden surge of power. Such fish as pike, for instance, tend to lie in wait, relying on lightning lunges to catch their prey. Here, acceleration is critical.

In a hypothetical model of a fish optimized for delicate maneuvering, thrust would be delivered by oscillating fins rather than flexure of the body itself. The body length would be minimized relative to other linear dimensions, and the fins distributed as evenly as possible around the center of mass. The result might look very like the butterfly fish and others that live in complex environments such as coral reefs, especially those that feed by browsing on organisms on the coral surface.

In sustained high-speed cruising, dragging emerges as the dominant factor. Drag is the sum of the backward forces exerted by the water in its resistance to being pushed aside. These forces are extremely complex, and cannot be removed entirely. Nevertheless, there are a number of design features that can combine to reduce drag to a minimum. There is, in short, an optimum shape. This can be seen as a

A FISH OF THE OCEAN DEPTHS

▲ The gulpers are ocean fish that live at extreme depths, typically around 2,000 to 3,000 meters (6,000 to 9,000 feet) below the surface, and are notable for the extraordinary size of their mouths. The long, snake-like tail ends in a small reddish light.

silhouette with maximum depth at a point a little more than a third of the total distance from head to tail, tapering gradually to a slender tail base, and a very deep and narrow tail fin. These features characterize the tuna, one of the fastest creatures in the sea.

All this suggests that extreme specialists in, for instance, delicate maneuvering must sacrifice a good deal of potential in acceleration and efficient cruising. But there are other ways of improving the compromise. Almost all fishes need to evade predators, but camouflaged fishes have correspondingly less need than conspicuous fishes to rely on acceleration to stay out of trouble. This may be, for example, why seahorses and seadragons, specialists in precise maneuver, are also highly cryptic in their form and unobtrusive coloration.

Body shape and fin arrangement are not the only factors of importance in efficient swimming. Increased speed means increased turbulence, which in turn means increased drag. Any means of reducing turbulence (that is, promoting laminar flow) will correspondingly increase speed or reduce the rate at which the animal tires. Whales and dolphins, for example, can control turbulence to a remarkable extent by sensing pressure fluctuations on their bodies and making constant minute adjustments to muscle and skin tone to compensate.

A further possibility in the control of turbulence is opened up by the recent discovery that extremely low concentrations of certain substances in the water can dramatically improve laminar flow. In one experiment, the swimming speed of fish was almost doubled by the addition of a high polymer ethylene oxide to the water, at a concentration of only 42 parts per million. It seems likely that the mucus exuded from the skins of fish reacts with the surrounding water, and that discharge from the lachrymal glands of dolphins plays a similar role to the fish mucus.

Wings

With their small size, insects are among the most efficient of all flying animals. It seems that insect wings arose as independent structures (that is, they are not modified limbs or similar structural components), and a number of anatomical features suggest that flight arose only once in the group. Insects have two pairs of wings arranged fore and aft, although in many groups one or other of the pairs has become secondarily highly modified. Beetles, for example, are characterized by the fact that the forewings have become rigid covers covering the hind wings at rest and playing little part in active flight. In many insects the two pairs are linked more or less closely together, as in butterflies, while in flies the hind wings have become mere knobs called halteres, functioning as stabilizers. Matters are not quite so simple, but the quick answer to why insects need two pairs of wings is to provide stability. Lacking tails, insects need two sets of wings rather than one.

▲ Millipedes may be found under fallen logs in forest and woodland almost anywhere. They differ from their relatives the centipedes in having two, not one, pairs of legs on each body segment.

IN THE AIR

vulture's wing:
full span

bat in full flight

moorhen

fruit bat's wing:
full span

hummingbird

bee

dragonfly

butterfly

fly

flying lizard

squirrel glider

moth

flying frog

Most insects are small enough, and the surrounding air therefore relatively viscous enough, that they are not bedeviled by the formidable problems of power-to-weight ratio that affects the much larger and heavier flying vertebrates. Until the present century, this defeated even human engineering.

The evolution of insect flight had to solve an entirely different problem, resulting from the fact that insects have external, not internal, skeletons. In insects, external wings must be driven by internal muscles, presenting substantial problems of linkage. Two methods of solving this have evolved, the so-called direct and indirect arrangements.

Large insects have relatively slow wingbeats, ranging from about 10 to 20 per second in

butterflies, locusts and dragonflies to about 50 to 70 per second in some moths. Smaller insects have faster wingbeats.

Insects much smaller than these are no longer concerned with lift. The relative viscosity of the air is so high that they effectively float in it like a fish in water, and progress is more a question of rowing through it than staying up in it. Such tiny insects typically have wings that through the microscope look more like combs or garden rakes than aerofoils, often with fringes along the leading edge. These liliputians often have very rapid wingbeats: the tiny midge *Forcipomyia*, for instance, has been found to vibrate its wings at an extraordinary 1,000 beats per second.

▲ An Indian dragonfly (*Trithemis aurora*) pauses to rest. Dragonflies are the hawks of the insect world, patrolling close to the surface of quiet waters in search of flying insect prey.

◄ (*facing page*) Animals like squirrel gliders are incapable of true flight, but their extended skin surfaces do influence the rate at which they fall. The greater the surface, the less the effects of impact with the ground, and the greater the potential for maneuvering. Even feeble flapping of the surfaces might work to improve these effects, and in the long run give rise to true, fully powered flight such as that exhibited by modern birds.

THE ORIGIN OF FLIGHT IN BIRDS

Flight for vertebrates is, in energetic terms, extremely costly, and requires a series of well-developed physiological, sensory and behavioral systems. Birds have several highly-developed mechanisms to enable flight—their intricate feathered wings, their unique respiratory system, and the ability to sustain several very different metabolic regimes, in flight and at rest.

The earliest known bird is *Archeopteryx,* which lived in Europe some 160 million years ago. This creature had feathers and may well have been capable of flight. One hypothetical model for the origin of flight in birds, sometimes referred to as the "trees-down" theory, suggests that the proto-bird may have begun to climb trees, perhaps to nest, to escape from predators, or to roost at night. Life in trees may have promoted endothermy (warm-bloodedness) and the development of feathers as means of improving temperature control, and might also have promoted improvements in agility, sense organs and co-ordination. Feeding in one tree then gliding to the base of the next can be shown to be energy cost-effective, and gradual development of elongated feathers might act to extend the glide and promote safe landings. The duration of the glide would be extended by flapping the forelimbs, which would also improve maneuverability in the air. Gradual improvements in these organ systems might result in powered, fully controlled flight.

An alternative hypothesis (the "ground-up" model) suggests that the proto-bird may have been a small and nimble bipedal creature that preyed on small flying insects, running them down on the ground and jumping after them as they flew. Enlarged forelimbs may then have evolved as stabilizers, improving the proto-bird's maneuverability during the chase, and promoting a gradual adaptation of the forelimbs as jumping, control and gliding mechanisms for improving the ability to capture insects.

▼A golden bowerbird (*Prionodura nutoniana*) flies from its bower in the highland forests of northeastern Australia. Ornithologists suspect that the avian feather may have evolved first as a device to promote temperature control, and only later became involved in the development of powered flight.

Hans & Judy Beste/Auscapes

Birds and bats

There are flying snakes, flying frogs and flying squirrels, but all of these are gliders—animals that have, in effect, merely found ways of falling slowly. Apart from insects, birds and bats are the only animals presently existing that are capable of true, sustained, fully maneuverable flight. These animals differ from insects chiefly in their larger size, but the overall effect of this is to make aerodynamics more important in the situation, and birds and bats must obey much the same design restraints that govern human-built aircraft.

The design of a bird's wing has much the same implications as the shape and arrangement of fins in fishes, and a good deal can be inferred about its lifestyle by examining the shape of its wings. For example, if a wing is long and narrow it is described as having a high aspect ratio, while if it is short and wide it has a low aspect ratio. A high aspect ratio implies less load-carrying capacity but greater efficiency. For example, eagles need load-carrying capacity and have correspondingly low aspect ratios. Swallows, on the other hand, spend a great deal of time on the wing but do not need to worry about the effects of payload.

One of the chief elements arising from the act of flapping is that, all things being equal, long wings are harder to flap than short wings.

Ground-dwelling birds that seldom need to fly, except to escape predators, need not fly far but must do so very rapidly. Such birds tend to have short, blunt wings to maximize acceleration. In aircraft and in birds, air spilling around the end of the wing sets up vortices that result in turbulence and drag—the wider the wing at the end, the greater this effect.

Thus birds that need long-range efficiency, such as migrants, tend to have more pointed wings than sedentary birds. Birds such as vultures, which need long broad wings for maximum soaring ability, evade the worst consequences of this effect by use of wide-splayed primary (outer wing) feathers. These effectively present to the air a cluster of pointed wingtips, rather than a single blunt one, decreasing the vortex effect.

Much the same might be said about bats. For example, bats that forage in cluttered environments such as forests tend to have shorter, broader wings than bats that feed in open areas, where they can fly more swiftly and maneuverability is less important. However, bat flight differs from bird flight in at least one very important respect. Bats can apparently dynamically alter the camber (the cross-sectional shape) of their wings, while birds, in general, cannot. This introduces an element of complexity still not fully explored.

▲ Lacewings are named for the intricate pattern of veins in their transparent wings. Here a strobe-flash exposure records the complete cycle of wing movements of the insect as it launches from a blade of grass.

Jany Sauvanet/NHPA

▲ The bill fits the flower and the flower fits the bill in a tandem evolution of mutual benefit: a long-tailed hermit (*Phaethornis superciliosus*) sips nectar from a flower. Many plants rely on hummingbirds for pollination, and have evolved flowers to match the length and curvature of the bills of their favored avian visitors. Confined to the Americas, most hummingbirds are active, pugnacious and conspicuous birds of vivid metallic hues.

becomes the recovery stroke instead of the power stroke, and the bird can hover, rise vertically like a helicopter, or even fly backwards. Wingbeats range up to 68 per second. In terms of energy output per unit of weight, the hummingbird outperforms any other vertebrate by a substantial margin. A hovering hummingbird generates about 10 times the output of a human running hard. They consume about half their total body weight of sugar per day.

The birds that fly forever

Many years ago, naturalists in England noticed that, towards sunset, flocks of swifts would congregate in the sky and begin a long, climbing spiral that ultimately took them out of sight. This presented a puzzle that only deepened when these observations were followed up by watching them again at dawn. Sure enough, the birds could be seen coming back down to routine foraging heights. Was it possible that they stayed up all night, sleeping on the wing? This possibility gathered strength with the subsequent use of radar, and it now seems established that swifts, especially the young and non-breeding birds, do indeed spend the night on the wing. In fact, a few strongly migratory species, such as the spine-tailed swift, may never land except when nesting, or when injured or ill.

Riders of the storm

Albatrosses and related seabirds (Procellariids) spend their entire lives at sea, coming to land only to breed. They are truly birds of the ocean, and individuals may spend years at a time far out of sight of land (some of the larger albatrosses do not breed until seven or eight years old, and even then only every alternate year). Their long, slender wings are supremely adapted to effortless flight in a windy, uncluttered environment. Albatrosses often use slope soaring along the face of waves, like hang-gliders along a clifftop, but they also exploit the fact that wind speed at the ocean surface is always somewhat less (because of surface friction) than it is several meters higher up. In other words, wind over water produces a velocity gradient that can be exploited to provide lift. The albatross uses this gradient to trade kinetic energy for potential energy and back again in an endless cycle that requires very little additional input by wing-flapping. So optimized and highly tuned are the seabirds to this flight style that they are almost helpless in a calm or over land, where such conditions do not apply. Procellariids avoid unprotected coastlines whenever they can, and may exhaust themselves seeking searoom against a storm.

Avian helicopters

Hummingbirds are in some ways the most remarkable of flying animals, and from a bioengineering point of view, they have more in common with a helicopter than a conventional aircraft, and operate at about twice the efficiency. Hummingbirds can rotate the wing through a full 180 degrees. The leading edge then becomes the trailing edge, the downstroke

THE FIVE SENSES AND OTHERS

Sense and sensibility

Interaction between an animal and its surroundings is one of the basic characteristics of life. But in order to make a response, an organism must first have some means of detecting changes in its environment. This is true even of single-celled organisms, but multicellular animals have evolved a fantastic array of sophisticated sensory systems to detect and analyze information about their surroundings. Most of these systems ultimately depend on specialized cells that are capable of responding to light (photoreceptors), chemical stimuli (chemoreceptors) or pressure (mechanoreceptors). Many animals are also sensitive to electromagnetic fields.

Jean-Paul Ferrero/Auscape

▲ Long slender wings spanning more than 2 meters (6 feet) signify an efficient glider that can stay aloft almost indefinitely. The shy albatross (*Diomedea cauta*) adapted to a pelagic existence in the Atlantic Ocean corridor known to early sailors as the "Roaring Forties".

Horizon /Franz Lanting

◄ Portrait of a bald eagle (*Haliaetus leucocephalus*), national bird of the United States of America. Large eyes (little smaller than those of humans) and beetling brows (functioning as a sort of sun-visor) contribute to its majestic glare, and are characteristic of those birds that soar high and scan great distances in search of prey. The bald eagle feeds mainly on fish and carrion.

Vision

Some chemicals have the property of releasing energy when exposed to light, and this is exploited by living things in a variety of ways. Plants use one such chemical, called chlorophyll, to manufacture food for themselves. Similarly, most vision depends on the photomorphic pigment rhodopsin.

An organ that exploits this property need be no more elaborate than a cluster of granules of rhodopsin embedded in the skin. While no image can be formed with such elementary systems, the animal concerned can at least distinguish between light and dark—a useful faculty in itself. Many animals improve on this system with clusters of photoreceptors inside a pit or depression in the skin. This means that a light beam entering the pit will strike one side but not the other, enabling the animal to make some estimate of the direction from which the light is coming. Again, this is not exactly full vision, but a useful ability nonetheless.

Further progress toward a full image-making facility involves progressively deepening and widening the pit while at the same time narrowing the opening. In this way, the ability to assess the direction from which light is coming becomes more precise.

The next logical step is to install a transparent lid across the opening to the cavity. If this lid is appropriately shaped, it can diffract the light entering the system in such a way as to form a true image, in much the same way as an image is thrown onto the film in a camera. Two such units arranged in parallel positions make full stereo vision possible.

Color vision is made possible by having photoreceptors that are differentially responsive to light of different wavelengths. In the vertebrate eye there are two main kinds of photoreceptors, called rods and cones. In essence, rods are sensitive to light while cones are sensitive to color. There are at least three kinds of cones, each most sensitive to a

◀ (*facing page*) A spotted owl (*Strix occidentalis*) dozes at a daytime roost. Most owls are nocturnal, and rely on acute hearing as well as vision to catch their prey. Many species have asymmetrical ear openings, which tends to emphasize the stereo effect and improve the precision with which a sound source can be located. Unable to tolerate disturbance, this particular species is found only in dense forests of the western coast and mountains of North America, and has become endangered.

▼ This portrait of a cuttle (*Sepia officinalis*) displays its large and remarkably expressive eyes. Nearly as sophisticated as the vertebrate eye, the eyes of these mollusks show distinct differences in structure, and it seems almost certain that they evolved independently.

Ken Lucas/Planet Earth Pictures

▲ A bushbaby (*Galago senegalensis*), photographed with electronic flash at night. The characteristic "eye-shine" of this and many other nocturnal animals is caused by a reflective layer, the tapetum, at the back of the eye, behind the sensitive or image-forming layer of cells. The tapetum improves light-gathering capability by reflecting light back through the rods and cones: any stray light that failed to register going in is thus offered another chance going out.

particular band of wavelengths. All this theoretical development represents a kind of model of how a visual system might have evolved in animals. Each step is useful to the animal, while at the same time opening the way to yet further development of the visual sense. Three basic architectures can be distinguished in animal vision, known as the arthropod, molluskan, and vertebrate models. Each of these has evolved to a very sophisticated level and together they suggest that vision was independently "invented" several times in the evolution of life. Our

own eyes are fairly representative of the vertebrate eye, in which the incoming light travels first through the nerve network, then strikes the photoreceptors. The remarkable eyes of squid and octopuses are also broadly similar to ours in structure, but differ most conspicuously in that the nerve network lies below the photoreceptors. In arthropods, the most characteristic form is a compound eye consisting of arrays of specialized photo-receptors called ommatidia.

Birds probably excel over all other animals in visual acuity. Firstly, the avian eye is huge in proportion to the rest of its body. Some eagles have eyes as big or bigger than those of humans (in absolute, not relative, terms).

Secondly, the retina is densely packed with photoreceptors: the Eurasian buzzard (*Buteo buteo*), for instance, boasts a density of 1 million cones per square millimeter in the fovea (the region of greatest acuity in the retina), compared to about 200,000 in humans. In the human eye each optic nerve carries about 1 million individual nerve fibers; in pigeons the total is about 2.4 million, while in the goldfish it is only about 53,000.

In all animals, the architecture of the visual system is strongly influenced by the animal's general mode of life. Predators, for example, tend to specialize in subtle analyses of their visual field in order to penetrate their prey's camouflage and other similar defenses, while animals that are heavily preyed upon tend to place the emphasis on prompt detection of danger. A good illustration of this trend involves a bird's field of view. Snipe, for example, have their eyes set in the sides of their heads, mounted high and well back, thus offering virtually a full 360 degree field of view. Owls on the other hand have eyes set side by side, much like our own, in an arrangement that allows full stereo vision and very precise judgement of distance. A snipe's depth-perception is probably not quite as good as an owl's, but a full scanning capability is more important for the snipe. This trend holds good for other animals in the universal predator–prey relationship, and much the same sort of thing might be said of senses other than vision. In Chapter Two we will see how visual acuity is put to good use for finding food.

The mere detection of light is not the whole story. Sensory input must be analyzed to be any use to the animal. In animals that rely on vision, a good deal of the brain is given over to processing the information, especially in an area known as the visual cortex. Indeed, much processing goes on in the eye itself and at various stages along the optic nerve, before the image ever gets to the brain.

One common example of "preprocessing" is known as lateral inhibition, and occurs within the eye itself. In this process, each photo-receptor triggers two responses when a light beam strikes it. The first is to send a response directly along the optic nerve, while the second is to prevent from firing (inhibit) those photoreceptors immediately surrounding it. We might think of this as a process in which each photoreceptor turns itself on, while at the same time turning its neighbors off. Because of this, those photoreceptors that (at any given instant) happen to be exposed to a dark area of the outside scene, do not fire because little or no light is falling on them. Similarly, those photoreceptors that are exposed to bright parts of the scene do fire, but not so vigorously as they might because each is also being inhibited by its neighbors. However, each photoreceptor that happens to be exposed to light-dark edges in the scene is surrounded by only half as many inhibiting neighbors as those other photoreceptors out in the lighter area (the other half are on the dark side, so they are neither firing nor inhibiting). The net result is that those photoreceptors exposed to edges are those that respond most vigorously, which means that the shape and contrast of objects are enhanced, and any movement within the field becomes easier to detect.

W. Moller/Ardea London

When light travels from one transparent medium to another (as from air to water), it changes direction at the boundary between the two and the amount of bending depends on the difference in density between the two. This means that an eye designed to see in air will not function as effectively in water, and an aquatic eye functions poorly in air. This factor presents difficulties for those animals that spend much of their time in either medium. The double-eyed fish, for example, has two sets of optical elements in each eye, the upper part designed to see in air, the lower in water. Some water beetles and a few other animals have eyes with similar structure.

▲ Many eagles and hawks, like this Eurasian buzzard (*Buteo buteo*), locate prey by soaring high in the sky, scanning the ground below for rabbits and similar small creatures. Perhaps the keenest-sighted of all animals, their visual acuity is so high it has been approximated to a human observer studying his or her surroundings through 20x binoculars.

In the final analysis, an animal sees things by detecting the reflection of light bouncing off objects and surfaces in its vicinity. Therefore, a comparable model could be constructed—in theory at least—from any kind of radiation that varies in wavelength and is differentially absorbed, diffused or reflected from objects. The amount of detail in such an "image" varies with the wavelength of the radiation involved. The longer the wavelength, the coarser the resulting image. In the ultimate sense, if all radiation is reflected, then no image can be formed from it. Similarly, if all radiation is absorbed, then again no image can be formed. The possibilities for vision lie in the wide spectrum in between. Thus some snakes have heat sensors concentrated in pits on the head in such a way that they pick up something very like an "image" from the patterns of heat radiating from warm-blooded prey.

Hearing

While sound is not radiation (it's a pressure wave), it behaves in some ways comparably to light. A "picture" of our surroundings reaching our ears can be constructed in much the same way as a visual image. Although they can never match the resolving power offered by vision, sound waves nevertheless present possibilities for extremely subtle analysis (we can form a clear impression of this by imagining ourselves listening to music).

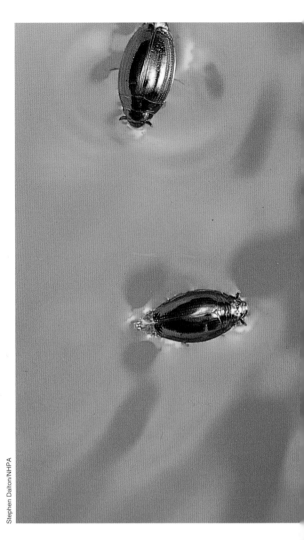

Stephen Dalton/NHPA

▼ Fossil scorpions are known from Silurian deposits some 400 million years old, which makes them the most ancient of terrestrial arthropods. Scorpions rely heavily on a highly developed tactile sense in their feet, and kill their prey by means of a venomous sting in the tail, normally carried arched over the back. A few species, like this *Centuroides exilicande* of Mexico and the southwestern United States, are dangerous even to humans.

It is difficult to directly compare hearing between animals, because so much depends upon the frequency. For example, a dog's hearing seems to be little better than our own if we "cheat" and consider only the frequencies to which we are most sensitive, but is vastly better if we consider higher frequencies. Our own aural sensitivity extends from about 20 to 20,000 hertz (cycles per second), but pigeons, elephants and a number of other animals are sensitive to frequencies ranging down to 1 hertz or even lower, while at the other end of the frequency spectrum, many small animals can hear sounds well above 50,000 hertz. The sound spectrum to which bats are sensitive extends from 5,000 hertz to 200,000 hertz.

Locating the source of a sound depends on several clues. Sound does not travel instantaneously in air, which means that, except when it originates from directly in front or behind, it must strike one ear a fraction of a second sooner than it reaches the other ear. This time delay can be used to judge the location of the origin of the sound. Similarly, any sound wave from a source off to the side reaches one ear directly, but travels through the skull to reach the other, which minutely changes its frequency and other characteristics;

this difference can also be used to detect the origin. One way of exaggerating the distinction between the two signals, thus allowing more precise analysis, is to have the receivers farther apart. Insects, for example, have their ears on their knees, which allows greater separation than if they were in their heads. Another way of increasing the distinction is to have one ear larger than the other or a different shape. Many owls have explored this possibility. The two ear openings in owls are asymmetrical and one is much larger than the other.

Taste and smell

Our own vision and hearing are fairly good compared to most other animals, but as we examine other senses in animals we move rapidly into an area of sensitivity we cannot share. Taste and smell are closely related, and it is often difficult to decide exactly which one is involved. Both are chemical senses—that is, they do not form an image, but involve the very precise and subtle examination of chemicals in the animal's environment.

In many animals this detection system is unimaginably sensitive. Eels, for example, are sensitive to some substances at concentrations well below one part in several billion.

THE BIOSONAR SYSTEM IN BATS

A typical bat feeds mainly on flying insects, which it locates and captures by sending out brief sound pulses and listening for the resulting echo. Biosonar also gauges a target insect's size, vector, bearing, azimuth, range, speed and behavior.

A sound wave has two basic components—amplitude (or loudness) and frequency. However, most natural sound is complex and consists of several frequencies together. Even otherwise "pure" sounds usually carry energy at frequencies that are multiples (harmonics) of the base frequency (the fundamental)—a phenomenon that is exploited by various musical instruments.

The size, texture and behavior of different target objects produce subtle variations in the relative strengths of these harmonics in the resultant echo. Bats are acutely sensitive to such variations in the harmonic "signature" of the echo, and many species can fine-tune both their sound pulses and their hearing while "on the fly" to emphasize or filter out one or other component. Some remove the fundamental entirely from their signals, broadcasting only the harmonics, while others broadcast only fundamentals. It is also common for bats to utter pulses that sweep (often downward) through a considerable range of tonal frequencies.

Air does not absorb sound equally at all frequencies, and a high frequency sound must be louder than a low frequency sound to carry the same distance. The louder the sound, the more the cost in energy to produce, and so the bat must consider a compromise. High frequencies offer more information but don't carry as far, while low frequencies are energetically cheaper to produce and travel farther, but provide less information for the bat to analyze.

Two characteristics of the pulse that the bat emits are also important—the duration of each pulse and the length of time between pulses. If pulses are infrequent, then an insect may have flown completely out of range between one pulse and the next, escaping detection entirely. Even at faster pulse rates, the direction to the target changes much more rapidly for near targets than for distant targets. Near and far objects have different angular velocities (that is, relative to the bat), even though their true velocities may be identical. The duration of the pulse itself is significant: because the behavior of the target continues during the pulse, the resulting echo is "blurrier" with a long pulse and sharper with a brief pulse. Thus the

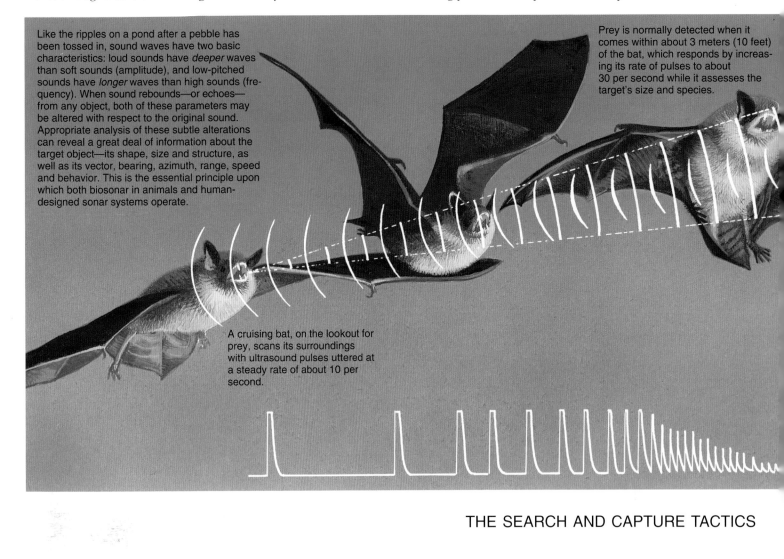

Like the ripples on a pond after a pebble has been tossed in, sound waves have two basic characteristics: loud sounds have *deeper* waves than soft sounds (amplitude), and low-pitched sounds have *longer* waves than high sounds (frequency). When sound rebounds—or echoes—from any object, both of these parameters may be altered with respect to the original sound. Appropriate analysis of these subtle alterations can reveal a great deal of information about the target object—its shape, size and structure, as well as its vector, bearing, azimuth, range, speed and behavior. This is the essential principle upon which both biosonar in animals and human-designed sonar systems operate.

A cruising bat, on the lookout for prey, scans its surroundings with ultrasound pulses uttered at a steady rate of about 10 per second.

Prey is normally detected when it comes within about 3 meters (10 feet) of the bat, which responds by increasing its rate of pulses to about 30 per second while it assesses the target's size and species.

THE SEARCH AND CAPTURE TACTICS

closer the target, the greater the need for short pulses rapidly repeated in order to intercept the target successfully.

Bats characteristically manipulate all of these parameters as they detect and close in on their prey. There are almost as many variations in capture strategies among bats as there are species, but a generalized or reasonably typical pattern has the bat in cruising flight traveling at about 2 to 5 meters (approximately 7 to 16 feet) per second, uttering pulses lasting about 4 milliseconds at a rate of about 10 per second. A potential target is picked up at a range of about 2 to 3 meters (7 to 10 feet), or about 400 to 600 milliseconds before interception. The bat then enters the goal-oriented phase of its attack, increasing its pulse rate to about 25 to 30 pulses per second. At the final interception, the pulse rate may increase to as much as 200 per second.

Efficiency varies widely and depends heavily on prey size, but the bat *Myotis lucifugus*, for example, seems to favor insects averaging about 2 milligrams (.05 ounces) in weight, at a capture rate of about 500 per hour, or 1 every 7 seconds.

Many flying insects have evolved countermeasures against the bat's biosonar systems. Some moths fold their wings and drop instantly to the ground on hearing the bat's approaching pulses. Others emit extremely loud high-frequency calls of their own, in an attempt to jam or swamp the bat's biosonar system and thus avoid being eaten.

Stephen Dalton/NHPA

▲ The biosonar system used by bats is so sophisticated that it can easily penetrate shallow water to detect fish and other small animals below the surface. Some bat species, like this fishing bat (*Noctilio leporimus*), even specialize in hunting such underwater prey.

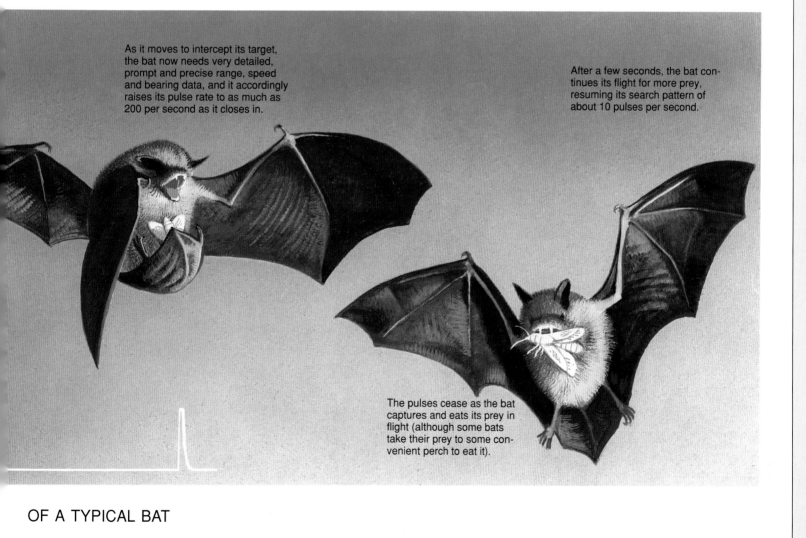

As it moves to intercept its target, the bat now needs very detailed, prompt and precise range, speed and bearing data, and it accordingly raises its pulse rate to as much as 200 per second as it closes in.

After a few seconds, the bat continues its flight for more prey, resuming its search pattern of about 10 pulses per second.

The pulses cease as the bat captures and eats its prey in flight (although some bats take their prey to some convenient perch to eat it).

OF A TYPICAL BAT

Other senses

The sand scorpion of the American southwest lacks well-developed olfactory, visual or auditory systems, but it uses vibrations in the sand to detect its prey. When a potential victim moves on or just under the sand, the scorpion reacts by turning to face the source and moving forward a few centimeters. It then waits immobile until the target moves again, progressively zeroing in on it until it actually touches; then it swiftly grabs it with its pedipalps (pincers) and stings it to death. Over distances of up to 30 centimeters (12 inches) or so, the scorpion seldom requires more than a few such re-orientation pauses to close in on its prey, and the whole thing is usually over within a few seconds.

The scorpion is using vibration-sensitive transducers (mechanoreceptors) in its "feet", and it locates its target by integrating the results from all eight of its sensors which, one on each of its feet, together constitute a sensory net about 10 centimeters (4 inches) across.

Relatives of the scorpions, spiders extend this concept of a sensory net by building webs of fine silk, spun from their own bodies and sometimes spanning several meters. The vibrations caused by struggling insects in the web are conveyed along the silken threads to mechanoreceptors in the spider's feet.

Other animals show a comparable sensitivity to this kind of stimulus. Flea pupae, for example, may lay dormant for months, but respond quickly to any vibrations in the ground

▼ Widespread in southern temperate seas, the lined catfish (*Plotosus lineatus*) favors sheltered inshore waters, where it frequently congregates in large schools. Most other catfish are freshwater species, where they feed on the bottom using a highly developed tactile sense in the feelers under their chin to detect prey.

that may signal the approach of a possible host. They quickly emerge, ready to leap onto the host as it passes. Some animals respond in a similar way to ripples on the surface of water. The whirligig beetle spends its life on the surface of quiet pools, relying on its low mass and relatively large spread of its legs to prevent it from falling through the surface tension of the water. Its antennae are forked, one prong bending downwards to lightly touch the water surface. It can thus "read" the ripples to gain information on nearby obstacles, prey or potential mates. The insect communicates in this way. It taps on the water with its legs to generate a sort of Morse code. Ten taps per minute means "I am female", while 90 taps per minute means "I am male".

Fish use vibrations under water in much the same way as we detect sound in air, but the main organ involved in this process in fish is called the lateral line, an array of mechano-receptors that arch strung out in a line along the fish's sides (as well as, in some fishes, elsewhere on the body).

Other animal senses are even more subtle. Disturbances in water, for example, generate minute voltage fluctuations as well as pressure waves, which a shark (and some other kinds of fish) can detect and use to build up a more precise picture of its surroundings. It is believed that the animal may even use this sense to navigate, responding to almost inconceivably subtle interactions between the earth's magnetic and electrical fields. Small granules of magnetite (a naturally occurring form of iron) have been found in the brains of a range of animals (even humans). The function of this material is still uncertain, but it seems a reasonable guess that its presence is involved in some way with navigation—a sort of built-in compass to steer an animal's direction.

▲ A platypus (*Ornithorhynchus anatinus*) cruising underwater. About the size of a cat, restricted to eastern Australia, and entirely aquatic, the platypus is so bizarre that early zoologists considered the animal a hoax when confronted with the first descriptions and specimens. Lacking any close relative, it is a mammal, yet lays eggs. In place of a conventional nose and jaws it has a supple, leathery-skinned structure resembling a duck's bill. Males have venomous spurs on their hind legs. And it has recently been established that the platypus can locate its underwater prey by detecting their electrical field.

Jean Paul Ferrero/Ardea London

Ron and Valerie Taylor/Ardea London

Communication: an active sensory system

The sensory systems we have looked at so far have one thing in common: they are all passive. The animal merely receives information from its surroundings. However, there are many ways in which the animal can participate in the process, by broadcasting signals and analyzing the resulting differences in the perceived environment in which it lives.

The nerves and muscles of active animals generate minute electrical impulses. These can be used by a predator to detect its prey, especially in water, which conducts electricity much better than air. A number of animals do just this. The platypus (*Ornithorhynchus anatinus*), for example, is capable of detecting field strengths of about 0.0005 volts per centimeter. This sensitivity is ample to sense the proximity of such small aquatic animals as crayfish or yabbies, which generate fields as intense as 0.001 volts per centimeter merely by flicking their tails. The platypus appears to be the only mammal that uses this detection system, but it has many counterparts in the sea. Sharks, rays and catfish have especially well-developed sensory systems of this kind for detecting prey.

A current flowing in one conductor will induce a current in any nearby conductor. Some fish, such as the electric rays, use this principle in their sensory systems. They emit an electrical pulse, and analyze the ways in which this current is modified by their immediate surroundings and the presence of other animals. At least one species, the notorious electric eel (*Electrophorus electricus*) of South America, goes one step further and uses its electric "battery" to stun its prey as well as detect it. The generating cells are large, disk-shaped, and arranged like stacks of coins in about 70 rows in the eel's tail. Over half of the eel's total body is given over to its battery, which can deliver a current of about 100 watts at nearly 600 volts. Such an incredible discharge could easily light up a row of common light bulbs.

Biosonar

Even at its most sophisticated, such a system is useful only at relatively short ranges of a meter (3 feet) or so. But there are other possibilities for what might be termed "active" sensory systems of this kind. Sound offers especially rich potential in this regard, even to humans, and medical technology is vigorously exploring

▼ A sand-tiger shark (*Eugomphodus taurus*). This rather sluggish shark inhabits shallow inshore waters in all oceans, with a habitual tendency to cruise slowly with its mouth open, exposing its ragged, formidable teeth. It will often approach skindivers and spearfishermen, and may attempt to steal their catch, but despite its formidable appearance it is not especially dangerous to humans.

its promise in such techniques as CAT scans and similar procedures. As is so often the case however, animals have already developed such systems to amazing levels of sophistication.

If we shout in a large, dark, underground cave the sound echoes. We can gain a good deal of information from assessing how the echo differs from the original sound—how large the cave is, how far up the roof is, and even some sense of whether it is empty or cluttered with stalactites or similar objects. We are using an elementary biosonar system.

The biosonar system used by bats is by far the most sophisticated of all such systems used by animals on land. When searching for prey, the bat utters a series of sound pulses at very high frequency, then listens for an echo. Some bats channel sound energy through the nose, others through the mouth, and the huge variety of facial adornments on the faces of bats can for the most part be viewed in terms of structures that modify the emitted sound in various ways, much like the design of a megaphone. It is also useful to regard the sound pulses themselves as being of two basic types: some bats (the so-called CF group) utter sound pulses at a constant frequency, while others (the FM group) utter pulses that sweep through a range of frequencies. Many bats mix both kinds, according to circumstances. Other critical components include the duration of each pulse and its harmonic structure. Much of the significance of these distinctions rests on whether the bat is operating in cluttered, "noisy" environments (such as a tropical rainforest), or more open environments, such as a grassy meadow or an open field.

The complexity of this system is extraordinary, and one bat species or another exploits virtually every conceivable nuance inherent in the behavior of sound reflections in air. Some bats exploit the Doppler effect to the full, and utter pulses that sweep through a range of frequencies; the bat analyzes the resulting phase shift to access the velocity, bearing and range of its target. There are even "whispering" bats and "noisy" bats.

Another way of visualizing the amazing precision of the system is to test the bat's ability in a three-dimensional laboratory "maze" of thin wires. The bat *Megaderma lyra*, for example, apparently experiences no difficulty in navigating safely through a maze of wires no thicker than a human hair. It can even go between wires that are so close that it must fold its wings briefly to get through.

However impressive the bat's biosonar, there are animals that may improve on it. Sound behaves differently in water than it does in air, and it is strongly influenced by such variables as temperature, pressure and salinity. Sound

Stan Osolinski/Oxford Scientific Films

travels about five times as fast in water as it does in air, which means that a water-based sonar system must be five times as efficient as an air-based system in order to provide the same information. Nevertheless, dolphins catch much of their food using biosonar and, like bats, can utter and detect sound at frequencies ranging up to 200,000 hertz. In fact it may be that some cetaceans may, like the electric eel, use their biosonar to finish the job. Some whales utter the loudest of all animal sounds, somewhere in the vicinity of 190 to 200 decibels (for comparison, we experience discomfort at about 150 decibels). Sound energies at this level must have devastating effects on nearby fish, and the whale may use such a blast of sound to stun or kill its prey.

Some animals, especially in the sea, use light in similar active sensory systems. The lantern-eyed fishes (family Anomalopidae) have a small pouch-like organ under each eye, which contains light-producing bacteria. These bacteria produce light constantly, but the fish can switch the light on and off at will by drawing a fold of flesh across the organ. Many other deep-sea fish, such as the bizarre gulpers (family Eurypharyngidae) and dragonfish, genus *Grammatostomias,* are equipped with light-emitting organs of various kinds. In some dragonfish the lights may be towards or at the

▲ Common across much of North America, the northern mockingbird (*Mimus polyglottus*) is only one of a number of bird species around the world that incorporate mimicry into their songs. One theory to account for such behavior suggests that in these birds the female might select her mate largely on the basis of the range and complexity of his song, and the simplest way a male can increase his repertoire, and thus increase his attractiveness to females, is to borrow other natural sounds.

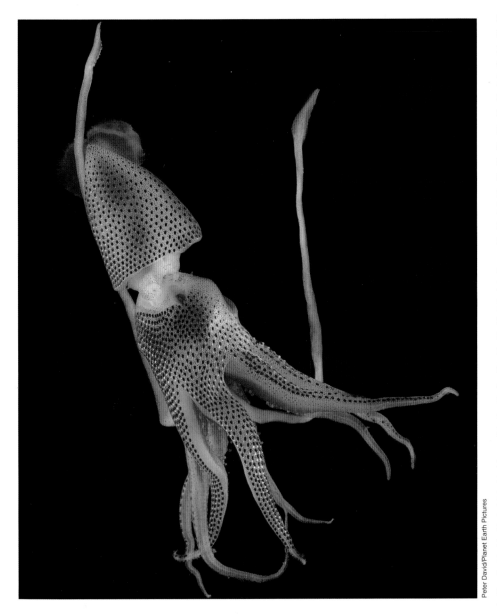

▲ Many squid have an unusual method of locomotion, being able to expel water from the body cavity, resulting in a sort of jet-propulsion. This species is *Histiotenthis bonelli*, which is also remarkable in having an array of light-emitting organs, of uncertain function.

Peter David/Planet Earth Pictures

controls the reaction by admitting or shutting off the oxygen supply to these cells, so that males and females are seen to communicate with flashes of light in a sort of Morse code. Each species has its characteristic code. Males of one species, for example, cruise around after dark, flying about a meter from the ground and signaling with 0.5 second flashes every 7 seconds; a receptive female responds with a 0.5 second flash about 3 seconds after the male. In some species, the insects congregate in huge numbers in particular areas to flash, covering bushes and trees with tiny flashing lights, resulting in a spectacle which has few equals in the natural world.

Communication: talking to others

It is in many ways a natural progression from passive sensory systems through active sensory systems to systems involving the broadcasting of signals with the particular intent of having them intercepted by other individuals of the same species. In short: communication. Animals broadcast a wide range of messages, especially of the general kind, "I want a mate" or "this land is mine", using almost the entire range of possible media: light, sound, smell.

Perhaps the oldest form of communication involves chemical senses. For example, the female of the silkworm moth (*Bombyx mori*) releases a chemical from a gland at the tip of her abdomen. Known as bombykol, this chemical attracts males when she is ready to mate. The male detects this chemical when molecules of the substance diffuse into fluid at the core of minute hairs that cover his antennae, a sensory system so sensitive that it responds to a saturation corresponding to 1 molecule of bombykol to 10^{16} molecules of air. What is more, the male moth can assess a concentration gradient of 10,000-fold, so he can hone in on the source of the scent with equally extraordinary precision. Many social insects, such as ants and termites, have evolved extremely intricate chemical codes.

Sound is a very common communication medium among animals. It is energetically costly, but has the considerable advantage that it can be turned on and off instantly at will (a useful characteristic if you're a very small animal and happen to suspect a very large predator close by!). Such broadcasts use sound outside the range audible to human ears. Elephants, for example, use infrasound to communicate over great distances.

The most complex of these systems is probably the song of the humpback whale. Males utter a range of sounds in "concerts" lasting 10 minutes or more; the same sequence of sounds is then repeated exactly, sometimes for hours at a time. In any given area all the

end of a wire-like barbel sometimes five times longer than the fish itself. Perhaps the most remarkable of all is *Pachystomias* sp., a deep-sea fish that is the true inventor of the sniperscope, or infra-red imaging system. This extraordinary fish spies on its prey in the red glow of its lights, to which its prey is blind.

For the most part, nobody really knows how these deep-sea systems work. Presumably they either attract prey, repel predators or attract mates, but the details remain obscure. Much more is known about bioluminescence in land animals such as insects.

The best known of these are beetles (fireflies) of the families Elateridae, Phengodidae, and Lampyridae, which actively use their lights in courtship. In these insects the last two segments of the abdomen contain a layer of light-producing cells (photocytes) backed by a layer of reflective cells. Light is produced in the photocytes by a chemical reaction between oxygen and a substance called lucerferin in the presence of the enzyme luciferin. The beetle males sing the same song, but the song changes through time and in all males. This means that the song uttered by any one male each breeding season differs from the song used the year before. Moreover, the behavior of sound in salt water is such that the sounds uttered by whales may carry for enormous distances—perhaps thousands of kilometers under some circumstances.

established. Others have two distinct repertoires of songs, one series used in territorial contexts, the other in sexual.

Among all animals on Earth, only humans appear to have a fully developed language able to convey abstractions and such intangibles as mood and tense from one individual to another. But some other animals come surprisingly close. In captive situations, several species have

Ken Lucas/Planet Earth Pictures

But the most familiar of all is bird song. It is useful to distinguish between two kinds of bird vocalizations, even though the difference resists precise definition. Some sounds are uttered by both sexes throughout the year, and have no link with courtship or breeding: such sounds are conveniently referred to as calls. Some sounds, termed "songs", are uttered only during the breeding season.

Some of these performances are very beautiful to human ears, and such notable songsters as the nightingale and the skylark have inspired some of the finest poetry in the world. But the true purpose of bird song is not to please poets; it is used to defend territory, or to attract a mate, or both. In some species, such as the European robin (*Erithacus rubecula*) and the rufous whistler (*Pachycephala rufiventris*) of Australia, both males and females sing the same songs more or less indiscriminately, and defend their mutual territory with equal vigor. Other birds sing chiefly to attract mates, using visual threat displays to deal with trespassers; these usually cease singing once the pair bond is

been taught artificial languages enabling a degree of communication between themselves and their human trainers. Dr Louis Herman and his team at the University of Hawaii, for example, have constructed two languages for use with trained bottle-nosed dolphins (*Tursiops truncatus*): one based on sounds, the other on gestures. These languages contain nouns ("ball", "hoop", and so on), verbs ("fetch", etc.) and such qualifiers as "up", "down", "right" and "left". Working with these languages, the dolphins appear to have some concept of semantics and syntax, and can construct and comprehend simple sentences. Similarly, other researchers have adapted Ameslan (an artificial human sign language for the deaf) to use with chimpanzees (*Pan troglodytes*). Through such media chimpanzees have learned to communicate not only with their human trainers but—perhaps more remarkably—with each other, and two chimpanzees have even been "overheard" using such a language to utter the approximate equivalent of "pass the hammer please".

▲ A portrait of *Photoblepharon palpebratus*, a member of the family Anomalopidae, or flashlight fishes. Aptly named, members of this extraordinary group have a pouch under each eye, in which live multitudes of luminescent bacteria. The fish can dim its "headlights", or even turn them off, by drawing a fold of skin across the entrance to the pouch.

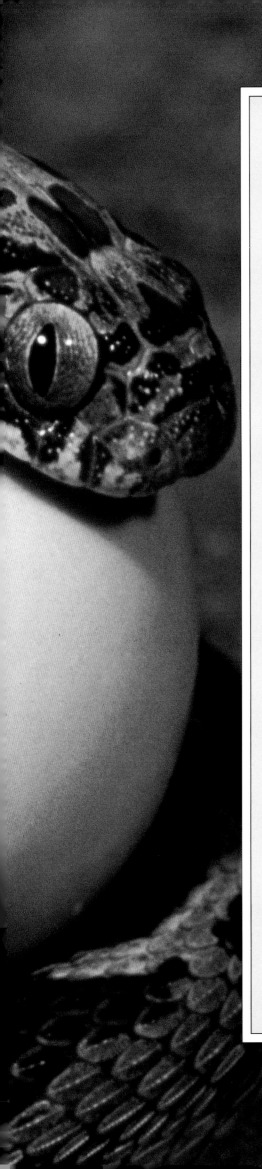

Chapter 2

FINDING FOOD

Tim Guilford

Driven by the inescapable need to be fed, the animal kingdom has developed a variety of marvelous responses.

PREDATORY SKILL
The most majestic of predators is the cheetah—the fastest hunter on Earth. It is a solitary hunter that carefully stalks its prey before launching into attack.

THE STAGES OF PREDATION
Ingenious predatory skills have been developed in response to the problems faced by animals. These come in four main stages: detection, identification, approach and subjugation.

DETECTING AND IDENTIFYING PREY
Most things in a predator's world are inedible objects, so prey have first to be detected among a welter of background confusion.

APPROACH AND SUBJUGATION
A variety of adaptations ensures the success of an animal's approach to its prey.

WELFARE STATES
Not all animals find their food through stealth, speed or sensory sophistication, and rely early in their lives on the goodwill of others.

LIVING OFF OTHERS
Animal parents find sustenance for their offspring. Some species work together, while others benefit through theft.

ADVANCED PREDATORY SKILLS
Over time, predators and prey have developed some formidable weapons. The simplest structures are the most effective.

ENERGY FROM THE SUN
Converting the sun's energy into carbohydrate through photosynthesis, plants are the Earth's food producers on which all animals ultimately rely.

PLANNING AHEAD
Humans were not the first to invent farming. Animal specialists like social insects have some very intricate plans.

FINDING FOOD

Tim Guilford

Right across the animal kingdom, predatory behavior has evolved in response to the problems faced by animals in the four stages essential to finding food: detection, identification, approach and subjugation.

PREDATORY SKILL

Grazing in huge herds on the grasslands of the Serengeti Plains in the midday heat of East Africa, wildebeest, gazelles, impala and other large herbivorous mammals may seem invulnerable to predation. But this is the domain of the fastest land predator on Earth, the cheetah (*Acinonyx jubatus*). The cheetah is a solitary hunter, and, with its coat camouflaged against the background, relies on the advantages of stealth. With keen eyesight, smell and hearing, it detects and identifies its potential quarry (a wildebeest calf perhaps) from a distance. The cheetah then carefully stalks its prey until it has approached, unseen, to within about 100 meters (330 feet). This slow approach can take minutes, or hours, and is in stark contrast to the next stage of the hunt: When the cheetah judges that it is close enough to stand a good chance of capture (half its chases will be unsuccessful), it breaks cover and accelerates toward the prey. With its

Gunter Ziesler/Bruce Coleman Limited

unusually flexible back, long legs, and sharp claws for traction like track-runner's shoes, it can reach a top speed of up to 100 to 110 kilometers (60 to 70 miles) per hour within seconds. As long as the prey is caught unawares, it will be outpaced before the cheetah tires. Powerful paws with semiretractable claws now fully extended, plus the force of impact, may bring down an animal easily half the cheetah's weight. And as the cheetah locks its jaws tight onto the prey's neck, breathing through specially designed nostrils to allow its grip never to slacken while the prey struggles, the animal eventually suffocates and is dragged into hiding to be eaten.

THE STAGES OF PREDATION

The cheetah is a supreme predator. But right across the animal kingdom, predatory practices have evolved in response to the problems posed by the four stages in the essential process of finding food before consumption: detection, identification, approach and subjugation. At

JM Labat/Ardea London

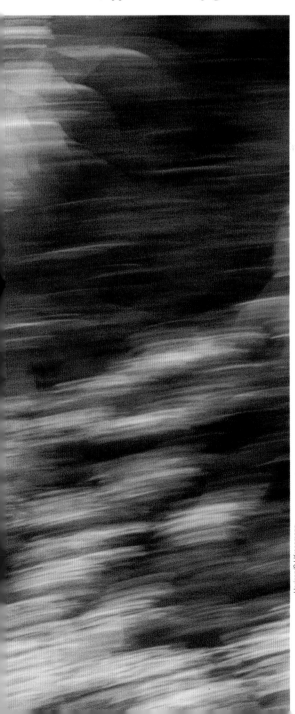

Horizon/SJ Krasemann

each stage of the process, animals have adapted their strategies to suit their own habits and environments. And the result has been a bewildering array of predatory practices.

DETECTING AND IDENTIFYING PREY

Most things in a predator's world are inedible objects, so prey have first to be detected among a welter of background confusion. Furthermore, no self-respecting victim will allow itself to be detected easily, unless of course it is dangerous and to be avoided anyway. Vulnerable prey themselves have evolved all manner of mechanisms to evade detection and identification: by keeping still, by camouflaging themselves, or by conducting business at times when predation is difficult. But the strategies ranged against them are awesome and highly skilled.

As we have seen in Chapter One, the keen eyesight of birds like raptors, great predators of the skies, is legendary. In the task of detecting and identifying prey, however, natural selection has equipped such predators with a range of advanced adaptations that go beyond mere acuity. Detection and targeting are further aided by one of natural selection's most ingenious

▲ A peregrine falcon (*Falco peregrinus*) mantles its prey, a pigeon, as it plucks and dismembers it. Falcons specialize in catching other birds in flight, overwhelming them by sheer speed like a sort of avian cheetah. The mantling reflex, partly spreading the wings over the victim, is well developed in birds of prey.

◄ (*facing page*) An Atlantic puffin (*Fratercula arctica*) returning to its Shetland Island colony with sand-eels for its young. Carrying the small fish neatly aligned in a row like this is typical of puffins, a neat trick considering how difficult it must be to catch a fish with a bill stuffed with three or four others.

◄ A leopard (*Panthera pardus*) runs off with its prey in its mouth. Leopards prefer to lug their prey up into trees for consumption at leisure, mainly to avoid losing it to lions, hyenas and others.

▲ Turkey vultures (*Cathartes aura*) sunning themselves on cardon cactus in Mexico. Broad wings make soaring easy but flapping them is hard work. So before setting out on the daily routine of scanning the ground far below for carrion, vultures usually wait until the morning sun has had plenty of time to warm the air and create vigorous thermals. Like elevators, these columns of rapidly rising air provide a free ride high into the sky. Until then, vultures sit idly on dead trees and perches.

inventions: binocular vision. Such "stereoscopic" vision allows the precise perception of depth and distance, which is especially important for a raptor on the wing hunting for fast-moving prey, or hovering in the sky above. Thus, in the Eurasian kestrel (*Falco tinnunculus*), the eyes are positioned toward the front of the head, giving a 50 degree overlap in the visual field. However, in a granivorous bird picking immobile grains from the background,

the eyes are positioned on either side of the head, allowing an almost spherical field of vision around the bird, ensuring that there is no blind spot from which a predator might approach unseen, but giving little ability to perceive depth and distance through binocular vision. Especially in owls, depth perception is further enhanced by frequent changes of head position, allowing the target to be compared from different angles.

Jen & Des Bartlett/Bruce Coleman Limited

Movement is a vital clue to the presence of live prey, and many visual hunters have become especially sensitive to it. Dragonflies and praying mantids, predators of the insect world, have large compound eyes which may not provide as distinct a picture of the world as in the vertebrate eye, but do provide excellent perception of movement. Work on amphibians shows that special groups of neurones in the brain are sensitive to the movement of prey-like objects across the visual field, and are involved in triggering the animal's predatory lunge-and-snap response. In toads that specialize on "worm-like" prey, such neurones are more responsive to the presence of horizontal edges than are those found in species of frogs that specialize on "fly-like" prey. It is almost as if these predators have specially tuned "prey detectors" appropriate for locating and recognizing the right kind of prey, although how exactly these are configured in the brain remains a mystery.

In some birds, and perhaps other animals as well, the problems of visual prey detection can be solved in a more flexible way. The ability to · detect particular types of camouflaged prey becomes enhanced by encountering a number of such prey in quick succession. As it is, insectivorous birds are excellent at picking out cryptic prey from the background—this is why insects have themselves evolved such an enormous variety of strategies for avoiding detection—but where a particular prey type is · especially abundant, it will pay to concentrate on searching for its distinctive characteristics. No one is yet sure exactly how they do it, but birds such as the blue jay (*Cyanocitta cristata*) get better at "seeing" a particular moth's pattern after just one or two successful captures. One idea is that this may occur through the formation of detection filters, or "search images", allowing the animal to concentrate the efforts of its visual perception system most

efficiently, and ignore less relevant stimuli. One problem with a search image is that while it may make one type of moth easier to detect, it may actually make detection of other dissimilar patterns more difficult. The bird solves this problem by allowing the search image to fade away as soon as it is no longer in use.

Visual prey detection and identification is sophisticated, but even in birds, those most visual of animals, it isn't everything. For a long time birds were thought to live without a functional sense of smell, but recently biologists have demonstrated that several species use olfaction to help them find their food. Nowhere is this ability more developed than in the kiwi (*Apteryx australis*), a flightless bird endemic to New Zealand where it hunts by night for invertebrates hidden in forest soils. Kiwis have tiny eyes, but, uniquely among birds, their nostrils are ideally located in the tip of their long beak for sniffing out the presence and position of what would otherwise be virtually undetectable prey. The kiwi has a relatively

▼ One of the most common owls over much of Britain and Europe, a tawny owl (*Strix aluco*) fetches home a rabbit for its young. On the whole, owls take similar prey to eagles and hawks, but hawks hunt by day, leaving owls to take the night shift.

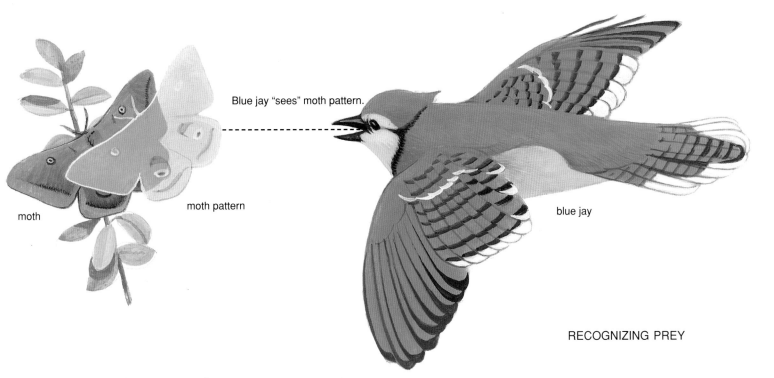

Blue jay "sees" moth pattern.

moth

moth pattern

blue jay

RECOGNIZING PREY

Melvin Grey/NHPA

large olfactory bulb area in the brain, thought to be important in the processing of olfactory information, and this feature is common to several other bird species with nostrils in a more normal position further back up the beak. One example is the snow petrel (*Pagodroma nivea*), an Antarctic seabird that can, under test conditions, distinguish a floating sponge soaked in fish oil at a distance from a control sponge that looks identical but does not smell.

In the often relatively featureless oceans, predatory sharks use their excellent odor sensitivity to detect and locate a distant blood source (perhaps an injured prey) by sensing tiny concentrations in the water (as low as 1 part per million). Many mammals, too, are famous for their olfactory ability, which often supersedes vision as the primary sense not only for finding food, but also in social communication and for detecting the proximity of predators. The humble rat (*Rattus norvegicus*), rarely admired, often feared, discriminates between foods with subtly different odors; learns to avoid those that may previously have caused sickness, and to prefer others. Such skills may be a nuisance to the farmer, contributing to the costly phenomenon of "bait-shyness", but they are part of the rat's great adaptability. Scientists have now shown that rats can also acquire food-odor preferences from each other, and by sniffing the face of a recently fed companion can gather information about what food sources are currently available. In a similar way, by sniffing they may even learn to detect and avoid substances that have poisoned companions.

▲ Experiments with blue jays (a common American woodland bird) shed some light on the prey-seeking mechanisms used by birds. After a few successful captures of a particular prey species, the blue jay behaves very much as though it had formed a mental "search image" based on the most prominent characteristics of the prey, using this image as a sort of mental template to filter out all extraneous information.

Similar stories could be told about the impressive hearing abilities of owls, or the extraordinary echolocation skills of bats (explored in Chapter One), but often the message will be the same. Hunters not only have spectacular sensory acuity, but use a whole range of adaptations in the process of detecting and identifying food, including special physical structures, sophisticated behavioral strategies, and even modifications of the brain itself.

APPROACH AND SUBJUGATION

The four stages of predation before consumption may not always be distinct, but it is intriguing to focus on the different stages and wonder at how the adaptations have evolved for their execution in different animals. For some hunters, approach is not a problem, for they simply keep still and lie in wait for their unsuspecting prey to come to them. They are the hunters by stealth, and their patient adaptations are curious and intricate. Herons (Ardeidae) stand waiting motionless in shallow waters, poised to strike with their lethal beak any small fish that swim within range. But why is it that herons can sometimes be seen leaning to one side? A strange sight indeed, yet it may have a perfectly sensible explanation. By casting a shadow the hunter can see into the water more clearly and block out the potentially confusing glare from its surface. Praying mantids, with their huge compound eyes mounted on rotatable heads, and powerful

MPL Fogden/Bruce Coleman Limited

▼ An Indian pond heron (*Ardeola grayii*). In the main, herons hunt by stealth and patient stalking, wading in water in search of fish, frogs and other aquatic animals.

GK Brown/Ardea London

claw-like front legs, are awesome predators of the insect world. Some are sit-and-wait predators, and the flower mantids, in particular, have perfected their stealth by camouflaging themselves with strange protuberances on the limbs that look like petals. But there is a puzzle. Flower mantids don't always sit completely motionless after all, but sway from side to side. Why? One possibility is that this advances their camouflage still further by mimicking the natural movements that plants make in a gentle breeze. The neotropical vine snake (*Oxybelis aeneus*) manages to camouflage its own locomotion in this way too, moving, as it were, one step back with each two forward in a pendulous motion that mimics the movement of surrounding vegetation and conceals the snake's progress. Furthermore, so as to approach its lizard prey undetected, the snake only moves when the vegetation is itself moving usually with a breeze.

Speed is the essence of approach and subjugation for many top predators. We have noted already the cheetah's high performance credentials, but for prey in the air danger can approach faster still. Having located and identified a small bird as potential quarry with its sharp eyes from hundreds of feet up, the peregrine falcon (*Falco peregrinus*) draws its relatively slender-tipped wings into its streamlined body and swoops at a top speed of 290 kilometers (180 miles) per hour. There is no faster animal on Earth, and as the falcon hits its prey near the head with its claws clenched to form a club, the unsuspecting quarry is inevitably stunned and drops to the ground. There it is later killed, sometimes with a neat, neck-breaking twist of the beak inserted between the vertebrae.

The approach and subjugation of prey may be further enhanced if hunters co-operate. This is particularly true where the prey is too large to be manageable by the solo predator. On the African savannas, for example, huge herds of migratory ungulates promise rich rewards for those hunters that can tackle the massive size and strength of the zebra or the buffalo. That most majestic of all predators, the lion (*Panthera leo*), lives in a "pride" of between perhaps 4 and 12 related females, and 2 or 3 adult males who may be half-brothers to each other but are likely to be unrelated to the females. It is the lionesses that do most of the hunting, often co-operating in subgroups,

A LION HUNT

The lioness separates a zebra from the herd.

The lioness is usually the hunter of the pride. Favorite prey are hoofed mammals such as zebras and wildebeests.

A lion and lioness observe their potential prey.

She gathers speed to catch her prey
and chooses her time to pounce.

The hunt is complete. Another member
of the pride helps with the kill.

The lion moves in to
share the feast.

The pride benefits from the hunt.
Cubs are the last to eat.

▲ A red-billed oxpecker (*Buphagus erythrorhynchus*) searches for ticks in a herd of hippos (*Hippopotamus amphibius*). Hippos are completely aquatic by day, congregating in herds of up to 150 or so, but they scatter ashore to feed on short grass at night.

usually at night. Lions are slower than cheetahs, but by partially encircling their prey they reduce the chances of being outrun before one of them manages to claw or swipe their quarry to the ground. By defending their kill as a group, they are also less likely to subsequently lose it to hyenas.

Hyenas also hunt co-operatively, heading out at nightfall onto the plains in groups comprising the appropriate number of hunters best suited to bringing down a particular target species. It is as if they discuss the night's hunting, and how best to succeed with it, before they leave for the kill.

Both lions and hyenas co-operate with members of their own species, often with individuals that are their blood relatives, so even if the benefits of group foraging are not always equally distributed this may be compensated for by reciprocation on later trips,

or by the advantages of helping kin. In some species, though, group associations are transient. Blackheaded gulls (*Larus ridibundus*), dive for small fish that shoal near the surface off northern shores around the world. Solitary birds find it hard to isolate fish from the shoal, perhaps because the fish can themselves follow the approaching gull's movements. So blackheaded gulls have conspicuous white and black plumage that helps others spot them from a distance and fly in to join the hunting when a shoal has been found. When gulls hunt in a group, fish seem confused by the birds approaching from all angles, and are easily separated and caught. There is no altruism in this co-operation because it benefits everyone to be in a larger group (up to a point at least), but nevertheless it too is predation expertise even though it is not as highly organized as that of lions and hyenas.

the kiwi spends most of its childhood inside the egg, buffered from the outside world, feeding off the carefully balanced diet provided for it in the enormous yolk sac.

In many fish, eggs are relatively small when they are released into the ocean currents, as in the coral reef dwelling blueheaded wrasse (*Thalassoma bifasciatum*), or into the shallow gravel beds of freshwater streams, as in the Atlantic salmon (*Salom salar*). Even after they have hatched and have consumed their small yolk sac of food, they are still tiny "fry", a fraction of adult dimensions. Yet now they must fend for themselves and find their own food as tiny predators or scavengers in their own right. The larvae of most invertebrates face forced self-sufficiency at a very early stage too. But it is those animals that take the duties of

▲ On sub-Antarctic islands, where other scavengers are few, southern giant petrels (*Macronectes giganteus*) fulfill much the same role as vultures and hyenas in other areas. The bird at center with its wings spread is a black-browed albatross (*Diomedea melanophrys*) ready for take-off.

▼ Hyenas are often thought of as solitary scavengers, but spotted hyenas (*Crocuta crocuta*) live in packs of up to 50 or so with a complex social system, and are in fact among the largest of carnivores. Hunting co-operatively, they are quite capable of bringing down prey as large as zebras or antelopes. Here a pack feeds in the Masai Mara Reserve, Kenya.

WELFARE STATES

Not all animals find their food through stealth, speed or sensory sophistication, and rely early in their lives on the goodwill of others. Parents must find food not just for themselves, but also for their offspring, and are the great providers of the animal kingdom. No animal, however good a survivor, however well designed, will make an impact on Earth without reproducing. In the kiwi, females lay a single egg some 20 percent as large as themselves, which is 60 to 65 percent energy-rich yolk (an "average" bird of the kiwi's dimensions would be expected to produce an egg a quarter the size, and nearer 40 percent yolk). This perhaps is not surprising when we learn that when the chick hatches, after two and a half months' incubation by the male, it is 8.4 percent of adult weight, four times that expected for a typical precocial bird, and already almost fully independent. It is as if

ECONOMIC DECISION-MAKING IN STARLINGS

▲ A flock of starlings congregates to bathe.

During the breeding season, European starlings (*Sturnus vulgaris*) have to face a rather formidable foraging task. Rather than simply finding food for themselves, they now have to find food for their chicks and bring it back to the nest hole. Parents hunt for prey, generally tipulid larvae, known as "leather jackets", in the fields around the nest hole, and collect them in their beaks. You might think that it would be a simple matter for a starling to decide when it was time to return to the nest with its load. After all, there is a limit to the number of prey that the bird can hold, or fly with. But the interesting thing is that starlings seem to return home before they have a full load. So why is this?

Biologists who have studied starlings in detail are convinced that there is a sophisticated economic logic behind the bird's behavior. As a bird collects prey in its beak, it constantly faces the decision of when it should stop hunting and return to the nest. As the number of prey items in the bill mounts up, the bill itself becomes a less effective foraging tool. Having a half-full beak makes it difficult to probe the grass in search of more prey, and may make them more difficult to pick up when they are found. Consequently, the bird faces diminishing returns before its beak is actually full. The really interesting thing is that if the journey between nest and field is short, then, according to the theory, a bird would maximize its total rate of prey capture by taking relatively small loads back to the nest, but if the journey is long, it would do better, waste less time, by being more persistent and collecting more before returning. And this is exactly what starlings do. By providing starlings with food items delivered at predetermined and diminishing rates into special feeders at different distances from the nest, biologists have managed to determine exactly when birds decide to stop foraging and leave for home. They leave earlier, and collect fewer prey at a time, if the journey is short.

We do not know how the starling makes its decisions. All we know is that those birds that make the right ones, economically speaking, will tend to be more successful breeders and leave more offspring to survive into the next season.

So, how far does the starling's flexibility and sophistication go when it comes to gathering food? The work load that each parent puts in depends on the number of chicks in the nest. What this means is that when, for some reason, they have only a small brood neither parent is working at full capacity. Why not, since this would surely increase the chicks' survival prospects? The answer seems to be that parents face a long-term trade-off. Working harder to find food for their young now brings diminishing returns for already well-fed chicks, but reduces the bird's capacity to survive the following winter to breed again next year (or, exceptionally, to breed again that same year). Biologists have shown that although both parents will normally work roughly equally to provision their young, by attaching tiny weights to their tail feathers one partner can be made to slow down. What is intriguing is that the other partner will now try to compensate by working harder. The economics of providing for the young is a sophisticated business.

Remarkably, birds also seem able to make sophisticated trade-offs with risks and dangers to survival that are more difficult to measure. As well as consuming energy and taking time, flight has another potential cost: it is dangerous. In one experiment, biologists demonstrated that starlings seem to be quite calculating about how risky a flight path they are prepared to take to find food. When starlings had to fly through gaps to collect rewards at a choice of feeders, they naturally preferred the feeders with wider gaps, even when these provided slightly less food at each delivery. However, when the birds were hungry, they switched preference and flew through the narrower gaps to obtain food at a higher rate. Natural selection seems to have provided birds, and other animals too, with a capacity to make quite sophisticated decisions in their quest to collect food efficiently, taking into account, amongst other things, diminishing return rates and travel times, the value of future against current reproductive investment, and the risks of starvation, predation and collision associated with particular foraging options. The starling, farmland pest, and favorite of few, turns out, nonetheless, to be a sophisticated decision-maker when the issue is that of survival.

parenthood more seriously that we are concerned with here. Even in fish and invertebrates we can find strange examples. In the mouth-brooding cichlid (*Astatilapia elegans*), a small tropical lake-dwelling fish from East Africa, the female incubates her egg batches by taking them up in her mouth until they hatch and become free-swimming (about two weeks). In other species it is sometimes the male that specializes in parental care, hovering around his offspring while they feed on plankton. When danger approaches, the male allows the fry to swim into his mouth.

Of course, provisioning can continue well beyond hatching or birth, where perhaps nature's most useful invention is milk, a carefully balanced liquid diet of water, proteins, fats and carbohydrates. There is no one milk, for in different species its composition seems to be adapted to the provisioning needs of a particular life history. Probably because of their need to survive the rigors of life in cold water from an early age, elephant seal pups (genus *Mirounga*), for example, take just three weeks to grow to four times their birth weight of about 45 kilograms (100 pounds). They do it by feeding on a milk extremely rich in fats. Kangaroos, on the other hand, are born weighing as little as 0.3 gram (0.01 ounce) and then crawl to the temperature-balanced safety

▼ A common turtledove (*Streptopelia turtur*) feeding its young at the nest. Unusually amongst birds, pigeons and doves feed their young on "milk", a nutritious secretion of the crop.

Melvin Grey/NHPA

▶ A clown anemone-fish (*Amphiprion ocellaris*) shelters among the poisonous stinging tentacles of a sea anemone. These coral reef fishes live in a peculiar relationship with sea anemones, cleaning debris from the tentacles in return for safe haven from predators. A secretion on the anemone's tentacles both repels and inhibits the stinging reflex of its neighbors, so that the animal does not sting itself to death instead of its prey. The anemone-fish avoids harm because the mucus that covers its body contains a chemical that mimics this same inhibiting substance.

Ken Lucas/Planet Earth Pictures

of the mother's pouch where they will stay, exclusively at first, for another 5 to 11 months (depending on the species). Even then, suckling may continue for a further 2 to 6 months after finally leaving the pouch. Initially, the mother provides a milk that is very low in fat content for her well-protected offspring, though this increases in a carefully controlled fashion as the baby grows and its nutritional requirements change.

Milk is not of course provided free. In the red deer (*Cervus elaphus*) living in the difficult conditions of the isle of Rhum off the coast of Scotland, lactation presents a greater drain on a mother's resources than the entire period of gestation. If she has produced a male calf one year, she may even have insufficient strength to breed at all in the next season.

It is not only young mammals that find their food by relying on their mother's milk. Pigeons and doves produce their own nutritious secretion known as "crop milk", with which to supplement their squabs' diet. About halfway through the incubation period, in both parents, the epithelium of the crop (a structure usually used for storing seeds immediately after a feeding bout) starts to thicken and eventually produces fat-and protein-rich cells which are sloughed into the crop and regurgitated for the young. Strangest of all, perhaps, are the nutritious skin secretions exuded by Amazonian freshwater cichlids known as discus fish. In the green discus fish (*Symphosodon aequifasciata aequifasciata*) the fry attach themselves to the skin of one of the parents as soon as their yolk sacs are exhausted, and feed exclusively on the nutritious white mucus the adult produces specially for the task. Parents take it in turn to feed the young, and when it is time to change over they swim beside each other, the one parent vibrating its body until the fry swim across to the other.

▼ Nocturnal like almost all bats, the South American vampire bat (*Desmodus rotundus*) feeds on the blood of birds and mammals, gently shaving layer after layer of skin with its razor teeth until the wound starts to bleed, then lapping up the resulting flow.

Merlin D. Tuttle/Bat Conservation International

Parents provide food for their young in other ways too. Many songbirds are hatched long before they are capable of finding food for themselves, and will sit in the nest offering their huge, brightly colored gapes to a parent returning from one of a continuous round of foraging trips throughout the day, trying to "persuade" that it is their turn to be fed. The noisy, conspicuous begging displays of nestling birds may seem anarchic, but recent theory suggests that the display may actually provide the parent with a reliable indication of which exactly needs food most, or which it would be most prudent to feed. Since the display is itself energy consuming, its intensity can give a combined indication of the chick's need and strength. Paradoxical, we might think, but we should not forget that in the long run it may not pay to feed the hungriest chick if prey is scarce and it is unlikely to survive anyway. It would be like throwing good money after bad. Indeed, in some birds of prey, it is quite usual for one chick to be hatched late and allowed to die early on. It's a kind of insurance policy: in the unlikely event that the season turns out to be exceptionally good for feeding chicks, two young may be raised instead of one.

In hyenas, providing food for the young may not be so frenetic, but it is equally arduous. As the great ungulate migrations across the African savannas progress, parents are forced to make longer and longer forays away from the den, and may sometimes leave home for ten days.

Exactly how they navigate over such distances is still something of a mystery. Insects are also experts at navigating home to provision their nests after foraging trips. Digger wasps, such as *Bembix rostrata*, stock individual underground cells with a larder of paralyzed fresh prey ready for the emergence of their hatchling larvae. The position of local landmarks around the otherwise inconspicuous nest entrance are memorized as useful cues.

Nowhere is provisioning taken more seriously than in the tiny mites of the genus *Adactylidium*, where the young not only hatch inside their mother, but also eat her from the inside out before they are ready to emerge and find food for themselves. Can such parental behavior really make economic sense in the harsh world of natural selection? At least where it has been studied in detail, as in the European starling (*Sturnus vulgaris*), it seems so.

LIVING OFF OTHERS
Adaptations for provisioning make good evolutionary sense for both provider and provisioned alike, but nature is not always so harmonious. In a myriad different ways, animals have evolved strategies for living off the enforced generosity of others.

We have seen already that group foraging can benefit everyone that takes part, but things are not always as simple as this. Dominant individuals may often gain more than their fair share, as if they were using subordinate

individuals as food finders. In New World Harris sparrows (*Zonotrichia querula*), foraging flocks consist of individuals with different skills. Some seem to be adept at discovering food, "the producers", and that is what they concentrate on. Other individuals are more skilled at stealing food that has already been found, so they make their living as perpetual "scroungers". In fact, life may not be so bad for

▲ A parasitic isopod (*Anilocra* sp.) on a shining puller (*Chromis nitidus*), Great Barrier Reef, Australia. In the marine equivalent of a tick on a dog, these isopods (a kind of crustacean) settle on a fish and bite a hole in its skin; specially adapted clawed feet then hold the wound stretched open while the parasite feeds on the blood and body fluids oozing from it.

THE WAYS OF THE SPIDER

▶ Spiders use silk to catch prey in an almost incredible variety of ways, of which a sample of three are shown here. Each drawing left to right illustrates successive stages in web construction. Many spiders weave their silk in complex patterns, forming webs of various designs, anchored to twigs, branches and similar points. Some of these involve ladder-like structures (top) that tend to funnel trapped and struggling insects to a special killing area, while others, like the familiar orb-web spiders (center), consist essentially of a structure of anchor lines across which a spiral of sticky silk is laid. Some, like the purse-spiders (bottom), use silk in the construction of cocoon-like lairs extending from their underground burrows. The spider lurks hidden within the purse until a careless insect happens to settle on it, when the spider quickly stabs it through the silk with its poison-fangs, then drags it through to be eaten.

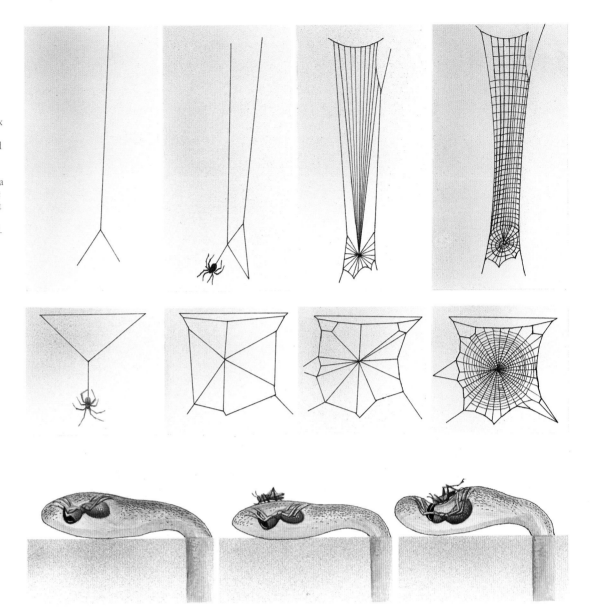

the subordinate producers because dominant scroungers may chase off other dominants, providing a kind of specialized defense of the food source for all concerned.

Stealing food from others is an occasional habit of many species, and for the blackheaded gull, other birds are usually the victims. Lapwings (*Vanellus vanellus*) search lowland fields in Britain hunting for worms. They are followed by blackheaded gulls that watch for when a worm has been caught and attempt to steal it before the lapwing has even had time to swallow. "Kleptoparasitism", as biologists call this kind of food-finding behavior, has been honed into a way of life by some animals. A particularly cunning example is to be found on the webs of *Nephila clavipes*, a spider from the Panamanian rainforest; when a *Nephila* catches its insect prey, it wraps it up in silk and suspends it from the non-sticky center nearby. An entirely different species of spider that lives as a specialist pirate at the web's edge, builds special "signal" threads to different parts of the

web down which it senses the web owner's movements. It knows when prey have been caught, and, remarkably, it can also read the distinctive vibrations associated with wrapping and storing prey. That's when it strikes, sneaking into the web's center, cutting the thread from which the prey hangs, and carrying the package away to the safety of the web's edge ready for departure.

As such relationships get more dependent and more intricate we move toward full parasitism itself. At least half the world's animal species are parasites, and few species are spared being hosts to several. And it is among parasites that some of the most sophisticated and sinister feeding techniques are to be found.

The life cycles of parasites can be immensely complicated. A common liver fluke (*Fasciola hepatica*) has two feeding stages, each infecting quite different animals. Up to 3 centimeters (1 inch) long, adults live in the bile ducts of domestic animals such as sheep and cattle, eating blood and surrounding tissue. They produce eggs sexually which are then excreted by the host and develop into "miracidia". These may infect a freshwater snail, such as *Lymnaea truncatula*, form another egg-like stage (an asexual "sporocyst"), then develop into the larval feeding stage (known as "redia"). Like the adult, this has a proper gut (though it may also take in nutrients through the skin) and feeds on the host's living tissues.

Many larval flukes feed first on the snail's gonads. This curious behavior actually serves the parasite rather well. By consuming the gonads, which are not part of the snail's life-support system, the larva initially enables the snail to continue living. What is more, the snail now loses hormonal control over its own growth regulation and rapidly increases in size, thus providing the parasite with a full larder once it starts eating the rest of the snail's considerably enlarged body.

Many parasites actually feed without a gut at all. Tapeworms, from the genus *Echinococcus*, for example, feed by attaching themselves to the host's own gut (a dog, perhaps) using a whole suite of specialized technologies. The tapeworm's "head" consists of a hook-bearing extension that inserts itself deep between the intestinal fingers (or "villae") that line the host's gut, and is armed with a terminal gland that secretes materials thought to assist in adhesion and in protecting the parasite from the host's defenses. Further down the head, special sucking pads grip the base of the villae, ensuring that the feeding segments of the parasite remain in a good position for feeding. With no gut, food is taken up directly through the parasite's surface by diffusion and active transport. It is here, outside the parasite, that digestion occurs as well—with digestive enzymes, which may have been stolen from the

▼ A pair of dung beetles (*Gymnopleurus virens*) rolling a ball of dung. The purpose varies with the species: some feed on it themselves, others first lay their eggs in it, then bury it in a burrow in the ground as food for their larvae on hatching.

THE LIFE CYCLE OF
A MOSQUITO

▶ Mosquitoes are carriers of several serious human diseases so a detailed understanding of their life histories is important in medicine. Malaria, for example, is caused by the single-celled parasite *Plasmodium falciparum*, which spends part of its life cycle in the bodies of mosquitoes of the genus *Anopheles*. Mosquitoes lay their eggs in water, either singly or in floating rafts, and the nymphs develop hanging from the undersurface tension, breathing through a tube at the tip of the abdomen or (in the case of *Anopheles*), through spiracles in the thorax. *Culex* and *Aedes* mosquitoes perch in a conventional manner, but *Anopheles* mosquitoes tilt their bodies in a characteristic manner at rest, the head, body and hind legs held in a more-or-less straight line.

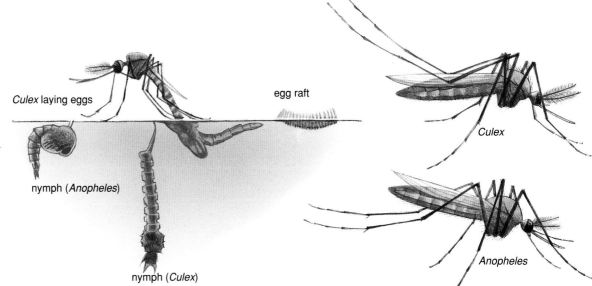

Culex laying eggs

egg raft

nymph (*Anopheles*)

nymph (*Culex*)

Culex

Anopheles

David Maitland/Planet Earth Pictures

host, bound to the surface. All in all, the tapeworm's way of life is as successful as it is bizarre: a dog with a severe infection may have its entire gut carpeted with worms.

The single-celled *Plasmodium falciparum*, which is responsible for the debilitating human disease malaria, has further refined feeding technology. The plasmodium parasite feeds inside the red corpuscles circulating in the host's bloodstream. Although the parasite reproduces asexually within the cell, eventually destroying it in an explosion of offspring, this is not before the cell's own nutrient uptake system has been hijacked into obtaining from the host plasma a whole series of nutrients.

There are other ways to live off others, but in a less intrusive or damaging way, by eating their waste. Scavengers and detritivores often form an important part of the food chain, and although their life may seem lowly, they can be very accomplished at it. The remains of a dead animal, such as a small mammal, may not seem an attractive meal to many of us, but to a carrion beetle (family Silphidae) it is a valuable prize. Males are quick to locate carrion, and will set up and defend territories on their quarry against rival males in the hope of attracting females. Once mated, a female will lay her eggs on the carrion and together they will bury them—a rich supply of food for their larval offspring. Dung beetles (family Scarabidae) lay their eggs on the fecal deposits of large African herbivores such as elephants, first rolling their quarry into a sphere with their specially elongated hind legs, then burying it.

We have already learnt that some birds can use their sense of smell to find food, and this skill seems to be especially well developed in the turkey vulture (*Cathartes aura*), a scavenger that can locate even hidden carrion over great distances with great precision.

Where waste is less concentrated, adaptations seem more directed towards picking up food items than to locating them in the first place. A strange example is that of the balyhoo (*Hemiramphus brasiliensis*), a fish of coral reefs and shallow marine bays where it scavenges on pieces of broken weed suspended near the surface. Balyhoo puzzled biologists for a long time. What was the function of their unusual jaws, the lower extending far out in front of the upper? In fact these jaws are well suited to collecting pieces of broken weed.

ADVANCED PREDATORY SKILLS

Over time, predators and prey have developed some formidable weapons. Perhaps the simplest structures, but by no means ineffective, are powerful jaws armed with sharp teeth. Predatory sharks can replace worn or broken teeth in a few days, with new rows constantly growing up from behind, and may use as many as 20,000 in a lifetime. Together with a potential biting force of 3,000 kilograms per square centimeter (43,000 pounds per square inch), their sharp teeth are used to cut and tear pieces from their prey. Jaws are often used in conjunction with powerful claws. Among cats, strong claws, used for holding and subduing prey, can be rapidly retracted by special muscles when they are not needed.

Colin Milkins/Oxford Scientific Films

When prey are armored too, finding food may require greater skills, or more sophisticated technology. Mussels (such as *Mytilus edulis*) are protected from predation, as well as the buffeting of the waves against the rocks to which they anchor themselves in thick

▲ The northern pike (*Esox lucius*) is a predatory freshwater fish that lurks in water-weed, capturing passing fish and other aquatic animals in sudden surprise lunges from cover. Here one swallows a captured newt.

Valerie Taylor/Ardea London

◄ (*facing page*) A female Sydney funnelweb spider (*Atrax robustus*) with its lizard prey. This is one of the few spiders truly dangerous to humans; unlike most spiders, it is willing—even eager—to bite when disturbed and, before the relatively recent development of an effective antivenene, bites generally proved fatal.

◄ Hammerhead sharks occur in warm temperate and tropical inshore ocean waters around the world. Remarkable for the extraordinary lateral lobes (of unknown function) on the head, the various species range up to about 4 meters (13 feet) in body length. They feed mainly on fish and squid. This is the great hammerhead (*Sphyrna okarran*).

◀ (*previous pages*) A male gerenuk (*Litocranius walleri*) reaches up to feed on an acacia bush in the Samburu Game Reserve, Kenya.
Richard Packwood/Oxford Scientific Films

beds, by strong shells kept tight with a single large muscle. Tiny impregnable fortresses they may look, but, like many well-armored mollusks, they are a nutritious food source too tempting for natural selection to have left alone. The European oystercatcher (*Haematopus ostralegus*) has developed two distinct techniques for preying upon mussels, with individual birds often specializing in one or the other. To feed themselves, mussels must open, and it is while their defenses are down that oystercatchers can stab their long, pointed beak between the shells and prize them apart. But the beak can also be used to hammer entry into a closed shell, if the right part of the mussel can be accurately struck. Northwestern crows (*Corvus caurinus*) can also feed on thick-shelled mollusks such as whelks (genus *Nucella*), but they use gravity to crack the shells by carrying them in their beak and dropping them from a height. In fact, using gravity is not as simple a

Kim Taylor/Bruce Coleman Limited

Michael Fogden/Oxford Scientific Films

▲ A common European toad (*Bufo bufo*) reaches out to swallow a tenebrionid beetle larvae. In the true frogs and toads the massive, fleshy tongue is attached at the front, not the rear, and can be extended a considerable distance outward.

matter as it may seem, because if the whelk is dropped from too high up, it will be sure to break, but so much energy will have been expended in making the drop that the strategy may become uneconomical. A further worry is that the shell may bounce out of sight and be lost. However, if the crow does not fly high enough, it may take too many drops to break the shell at all. Biologists have calculated that if the probability of having to repeat drops with unbroken shells is taken into account, the best height for dropping shells is close to the 5.2 meter (17 foot) drops that crows usually make. Somehow, instinctively, the crow "knows" which height is going to be most successful for its particular drop.

Birds may be clever predators of mollusks— the behavior of the song thrush (*Turdus philomelos*) beating a beak-held snail against a special anvil stone is almost legendary—but perhaps the greatest array of tricks for gaining entry to these nutritious armored nuggets is to be found among mollusks themselves. The simplest method of all belongs to members of the bubble shell family which swallow small bivalves whole and crush them with their powerful gizzard plates. Gastropods in the genus *Busycon* chip away at their prey's armor, whilst *Buccinium undulatum* forces the valves apart by using the lips of its shell. Both then reach inside with their proboscis armed with a saw-toothed tongue, or "radula", with which

they rasp at the prey's now defenseless flesh. Although the radula is primarily a grazer's tool, it has become an advanced piece of predation technology in several mollusk lineages. Some *Murex* gastropods use their radula as a drill which, when lubricated with an acidic secretion to help dissolve the shell, bores a neat hole through its prey's armor. It is a slow process, and may take days, but against it there is no defense, and death must eventually follow. Cone shells, however, have gone one step further in this predation stategy, using their radula as a harpoon loaded with poison darts made from radula teeth which carry a peptide neurotoxin capable of paralyzing a passing fish in seconds.

Fast, effective and economical, venoms are the chemical weapons of the animal world. With no claws for manipulation, many snakes have developed chemical weaponry for subduing their prey. Most sophisticated are the vipers, with tubular "hypodermic" fangs in the front of the upper jaw that can be flicked forward to strike and withdraw with incredible rapidity. Venom is pumped through special canals from poison glands that produce what is really a modified saliva, and once inside the quarry, many snake venoms start their lethal proteolytic digestive activity immediately.

Some of the most toxic compounds of all are aimed not against prey at all, but as a defense against predators. Thus the skin secretions of

▲ A hog-nosed viper (*Bothrops nasutus*), common in tropical American forests, swallows an ameiva lizard (*Ameiva festiva*). Snakes have a metabolic rate much lower than that of birds and mammals, and a correspondingly reduced need for food. Few feed more often than once a week, and the larger species, like some pythons, can survive more than a year of fasting.

▲ A venus flytrap captures a fly. Special cells along the central rib of the modified leaf act quickly to fold the two halves together, while long spines interlocking along the opposing rims form a cage from which there is no escape.

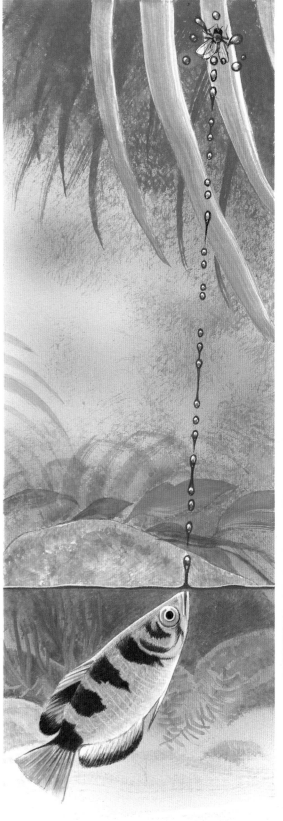

Frieder Sauer/Bruce Coleman Limited

South American dendrobatid poison-arrow frogs, or the poisonous spines of the strangely cryptic stone fish (*Synanceia verrucosa*) can cause serious trauma to a human.

The orb-weaving spiders, such as the garden spider (*Araneus diadematus*), are something of folk heroes for the meticulous way in which they spin their intricate web. But the orb web is not just a natural structure of great beauty as it glistens in the early morning dew; it is a trap, precision-built and deadly. During the day, the female sits, usually at the center, with legs tuned to the web like antennae, waiting to detect the signature vibrations of small insects that have become ensnared on the sticky lines of the trap. From these signatures alone she can identify different kinds of prey, and will decide immediately the appropriate attack strategy. A moth, whose wing scales will disable the web's glue, has to be bitten quickly, whilst a wasp which itself carries a dangerous sting has to be well wrapped before being eaten.

Strangely, one of the most sinister traps of all is to be found in the plant kingdom. Like many carnivorous plants, the venus fly trap (*Dionaea muscipula*) can survive in nitrate-poor substrates by augmenting its supply from the breakdown products of insects it has caught and digested. So how on Earth does a plant manage to catch animals? The trap consists of two flat, semicircular plates each with long spines around the outer edge which act as bars when the plates close together. The plates are hinged together in a region where special cells use rapid changes in pressure to close the trap.

THE ARCHER FISH

▲ The archer fish captures insects by unleashing an unexpected spray in an upward motion. Stunned, the insect falls to its predator.

Each plate is also equipped with a series of sensitive hairs that trigger the trap when disturbed by a fly crawling on the plates. So far so good, but we haven't explained why flies are attracted into the trap in the first place. The traps are not colored green like the rest of the plant, but are a lurid red which may fool flies into mistaking them, if only temporarily, for flowers or perhaps even flesh. The trap is not just a physical one, but psychological too.

Psychological traps abound in the animal kingdom. One of the best known belongs to the angler fish, which, whilst predominantly cryptic in its coloration and movements, has a long, fine protuberance sticking out over the top of its head which it uses as a kind of fishing rod. On the end of the rod is a conspicuous, worm-like lure which, when jiggled, deceives small fish into thinking they have spotted a prey of their own. They are attracted toward the lure, and so toward their death for, once in range of the angler fish's mouth, they become sucked up with the in-rush of water as the predator's jaws are speedily opened, and then shut. There is no room for escape.

Amongst insects, deception is commonly used in self-defense, with camouflage and mimicry the most widespread examples.

Those who have witnessed it will have marveled at the strange light produced by a controlled chemical reaction in bioluminescent animals. Bioluminescence is used in a variety of ways by different animals: to court, to startle, to lure and to warn. But in a strange-looking deep-sea fish called *Aristostomias scintillans*, it has been honed into a bizarre piece of advanced predation technology. This fish lives where precious little light penetrates from the surface. Because water absorbs red light more than blue light, there is virtually no red light at these depths at all. As a consequence of this, several strange things have happened.

▼ Otherwise known as frogfish, angler fish of the genus *Antennarius* lie quietly on the seafloor and tempt other small fishes to within capture range by jiggling a long, worm-like lure on the forehead.

G.I. Bernard/NHPA

▲ Snakes have neither pectoral girdle nor sternum, and the various bones of the jaw are connected to the skull and to each other only by muscles and elastic ligaments, not joints. The swallowing of large prey is aided by backward-pointing teeth and alternate shuffling movements of the jaw bones. Here a fer-de-lance (*Bothrops atrox*) demonstrates by swallowing an agouti in a Costa Rican rainforest, while mosquitoes swarm about it.

▶ Fanworms and feather-duster worms of the family Sabelidae are polychaete worms that live, often in massed colonies like this group in the Bahamas, in protective tubes of cemented sand and coral fragments. When undisturbed they evert a delicate, fan-shaped mass of feathery tentacles, serving as gills and food-gathering organs, filtering planktonic organisms from the water. When disturbed they snap them suddenly back into the tube.

Many fish and crustaceans are colored red. This does not mean that they look red at such a depth: on the contrary, the absence of red light means that they are virtually invisible, which is of course exactly the point. Similarly, most fish have lost the red-sensitive receptors in the eye because, understandably, they are useless. But *Aristostomias* has taken advantage of this and has developed flashlights, powered by bioluminescence and located below each eye, which emit beams rich in red light. In the beams, prey must not only show up brightly, but they are probably also unaware of the light themselves. So why is the light not invisible to *Aristostomias* as well, and with it the prey? *Aristostomias* breaks the rules completely, and has eyes containing red-sensitive receptors that are used to full advantage.

It is usual to think of predatory practices as active, aggressive, even sinister. But there is a diverse group of animals which find food by catching prey in a more passive way: by "filter feeding". Filter feeders are not true predators, but survive by trawling for small planktonic animals using trap-like structures or nets that are usually living extensions of their own bodies. Passive trawlers position themselves so that large volumes of water pass through their

Doug Perrine/Planet Earth Pictures

traps every day. Many marine fan worms, such as *Sabella pavonia*, the peacock worm, extend a fan-like array of filaments out of their protective sheath-like homes, each filament covered in a mucous train to which food particles in the passing water stick. These fans are beautiful structures in their own right, but view them with sufficient magnification and they become much more. Each filament is lined with tiny motorized hairs, or "cilia", that power the mucal train in a slow, steady movement toward the center of the fan, and the mouth.

Mucal strands, many times their body length, are thrown out by snails of the genus *Vermetidae*, then drawn in and eaten along with the microscopic food particles that they have pulled out of suspension in the quiet waters where they feed. Mussels and other bivalve mollusks are also more active in their feeding. They draw a current of water over ciliated, mucus-covered web structures derived from their gills where unicellular algae and other suitable food particles are sorted and separated from waste.

Most literal trawlers of all, perhaps, are the sea butterflies, mollusks too, that drag huge mucus nets up to 2 meters (6 feet 6 inches) in diameter behind them as they swim.

There are trawlers amongst birds too. Swifts pick up tiny insects borne on the air currents using whisker-like extensions around the

Kenneth W. Fink/Ardea, London

mouth to funnel prey into the beak and so increase their catchment. Other birds have specially adapted, laterally flattened beaks for filtering food from shallow waters with systematic side-to-side movements of their heads. The greater flamingo (*Phoenicopterus antiquorum*), for example, partially opens and

▲ A greater flamingo feeding. Intensely gregarious, flamingos usually occur in vast flocks on extensive saline lakes and lagoons, feeding on algae and aquatic invertebrates such as brine shrimp.

▶ (*facing page*) Other New World monkeys have long tails, often prehensile, but the uakaris differ in having short, bushy tails. The three species show a distribution pattern unusual among mammals: each is restricted to a distinct, comparatively small area of Amazonian forest, with no overlapping. This is the red uakari (*Cacajao rubicundus*).

closes its beak repeatedly, pumping muddy water through a mesh of hooks located along the inner edges of the jaw, drawing inward the tiny invertebrates it has trapped with special spines on the tongue.

What is most surprising of all about this most unassuming method of feeding is that, despite the tiny size of each food item caught, it can support animals with huge body mass. Indeed, the largest animal on Earth, and probably the largest that has ever existed, the blue whale (*Balaenoptera musculus*) which reaches a staggering 150,000 kilograms (330, 700 pounds), is a filter feeder. With sieve-like structures made from flexible whalebone, blue whales filter "krill", often single species of pelagic shrimp which live in huge numbers off the plankton that thrive in the nutrient-rich upwellings of cold Antarctic seas. Whenever the whale closes its mouth and forces water out through the long, parallel "baleen" plates with its powerful throat muscles, food is trapped on the matted, hairy inner edges of the plates.

Francois Gohier/Ardea London

▲ Unlike other baleen whales, the gray whale (*Eschrichtius robustus*) is a bottom feeder. It plows the sea floor, stirring up minute crustaceans, mollusks and fish from the ooze, sucking the turbid water into its mouth, then straining it through the comb-like plates of baleen fringing its jaws, here seen in close-up. Barnacles encrust its head.

ENERGY FROM THE SUN

Converting the sun's energy into carbohydrate through photosynthesis, plants are the Earth's food producers on which all animals ultimately rely. In their exploitation and harvest, animals have evolved a huge diversity of techniques, and it is these that we will explore next.

On Aldabra atoll in the Indian Ocean, water is scarce and, despite its tropical location, plant growth is therefore quite limited. Because of its remote location, land mammals failed to colonize Aldabra until very late when rats, cats and goats arrived with mariners' ships and

escaped. Nonetheless, this tiny ecosystem is dominated by large herbivores, just like any other. They are Aldabran giant tortoises (*Geochelone gigantea*), less well known than their Galapagos relatives, but more numerous. Their main food source is a sparse sward that they can crop down to a height of less than 1 centimeter (0.4 inch) with a strong keratin beak mounted on jaws that are built to be capable of a powerful grinding motion. This grinding motion, and the possession of hind teeth with complex grinding surfaces, rather than the sharp cutting edges characteristic of carnivores, are hallmarks of the grazer's success. Whether in the tortoises of Aldabra or the ungulates of the great African plains, they allow the thorough mastication of plant material that is essentially less nutritious than animal flesh, and far tougher to digest.

The problem with plant material is that much of its energy-producing carbohydrate is locked-up in a structural material called cellulose, in a biochemical configuration that is hard for animals to break down. There are solutions, of course, and they are often quite curious. When we pour cow's milk in our coffee we should not forget that this nutritious food has been produced by an animal which has had to face this very problem.

Ruminants, such as the domesticated cow, have a special stomach chamber (called the "rumen"). Here ground-up material is allowed to ferment in the presence of bacteria that secrete enzymes capable of digesting cellulose directly. Material in the rumen is repeatedly regurgitated, mixed with saliva and rechewed: an activity often referred to as "chewing the cud". Once partially digested, food and bacteria continue back through a further series of stomach chambers, bypassing the rumen, where nutrient absorption is completed. Some herbivorous mammals, known as "hindgut fermenters", have just one stomach and a nutrient-absorbing "cecum", but as with the ruminants cellulose digestion depends on the fermenting action of micro-organisms. Similar mutualisms have been exploited in the insect world. Termites, for example, build their elaborate societies and complex living structures from an economy based entirely on the consumption of dead wood. They too do it by relying on the digestive powers of micro-organisms in the gut.

Plants have counter-attacked. Many have defenses against herbivores. The spines of the acacia tree are a physical defense against the actions of large browsers, while the oak tree (*Quercus quercus*), in common with many plants, produces leaves that soon develop tough cuticular surfaces laced with toxic tannins to deter smaller herbivores such as insect larvae.

▲ A giraffe (*Girrafa camelopardalis*) browsing on the foliage of an acacia tree, its staple diet. Plants have evolved many ways to discourage herbivores, including the growth of long, sharp thorns, depositing hard mineral salts in the leaves to increase tooth wear, and storing nutritious components in underground tubers rather than in the leaves.

Of course natural selection does not sit still, and animals have themselves evolved a range of responses. Take the deciduous oak tree of temperate Europe. Every spring it emerges from the relative inactivity of winter in a flourish of leaf production. Within a matter of days, the leaves have opened to full size, toughened, and armed themselves with their defensive chemicals. But during the brief period of bud-burst they are a huge and vulnerable source of food. It is then that the winter moth larvae (*Operophtera brumata*) must hatch and feed, requiring a careful act of predictive timing that can make the difference between success and

reproductive failure for the moth, for if they emerge too late the caterpillars will grow slowly or not at all, or if too early will find no food at all.

Other insects have evolved more cunning strategies still, bypassing the need for such precarious timing by feeding only on the undefended mesodermal tissue right inside the armored layers of the leaf. These are tiny leaf-mining insects, such as moths from the genus *Stigmella*, whose larvae hatch from eggs laid on the outside of the leaf and burrow inside to form narrow private galleries providing not just an ample supply of food but offering physical protection too.

Some other insects get the tree to feed *them*. Thus, sucking insects such as aphids simply insert their specialized hypodermic mouthparts into the plant's nutrient transport system, or "phloem", and allow the system's own pressure to pump food directly through their bodies. Technically, they do not really have to suck at all. Amongst both aphids and wasps are species that tamper with the tree still further by irritating the developing leaf in such a way as to induce the formation of a characteristic "gall", which provides the larvae with a well-protected private larder.

Not all plant material is as indigestible to animals as cellulose. Seeds, flowers, fruits and storage organs such as tubers can offer more manageable sources of nutrition in the form of starch and sugars. It is for their exploitation that some of the most intriguing food-finding adaptations have evolved. The exploitation of plant storage organs as food is not unusual. In fact potatoes were such a common food in some areas that diseases have caused famine, and even with today's sophisticated technology its pests are of serious economic concern.

Under the harsh, arid East African plains, however, conditions are different. Many plants there buffer themselves against difficult conditions by storing starch in huge tubers, safe from most herbivores under the rock-hard earth.

Of course, no potential food source is ever safe in nature, and in this case it is a strange, blind, burrowing mammal that has evolved the requisite skills. The naked mole rat (*Heterocephalus glaber*) lives its entire life underground, as far as we know, in huge colonies where individuals spend much of their time specializing in one function or another. While larger, and probably older, individuals tend the single breeding female at the nest, smaller individuals dig exploratory tunnels with their specially protruding teeth, shoveling earth back down the tunnel behind them. They dig in search of tubers, and when they find one it is systematically transported piece by piece back to the nest area to be shared with others in the colony.

Puzzling as it may seem, this extreme social system, unique among vertebrates, is

▼ The naked mole rat lives its entire life underground in huge colonies.

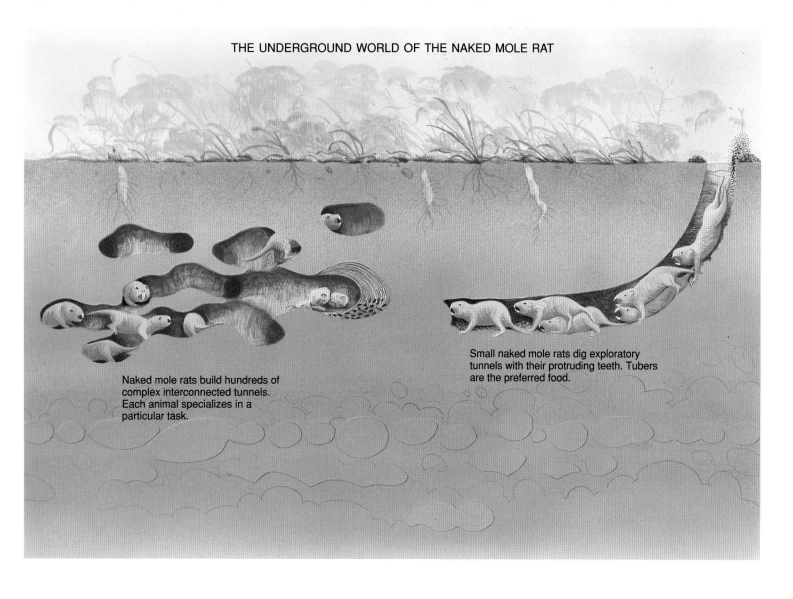

THE UNDERGROUND WORLD OF THE NAKED MOLE RAT

Naked mole rats build hundreds of complex interconnected tunnels. Each animal specializes in a particular task.

Small naked mole rats dig exploratory tunnels with their protruding teeth. Tubers are the preferred food.

▲ A lesser long-nosed bat (*Leptonycteris curasoae*) extracts nectar from a saguaro cactus in the Sonoran Desert of Mexico. Nectivorous animals have developed a range of physical adaptations to enable them to reach their sometimes elusive food source.

▶ (*facing page*) The 340-odd species of hummingbirds have evolved an intricate relationship with the flower species at which they feed, a relationship hinted at by the range of shapes and sizes of their bills. Both flower and hummingbird benefit from the relationship: in essence, the hummingbird (unwittingly) carries pollen from one flower to the next in return for a reward of nectar.

itself at least partly an adaptation for finding food. Each tuber constitutes a rich food patch, but only to the animal that can find it. Because each patch is hard to find, a solitary animal the size of a naked mole rat would probably starve before it ever found one. Consequently, in order to make sure that the risks of failure can be spread across many individuals, so that they are more than balanced by the average rewards, it has paid mole rats to co-operate in finding food. Even if one should be unlucky and never find a tuber in its life, other members of the colony will, by chance, find more than their share, and the colony will thrive. It is almost as

if the colony were a single super-organism, with each worker a tentacle reaching out into the substrate in search of food.

The reward from exploiting unpredictably distributed food sources has contributed to the evolution of advanced social behavior in other animals too. Nowhere is it more developed than in the social Hymenoptera: ants, bees and wasps. As with naked mole rats, the evolution of such a degree of social co-operation in these groups has been catalyzed by the unusually close relatedness of the group members. In effect, by helping others they are helping their own genetic future, not through their own

HUMMINGBIRDS

violet-bellied hummingbird
Damophila julie

Groups of hummingbirds can feed at one flower.

mountain velvetbreast
Lafresnaya lafresnayi

sword-billed hummingbird
Ensifera ensifera

white-tipped sicklebill
Eutoxeres aquila

Some hummingbirds feed alone.

A variety of bill shapes cater
to various flower shapes.

blue-throated sylph
Aglaiocercus kingi

beautiful hummingbird
Calothorax pulcher

Others disperse between a
group of flowers.

violet sabrewing
Campylopterus hemileucurus

▼ A mudwasp (*Eumenes* sp.) returning to its nest with a paralyzed caterpillar. Depending on the species, solitary wasps of this group excavate burrows in the ground, or build vase-shaped nests of fragments of mud cemented with saliva, stocking them with caterpillars or similar prey. Carrying the victim—paralyzed but not killed—back to her nest, the wasp lays her egg upon it, seals the chamber, then departs for ever. The wasp larvae thus have a supply of fresh food available for them when they hatch.

Anthony Bannister/NHPA

offspring but through the offspring of their close relatives. Nevertheless, such social behavior is again only rewarded because it enables the exploitation of a food resource that would otherwise be beyond the reach of so small an organism: patchily distributed "explosions" of flowering plants that can provide them with energy-rich nectar.

The purpose of nectar is to attract animals to flowers with a rewarding food source. Most striking is the effect that this "coevolution" has had on the design of the hummingbird pollinators of the Americas. In Costa Rica, the scarlet passion-flower (*Passiflora vitifolia*) has deep, inaccessible flowers that only hummingbirds with long, curved bills can reach right into. Consequently, flower visitation is largely restricted to the buff-browed hermit (*Pheothornis superciliosus*) which acts as a rather specialized courier of pollen between plants of the same species. It would seem that through such specialization both flower and the hummingbird benefit.

Not all nectivorous animals play by the rules however. Among birds and insects there are robbers which break in to reach the nectar, by-passing the orthodox route down the corolla where the organs for picking up and delivering pollen are located. Carpenter bees saw their way into the flower base to get at the nectar, while the bananaquit (*Coereba flaveola*), a small nectivorous bird from the Caribbean, seems to push its short, curved beak through the base of the corolla, puncturing the flower it is robbing.

Plants have also enlisted the help of animals in the all-important task of dispersing their seeds. The European blackbird (*Turdus merula*), for example, collects the brightly colored berries of trees such as yew and holly, devours the nutritious fruit, and later expels the indigestible seeds well away from the tree that produced them. This is, of course, the point. Because the frugivore is rewarded with a nutritious coating, it is enticed into carrying the seed away. Indeed, some plants have become so dependent on the activities of frugivores that their seeds will only germinate after passing through the gut.

Nevertheless, there is a good living to be made from eating seeds, and animals have evolved special technologies to aid them. Granivorous birds, such as the pigeon (*Columba livia*), enhance the grinding capacity of their muscular gizzard by eating small stones as well. The combined abrasive and enzymic action with the stones included prepares even the toughest grass seeds for digestion.

Some of the largest seeds in the world, those of the coconut palm, are not immune from attack. The robber crab (*Birgus latro*), a large land crab of tropical islands, drags fallen coconuts into the sun, shreds the outer coat with its immense claws, and waits for the nut to crack to release the nutrients.

The robber crab's claw, the hummingbird's bill, and the pigeon's gizzard are all impressive physical pieces of feeding technology. But the more biologists study the workings of natural selection, the more it becomes clear that animals do not just use their technology

THE HONEY-BEE DANCE

NA Callow/NHPA

▲ A honeybee gathers nectar to take back to the hive. If the source is particularly rich, she will communicate the location and distance of her find to others at the hive by means of a specially coded pattern of dance movements, thus encouraging others to return to help harvest it.

Place a droplet of sugar solution on a flat surface and eventually a honey-bee will find the food source and drink. Within minutes of the bee departing, many others will return. The first has somehow told its nestmates where to go. How?

If a worker bee discovers food near the hive, she will return, regurgitate a little food to attract the attention of others, and then perform a "round dance" on the vertical surface of the comb: a vigorous series of tight, alternating clockwise and anti-clockwise circles. By watching the dance, and perhaps smelling as well, other workers learn that they should search nearby for a new food source. When the new food source (perhaps a tree that has just started to blossom) is more than about 50 meters (165 feet) from the hive, the scout performs a straight section in the dance,

during which she waggles her abdomen. The duration of the waggle run, the number of waggles, and the time it takes to complete the dance, all provide information about how far away the food is. Similarly, she emits high-pitched sound bursts whose duration also correlates with distance. More remarkable still is the fact that she can communicate direction too, by orienting her dance at an angle to the vertical that corresponds to the horizontal angle to the sun that must be flown to reach the food.

▲ A young ground squirrel (*Xerus inauris*) cautiously investigates a dangerous Cape cobra in the Kalahari Desert, South Africa. In characteristic cobra style, the snake has its hood extended in warning.

blindly; they are not just well-equipped, opportunistic foragers; they often employ sophisticated behavioral strategies too. Animals, like humans, plan ahead.

PLANNING AHEAD
Humans were not the first to invent farming. The social insects are specialists at it. Many ants not only "milk" sap-sucking aphids for the sugar-rich excreta known as honeydew, they even tend them as if they were herds of valuable cattle. *Lasius neoniger*, for example, keep eggs of the American corn-root aphid (*Aphis maidiradicis*) in their colonies over

winter, then place the nymphs on the roots of plants close-by when they hatch. In many cases, the bugs have become to some extent domesticated, with reduced defensive systems and special hair-baskets around the anus for holding the honeydew droplets ready for their masters. The relationship is mutualistic since the ants will fight off potential predators, and in one genus of extraordinary pseudococcids from Java (*Hippeococcus*), endangered individuals climb onto their host's back with modified legs and wait to be transported to somewhere safer.

When it comes to defending "feeding territories", animals indulge in farming of a sort

defending a territory against other individuals, a sunbird ensures that the flowers it feeds on contain more nectar per visit than they would otherwise. This is because flowers produce nectar during the day, so they are always gradually refilling. The catch, of course, is that defense is energetically expensive, and costs the bird about three times as much as feeding behavior. However, if the bird manages to make sufficient gains from each flower, it can spend more of its time resting, which is the most energy-saving behavior of all. By measuring the actual nectar production in the wild, biologists have calculated that the balance is a delicate one, but where the foraging rewards are sufficient to outweigh the costs, sunbirds do indeed become territorial.

Subsistence farming of this sort is found in many animals, but some have taken things a stage further and store their food. Storing is generally an adaptation for dealing with

too, and the economics of defending and harvesting such territories can be a finely balanced thing. One of the best studied belongs to the golden-winged sunbird (*Nectarinia reichenowi*). The sunbirds are in many ways the Old World parallel to the hummingbirds of the New World. They too are tiny, often brightly colored creatures serving similar ecological roles as specialist nectivores. The golden-winged sunbird feeds on *Lenotis* flowers in East Africa, and not only is it physically suited to the task of probing the nectar-producing florets, with a fine, curved beak, it uses the behavioral adaptation of territorial defense as well. By

changes in the availability of food relative to the animal's predicted needs. Outside the tropics particularly, the Earth's seasonal weather forces plants and animals themselves to respond with seasonal behavior. During winter, days are shorter, the sun's penetration is weaker, and temperatures drop. For a host of related reasons plant productivity drops, and many species concentrate their growth in the summer months, culminating in a burst of reproductive output in the autumn. This is when most trees produce their fruits, and consequently for many animals the harsh conditions of winter are preceded by a glut of food. Of course, most of

▲ A red ant (*Myrmica rubra*) "milks" its colony's herd of aphids for honeydew. Ants of numerous species protect aphids from predators in return for a sugary solution (honeydew) excreted by these tiny insects. Some will even store their eggs over winter and take them out to pasture, like dairy cattle, when they hatch.

▶ (*facing page*) A dormouse (*Muscardinus avellanarius*) investigates a snack of berries. Feeding mainly on nuts and insects, this tiny European rodent is active mostly at night, spending the day in small "dormitory" nests woven of grass, moss and twigs and stuffed in grass tussocks or cavities in fallen timber.

▼ An acorn woodpecker clan's communal larder. As its name indicates, acorns are the staple diet of this resident of the American southwest. The acorn woodpecker lives in groups which maintain permanent food stores, contributed to by all members of the group, against winter shortage. The acorns are wedged, like pegs in a board, in small holes.

this is useless to them unless they can have access to it during the winter months.

Birds, for example, can be adept food storers. During the Californian autumn, colonies of acorn woodpeckers (*Melanerpes formicivorus*) store thousands of acorns in specially drilled holes in the bark of large trees near their nesting sites. These "granaries", which are the cumulative result of many years' work, provide a valuable source of food for the birds as they survive the lean winter and labor to reproduce during the following spring. So why don't other animals plunder the highly visible stores? One reason is probably that the acorns, which are meticulously positioned, are not physically easy for other animals to remove. This is not true for the stores of the marsh tit (*Parus palustris*), which uses a different trick to keep its food supply relatively safe.

Marsh tits face a rather different problem. Because of their tiny size (about 11 grams; 0.4 ounces) and high metabolic rate they cannot survive long without food, especially in the cold winter months. To buffer themselves against the risk of starvation that confronts them every day, they store sometimes hundreds of seeds during the morning, then collect them again later in the day. Rather than store them all in one place, where they will be vulnerable to plundering by other hungry creatures such as shrews, they secrete them singly in hidden locations all over their woodland territory. "Scatter hoarding", as it is called, may be a neat solution, but actually it presents the marsh tit with a formidable problem: how to retrieve the seeds once they are stored. Perhaps the bird could use a simple rule in the hiding, so that, you might think, recovery would be a simple

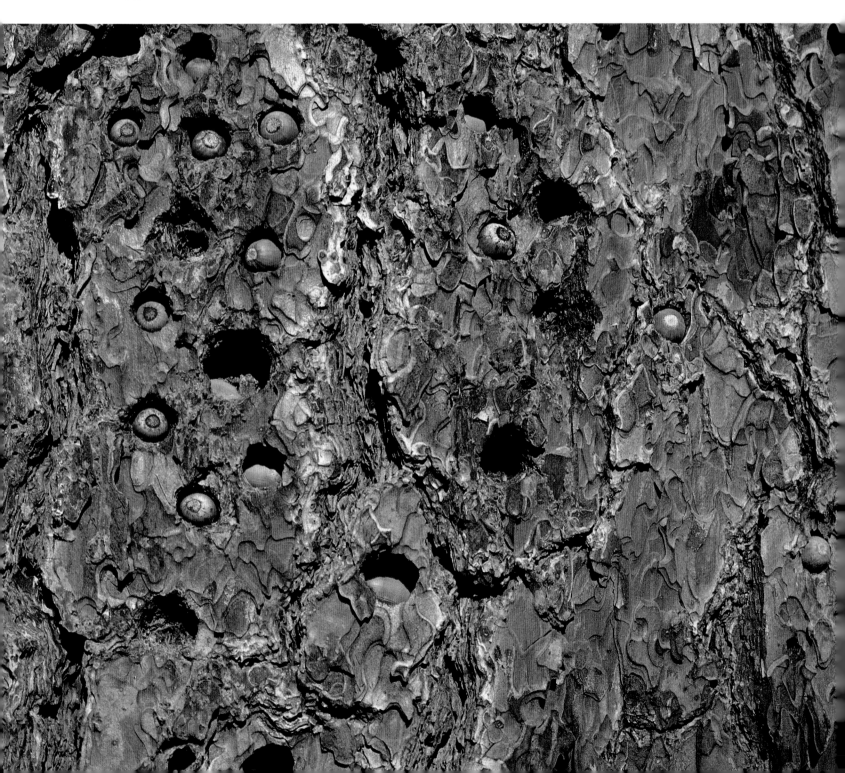

matter of rechecking every "suitable" site later in the day. In fact, biologists have now discovered that marsh tits remember the locations where they have stored an item, which change from day to day, probably recognizing each by its unique combination of visual and spatial cues with commendable accuracy. Indeed, there are now tantalizing indications that it is not just the marsh tit's behavior that has been specially adapted for this unusual food-finding technique, but the very structure of its brain as well, with its "hippocampus", an area thought to be involved in spatial memory, unusually enlarged. This is animal feeding technology at its most advanced and sophisticated.

Many animals plan ahead in a seemingly less precarious way, by laying down fat stores on their own bodies in readiness for lean times ahead. At the start of winter a house sparrow has put on 14 percent of its own weight in fat, while gannet chicks, which must endure an extremely unpredictable parental feeding regime, can store 1 kilogram (about 2 pounds) of fat, about one-third of their body weight, as a mechanism for survival.

If the shortage of food, or the cold, or both, prove too much, there is one last option which is, in a sense, the most incredible piece of food finding technology of all: migration. For the acorn woodpecker, conditions are not always good enough to maintain their colonial, sedentary, storing way of life. In Arizona, acorns are less plentiful than they are in California, and the woodpeckers migrate south for the winter instead.

The swallow (*Hirundo rustica*) is, of course, legendary for its migration abilities. The autumnal disappearance of swallows from British skies not only saddens the hearts of rural folk, foreshadowing as it does the coming of winter, it is also a phenomenon that once confounded even the best naturalists. Only with the advent of systematic ringing studies did it become apparent that swallows, which spend the European winter in Africa, make the staggering journey thousands of kilometers north to capitalize on the rich abundance of the temperate summer. It is here that conditions are best suited to feeding young.

Many animals migrate between summer and winter feeding grounds, and often it seems that the young learn the characteristics of the route from more experienced adults. But in the monarch butterfly (*Danaus plexippus*) this solution is impossible. Monarchs overwinter in vast aggregations, numbering tens of millions of individuals, in the upland forests of Mexico, where their relative torpor conserves energy. But in the spring, the monarchs start to migrate

Stephen Dalton/NHPA

JA Bailey/Ardea London

▲ A common resident of Europe, a marsh tit (*Parus palustris*) fetches food for its nestlings. Especially in winter, marsh tits practise "scatter hoarding", storing dozens or even hundreds of seeds one by one in the morning for retrieval later in the day, thus buffering themselves against possible shortage in the evening when extra energy is needed to see them through the long bitter night ahead. Studies confirm that the birds memorize the location of each individual cache.

▶ Seen from an aircraft, a migrating flock of snow geese (*Anser caerulescens*) passes over Canada's northern wilderness. At its most extreme, migration may require adjustments at every level of the traveler's daily routines.

north to Florida where the ageing adults mate and lay eggs on the fresh growth of milkweed plants on which their larvae feed. Many then die. As summer gradually creeps north, the next generation of butterflies heads north too, utilizing milkweeds as far as Canada. Several generations may thrive before the days shorten again, temperatures drop, and plant growth slows. Then the adults, which have never been south in their lives, build up their fat stores and migrate the thousands of kilometers to Mexico, where they will occupy the same overwintering roosts as their ancestors. How they do it biologists are only now beginning to understand, but it seems certain that they are fulfilling one of nature's most extraordinary strategies for finding food.

Jen & Des Bartlett/Bruce Coleman

Chapter 3

COURTSHIP AND FAMILY LIFE

Timothy Halliday

For animals, courtship and family life can be as varied as the millions of species in existence. While mayflies meet only as a pair for a few seconds, other creatures, such as pigeons and parrots, pair for life and become inseparable.

COURTSHIP AND MATING

With all his show and finery, the male of the species is usually the more active partner in courtship. He is typically more brightly colored and usually has some outstanding anatomical feature, such as elaborate plumes, horns or enlarged fins. However, nature does provide exceptions to the rule and the roles can be reversed.

THE TIMING OF MATING

Courtship synchronizes the behavior of males and females to exactly the right moment so that mating will be a success. But there are other factors that affect the timing of mating. Birds, insects and amphibians mate and breed in the spring. In desert habitats, where the seasons are not very regular, many animals breed opportunistically, often after periods of rain.

PARENTAL BEHAVIOR

Animal parents exhibit diversity in rearing their young. It may be the female, the male or both parents that assume parental duties, varying with the species. One problem faced by all animal parents is how to look after the young in their particular environment.

COURTSHIP AND FAMILY LIFE

Timothy Halliday

▲ A male blue peafowl (*Pavo cristatus*) in display position.

▼ Southern elephant seal (*Mirounga leonina*) prepares to mount one of his harem. Males arrive first at the breeding colonies, and dispute for the largest territories they can successfully defend against rivals. Mating takes place indiscriminately with any females within this territory, who are treated as members of a harem that may number 50 or more.

One of life's great ironies is that in spite of the tremendous diversity of animals on Earth, their passage of entry into this world is essentially the same—through fertilization and sexual reproduction.

For all animals that reproduce sexually, the most crucial event is when an egg meets and is fertilized by a sperm. For some animals living in the sea, neither courtship nor family life has anything to do with this process. Males and females are simply brought together at random by the vagaries of water currents and shed their eggs and sperm into the water, wherever they are at the time. However, for a great many animals, fertilization results from mating, in which a male and a female interact with one another in an intimate and direct way.

The nature of the behavior that precedes, accompanies and follows mating, called courtship, varies enormously from one species to another. Whereas some species, such as mayflies, meet as a pair for only a few seconds, others, like pigeons and parrots, pair for life and become inseparable, even when they are not engaged in reproductive activities.

Family life, in which the young interact with their parents, is equally diverse and variable between species. Many fishes and insects, for example, have no contact with their parents after they have been left, as eggs, to fend for themselves. However, for many young, a prolonged period of weeks or months, in which they are cared for, and protected by their parents, is essential for survival.

Why is there such diversity and variety in sexual and parental behavior when, for all sexually reproducing animals, the starting point of the process—fertilization—is essentially the same? To understand the answer to this question, it is necessary to appreciate two important general principles. Firstly, during the course of evolution, nature has found many different solutions to the same problems. And secondly, in any species, the nature of one phase in the reproductive process, such as courtship, is largely determined by the nature of the others, such as mating or parental care.

As an illustration of these two principles, consider just one specific aspect of reproduction, the production of eggs by a female.

The most successful female in a species, you could argue, is the one that leaves the largest number of eggs—she will have the greatest number of offspring surviving into the next generation. Natural selection will favor those characteristics that have enabled her to produce large numbers of eggs, and those strengths will become typical of the species.

However, that is not the end of the story and there are other aspects of a species that evolution might favor. In most species, for example, eggs contain yolk on which the developing embryo feeds during the first few hours or days of its life. The more yolk that goes into an individual egg, the better the start in life that egg has and so the more likely it is to survive.

▲ Unique among insects in being able to rotate the head, praying mantids are formidable predators that will eat anything that can be subdued by their powerful spiked forelimbs—even other mantids. Most males mate only once, since they are usually eaten by the female during copulation.

makes a demand on a parent's limited energetic resources so that there is a trade-off between investing a large amount of care in a few eggs, or rather less care in many eggs at once.

A second major factor that has led to courtship behavior being so diverse is the fact that the reproductive make-up of females and males is fundamentally different—namely, the size of their gametes (see section on Sex Differences). Females produce relatively few, large eggs, whereas males produce millions of tiny sperm. An important consequence of this difference is that males can increase their reproductive success by mating with more than one female, while females generally cannot. As a result, evolution has favored characteristics in males that allow them to attract and compete for females, and in females has favored characteristics that will enable them to produce more

▲ One of the most impressive animals of the North American Rockies, a male elk, or wapiti, bugles in rut. Many mammals, like the elk, use a courtship and mating system otherwise uncommon among vertebrates: males contend with other males in order to accumulate a harem consisting of the largest possible group of females.

Natural selection would, therefore, also favor the egg with a high-quality yolk. What we have already are two alternative ways of maximizing reproductive success in terms of the number of surviving progeny—producing a large number of small, sparingly yolked eggs, of which only a few survive; or producing a few large, generously yolked eggs, of which a high proportion will survive. Obviously these are alternative types of behavior for animals—they are not equipped to do both.

The pattern of egg production shown by a species thus involves what is called an evolutionary "trade-off". The compromise between the number and the size of eggs that a female produces is one such trade-off, but there are many others in the process of reproduction (see section on Reproductive Allocation). Another involves parental care. The chances that eggs survive can be increased in many ecological situations, if one or both parents defends and cares for them. Parental care

Erwin & Peggy Bauer/Auscape

Charlie Ott/Bruce Coleman Limited

eggs and to develop attributes that enable them to provide for and look after the young. This suggests that, generally, males need to be large, aggressive and conspicuously decorated, while females are smaller, more passive and devote much of their time to parental care.

While some animals fit this crude stereotype, many others do not. The male elephant seal (*Mirounga angustirostris*), for example, is up to three times heavier than the female, is highly aggressive and takes no part in parental care. On the other hand, however, male jacanas or lily trotters (*Jacana spinosa*) are dominated by larger female mating partners and are the primary providers of parental care. There are many other examples of animals that depart in various ways from the stereotype and one of the greatest challenges of biology is to try to understand why this is so.

The fact that the two sexes typically play different roles in the reproductive process profoundly influences the nature of courtship between them, in two principal ways. First, it creates an inherent conflict of interests between the sexes. In many birds, for example, a female will enjoy greater reproductive success if her mate remains with her and shares in the care of their offspring, but the male may do better if he leaves her and mates with other females. Secondly, courtship provides the opportunity for individuals of each sex to choose a mating partner; but on what basis should they base their choice? The answer varies from species to species, and depends on the role played by the partner in reproduction. For example, where the role of the male is to provide food for the young, females are expected to prefer as mates those males that are most adept at finding food,

▼ Western grebes (*Aechmophorus occidentalis*) in California performing the courtship display known as "rushing". Grebes are typical of those birds in which courtship is a mutual affair. Both partners establish their bond by means of virtually identical displays, and females will even occasionally mount males.

▲ Southern right whales (*Eubalaena australis*) mating, Valdes Peninsula, Argentina.

but in species where the male's role is to protect the young against predators, females should prefer larger, more aggressive males.

COURTSHIP AND MATING

In the great majority of species, the male is the more active partner in courtship. He pursues the female or produces signals, in the form of postures, calls or odors, that attract her from a distance. He is typically more brightly colored and usually has some outstanding anatomical feature, such as elaborate plumes, horns or enlarged fins. By his behavior, he must overcome the female's apparent reluctance to mate with him. In the three-spined stickleback

(*Gasterosteus aculeatus*), the male alone cares for the eggs and, during courtship, he leads the female to his nest and displays in front of it. At this point, females may reject their male counterparts if they have built unsatisfactory nests, because in doing so they have failed to demonstrate their suitability as fathers. In the common tern (*Sterna hirundo*) the male brings fish to the female during courtship, which is known as courtship feeding, and during parenthood provides much of the food for the chicks (see section on Courtship Feeding). In another species, such as the peacock (*Pavo cristatus*), the females prefer to mate with males that have the most highly developed trains. As the development of a peacock's train is related to his age, the peahen's preference means that she is more likely to mate with an older male, because he has proven his ability to survive.

There are, however, exceptions to the general rule that the male is the more active partner in courtship. In many insects, females produce airborne secretions, called courtship pheromones, that attract males from a distance. In the silkmoth (*Bombyx mori*), the male has huge feathery antennae covered with millions of tiny pheromone receptors, each so sensitive to the pheromone called bombykol that a male can detect a female from a distance of several kilometers. In some animals, the reversal of typical courtship roles has occurred, because the division of parental care between the sexes is reversed. In the dendrobatid frog (*Dendrobates auratus*), the male cares for the eggs and tadpoles, while the females have to seek out and solicit further mating from other males (this is achieved by tapping their hind limbs on the male's back). In some birds, both sexes care for the young and courtship may be mutualistic, to the extent that it is impossible to tell the sexes apart. In the great crested grebe (*Podiceps cristatus*), males and females are identical in appearance and perform a series of elaborate displays in which each sex behaves identically. In mating, the female even frequently mounts the male.

Apart from its major role, courtship behavior also fulfills an interesting variety of secondary biological functions. One such function is that it may enable potential mating partners to locate one another, often over a considerable distance. Messages may be carried, for instance, in the form of a courtship song. In some species, such as the great tit (*Parus major*), the cessation of singing in males marks the end of courtship, and infers that they have acquired a mate. However, song can also be used in territorial defense, and acts as a "keep out" signal to rival males. Males in many frog and

▼ A pair of mandarin ducks (*Aix galericulata*), a striking example of the breeding regime, common in birds, in which the courting male is spectacularly plumaged but the female is dull and unobtrusive. In many duck species, once courtship is over and the pair bond established, the male promptly molts into an eclipse plumage, thus evading much of the obvious predation risk.

Eric Sodes/NHPA

jerboa

raccoon

prarie dog

puff adder

bat

sealion

louse

platypus

cat

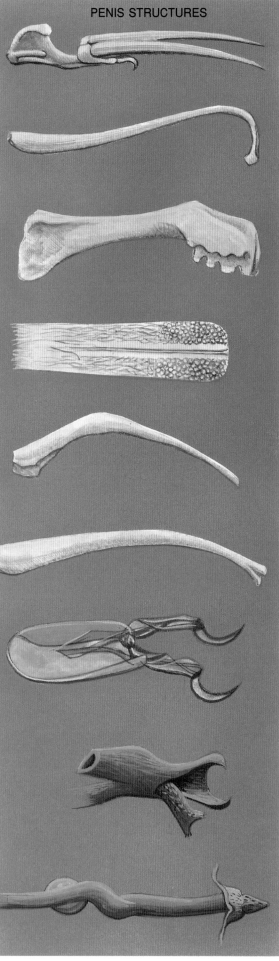

PENIS STRUCTURES

insect species also produce sounds to attract females. In frogs, these sounds are produced by the vocal chords and are enhanced by one or more inflatable vocal sacs. In insects, on the other hand, sounds are generated by rubbing the wings (for example, crickets) or the legs (for example, grasshoppers) together. Like the songs of birds, these sounds are also used in aggressive interactions between males. Other senses used in male attraction and location include electrical signals in certain fish that live in murky water and vibrations in some types of insects and spiders.

Obviously, mate attraction by males is an inherently competitive exercise. So, naturally, any male that displays more effectively than its rivals will tend to enjoy higher mating success. Competitive behavior may call for displaying more often, calling louder, or producing more odor. While this behavior confers obvious benefits on a male, in terms of greater mating success, it also tends to increase a number of costs. For example, males may attract not only mates, but also enemies that "eavesdrop" on the communication system of their prey. The tungara frog (*Physalaemus pustulosus*) is preyed upon by the fringe-lipped bat (*Trachops cirrhosus*), which swoops down over a frog pond and scoops a calling male up in its open jaws. The male pheromone of the southern stink bug (*Nezara viridula*) and the calls of the American field cricket (*Gryllus intiger*) attract particular kinds of flies that are parasitic on these insects alone.

A particularly remarkable example of exploitation of one species' sexual behavior by another predatory species is seen among American fireflies. Females of the genus *Photuris* display aggressive mimicry, and imitate the distinctive flash patterns of other female fireflies, particularly those of the genus *Photinus*. Unsuspecting *Photinus* males fly around, emitting their species-specific flash pattern, in the hope of attracting the attention of females of the same species, but may attract *Photuris* females who make it their business to intercept and lure the *Photinus* males down to the ground, where they eat them! With a great deal of versatility, these "femme fatale" predators are able to mimic the female flash patterns of not one, but several different prey species and can vary their behavior according to which kind of prey is most abundant.

A second danger to signaling males is that their emissions may also attract rival males of the same species. As a result, many animals that call to attract females, such as crickets and frogs, band together to create dense "choruses", in which competition for females is intense. Guppies (*Poecilia reticulata*) tend to form groups

of displaying males and the presence of rivals causes each male to increase the frequency with which he performs the various fin and tail movements. In several species of frog, calling males attract one or more non-calling "satellite" males that sit close to a caller and attempt to intercept females that approach him. In the European smooth newt (*Triturus vulgaris*), males approach a rival as he displays to a female and interrupt his courtship at a critical stage.

A third kind of cost relates to the fact that courtship signals are energetically expensive. After a time, signaling males may simply become exhausted and have to stop. In the American green treefrog (*Hyla cinerea*), individual males call only on some nights. On the intervening nights, while they recoup the energy necessary for calling, they adopt the silent "satellite" strategy and attempt to "steal" females away from calling males. In the case of the red deer (*Cervus elephas*), males roar repeatedly and frequently during the autumn mating period (called the rut). By the end of the rut, the males will have lost a great deal of weight and may be so exhausted that they are unable to survive the rigors of a severe winter.

Another function of courtship behavior, which becomes important once potential mates have come together, is called "persuasion". This occurs when one sex of the species, usually the male, endeavors to stimulate his partner until she becomes sexually receptive. This may be achieved via the adoption of elaborate postures, the production of sounds, the secretion of odors, and various forms of tactile stimulation in which the female is stroked or prodded repeatedly. A bizarre and extreme example of tactile stimulation is provided by certain snails, in which the male produces hard, sharp love-darts that he shoots into the female's body. More familiar examples of visual stimulation are the elaborate postures of the peacock and the birds of paradise, in which the brightly colored

▲ Conspicuous display features are not necessarily carried only by the male. In the royal flycatcher (*Onychorhynchus coronatus*) of South America, for example, both sexes are characterized by a large fan-shaped crest, yellow in females and vermilion in males.

◄ (*facing page*) Not all animal species have a penis, but in those that do, the shape and size of the organ varies enormously. From top to bottom: jerboa, raccoon, prairie dog, puff adder, bat, sealion, louse, platypus, and cat.

► (*following pages*) The comb-crested jacana (*Irediparra gallinacea*), also known as the lotus bird or lilytrotter, is a long-legged wading bird of northern Australia. *Horizon/Mark Hanlon*

REPRODUCTIVE ALLOCATION

M. Iijima/Ardea London

▲ A Japanese macaque (*Macaca fuscata*) suckles her cub. One general characteristic of mammals is a relatively low reproduction rate coupled with a high investment in parental care.

In the course of their lives, animals acquire all the nutrients and energy they need through feeding. Nutrition provides a species' resources which are then allocated to support various activities for survival, growth and reproduction. In their daily activities, animals must somehow take into account the fact that once energy has been expended, it is lost and cannot be used again for another activity. To ensure that animals achieve everything they need to in a lifetime, they have to trade-off one activity against another—to put too much energy into breeding may lead to an early death, to put too little may ensure survival but would not leave any descendants.

The fundamental trade-off that all animals (and plants) must make is between survival and growth on the one hand and reproduction on the other. As young animals grow and develop, they typically allocate very little energy to reproduction, but once they reach reproductive age, their gonads mature and, in many animals, growth ceases. In species that reproduce only once in their lives, such as the salmon, the shift in resources to reproduction may be almost total and the individual dies after breeding. In species that breed several times in their lives, there must be a trade-off each breeding season, between reproduction and survival.

Resources that are allocated to reproduction, called "reproductive effort", may be divided into three principal activities: the production of gametes (eggs and sperm), mating, and caring for the young. Between these three aspects, innumerable trade-offs are made by many species in a variety of ways. For example, some female animals, such as many fish species, produce huge numbers of eggs but devote little or no effort to caring for their young. Female mammals, by contrast, produce litters containing relatively few young but, in terms of sustaining the fetuses in the womb and feeding the newborn young on milk, their investment in parental care is large.

The pattern of trade-offs between different categories of reproductive effort within any one species has evolved largely in response to the nature of its environment. If the environment is very hostile to animals during the early stages of their lives, and it appears that they will only survive if looked after by their parents, selection will favor parental care at the expense of producing large numbers of offspring.

and greatly elaborated plumage of the male is spread and displayed to maximum effect. Among salamanders, the predominant mode of stimulation is olfactory and different species show different postures in which pheromone-secreting glands on the head or around the cloaca (sexual opening) of the male are pressed or rubbed against the female's nostrils. In the two-lined salamander (*Eurycea bislineata*), the male rubs courtship glands under his chin over the female's back and then lacerates her skin with two sharp protruding teeth. This causes his pheromone secretions to pass directly into her bloodstream.

If a male is to successfully attract, stimulate and mate with a female, he must also reduce

◀ In many moths, like this Australian emperor gum moth (*Antheraea eucalipti*), it is the female which initiates courtship. She signals her readiness to mate by releasing into the air a chemical that a male can detect from several kilometers away, using sensors in his elaborately branched antennae.

▶ Like the peacock, the birds of paradise of New Guinea perform spectacular displays to attract females, but in several species the males congregate in groups, known as leks, to do so. Here a male Raggiana bird of paradise (*Paradisaea raggiana*), at the climax of his display, is studied by a female (upper right).

Bruce Beehler/NHPA

any tendency that she has to behave in ways that are incompatible with mating. In many birds, for example, individuals of both sexes are in continual competition for food, roosting sites, and so on, and so there are frequent aggressive interactions between them. If a male and a female are to mate, their natural tendency to be aggressive toward one another must be overcome. The courtship behavior of many male birds incorporates postures, the function of which is to pacify or to appease the female, reducing any tendency in her to flee from, or to attack the male. During courtship in the black-headed gull (*Larus ridibundus*), both sexes turn their heads away from one another, concealing the dark brown "mask" on the face which, in other contexts, is presented as an aggressive signal to an intruder.

In many spiders, the male faces a different kind of problem. Female spiders are commonly much larger than the male and there is a very real risk that he will be mistaken for food and eaten when he approaches the female. However, male spiders possess a variety of behavior patterns that prevent this. Some vibrate the female's web with a characteristic rhythm that signals to her that a suitor, and not a prey item, has landed on her web. In other species, the male presents the female with an insect that he has caught previously; this keeps her dangerous

A male uses his bright colors to attract the attention of a passing female.

THE COURTSHIP

If the female is receptive, a courtship dance ensues.

The male then entices her to a nest he has built among the waterweed.

mouthparts busy while he mates with her. Some spiders increase the period of safety that this affords them, by wrapping the insect in layers of silk before presenting it to the female. There are even some spider species in which the male entangles the female in silk threads, apparently immobilizing her or her mouthparts, but this may also be looked upon as a "symbolic" form of behavior because, after mating, the female escapes easily.

The third function of courtship is to bring about precise synchronization of male and female activities. This is especially important when eggs are fertilized outside the female's body. If eggs and sperm are not released very close together, in time as well as in space, there is often a considerable risk that the eggs will be dispersed before the sperm can reach them. The complex courtship sequence of the three-spined stickleback (*Gasterosteus aculeatus*) is a good example of a behavioral mechanism that ensures precise synchronization of male and female behavior. It consists of a series of interactions between male and female, in which each activity by one partner is both a specific response to what the other partner has just done, and also the stimulus for the partner's next activity. It is thus a chain of stimuli and responses, in which each reaction acts as the stimulus for the next response. When a female

stickleback swims into a male's territory, where he has built a nest, he responds by performing a "zigzag" dance in which he alternately swims toward and away from the female. He persists in this display until she responds by turning toward him in a "head-up" receptive posture. This is the stimulus for him to lead her to his nest and, if she has followed him, he takes up a "head-down" posture just outside the nest entrance. The female inspects his nest and, if she is receptive, her response to the male's behavior, and to his nest, is to wriggle her way head-first into the nest. The male then nudges the base of the female's tail with his snout and she responds by laying her eggs inside the nest. Finally, she swims forward out of the nest and the male immediately follows her through it, shedding sperm onto the eggs when he is inside.

The requirement that each stage in one partner's behavior must receive an appropriate response from the other partner before that fish can perform the next ensures that neither stickleback can "get ahead" of its mate. Instead, each fish reaches its peak of sexual arousal, expressed in the production of eggs and sperm, at almost the same moment. If one fish is initially more strongly motivated to the mate than the other, the stimulus–response pattern of their courtship gives the less motivated partner time to catch up.

▼ The complex courtship sequence of the three-spined stickleback (*Gasterosteus aculeatus*).

OF A STICKLEBACK

He guides and coaxes her inside, nipping at her fins if she turns aside.

Once inside the nest, the female lays her eggs.

As she swims away, the male promptly enters the nest to fertilize the eggs. He remains to guard and care for his brood until they hatch a few days later.

SEX DIFFERENCES

Within any animal species, males and females show marked differences in their anatomy and behavior—this is known as sexual dimorphism (the occurrence of two distinct types of individuals in an animal species). The idea behind sexual dimorphism is that, whereas females produce relatively large, immobile eggs, males produce tiny, mobile sperm. Because eggs are larger than sperm, they are produced in smaller numbers than their more mobile counterpart.

This means that, whereas a male can increase his reproductive success by mating with several partners, a female usually cannot. Males and females thus typically pursue fundamentally different reproductive strategies. Males have evolved patterns of behavior that enable them to compete with other males, for example, by fighting, and to be attractive to females in courtship. Associated with these patterns of behavior are specialized anatomical features, such as horns and other weapons for use in fighting, and elaborate plumage that enhances the effectiveness of sexual displays. The emphasis on competition among males has often favored the evolution of larger body size than females.

▲ Two male impalas struggle for domination of the herd. In this African species males have horns but females do not.

Precise synchronization is also important in the courtship of newts and salamanders and for such arthropods as scorpions and pseudo-scorpions, in which sperm is transferred from male to female in a capsule called a spermatophore. Following some preliminary courtship, in which the male stimulates the female, a male smooth newt turns away from the female. She touches his tail, a stimulus to which he responds by depositing a sperma-tophore. As he then moves away from it, the female turns to follow him and, as she passes over the spermatophore, it becomes attached to her cloaca, completing the process.

Another major function of courtship behavior is reproductive isolation, which ensures that individuals mate only with members of their own species. This insurance is necessary because if individuals mate with members of other species, total reproductive failure may result. If any offspring (called hybrids) do result, they are typically unlikely to survive or, if they do survive, they are generally sterile or have very low fertility. To reinforce reproductive isolation within a species, there are courtship signals which are used to identify

and attract potential mates. Naturally, between species, the signals differ markedly. As a result we, as humans, are able to identify many birds, frogs and insects solely on the basis of the different sounds that they produce. The visual displays of the different species are also generally associated with distinctive color patterns. For example, the males of many species of ducks are brightly colored and highly distinctive, so that males of different species are readily identified by humans. By contrast, female ducks typically have speckled plumage that provides camouflage, and females of different species are often much harder to tell apart than males.

For effective reproductive isolation to take place, not only do the males have to present a distinctive appearance and behavior, but the females must be highly selective in their choice of mates. In frogs and many insects, females identify males of the same species by particular features of the calls they produce. In fact, the ears of the females contain receptor cells that are "tuned" specifically to the males' sound frequencies. At the same time, the females are also "deaf" to the sounds produced by males of

▲ Two Surinam toads (*Pipa pipa*). One of the implications of external, rather than internal, fertilization is that the male can do nothing until the female chooses to lay her eggs. In these circumstances, holding her tight and refusing to let go is the simplest strategy by which a male might ensure that, when his mate is ready, he is on the spot and rival males are not. The embrace is called amplexus, and is adopted by many frogs and toads.

The male seahorse has a marsupial-like
pouch in the belly, into which the female
lays her eggs during mating.

The female then leaves, abandoning
her eggs to the care of the male.

another species, so that the risk of their engaging in hybrid matings is very low.

While the ability of individuals to discriminate between their own and other species is determined by the properties of their sense organs in insects and frogs, for many birds experience in early life also plays a vital role. While they are being looked after by their parents, the chicks of some birds, such as chickens, ducks and zebra finches learn the specific characteristics of their species through their parents. This process, called sexual imprinting, enables them to recognize birds of their own species when they reach breeding

age. If young zebra finches or geese are reared by "foster parents" of another species, they develop a sexual preference for the foster species, not their own. As a classic example, geese that were hand-reared by the ethologist Konrad Lorenz developed a strong sexual preference for him!

The last major function of courtship is that it provides potential mating partners an opportunity to assess one another and to exercise mate choice. Individuals within a species show variation in numerous characters and, in general terms, it will be to the benefit of each individual, in terms of maximizing their

The eggs are incubated in the male's pouch
until they hatch as miniature seahorses, and
are released from his pouch.

THE BIRTH OF A SEAHORSE

reproductive success, to mate preferentially
with a high-quality partner. In a number of
insects, fish and salamanders, for example, it
has been found that males prefer to mate with
larger females. In these animals, a female's size
is typically a good indication of the number of
eggs that she will produce. Thus, by choosing
larger females to mate with, males may increase
the number of their offspring.

For the smooth newt, mate choice is a
complex and subtle process that appears to be
based, in both sexes, on more than one feature
of the partner. Presented with two females, a
male newt, like certain fish and insects, will
usually direct his courtship toward the larger of
the two. If he finds himself in the presence of a
single female, he will display to her as
vigorously as he can, apparently without
discrimination. There is, however, one variation
in his behavior, in that he produces more
spermatophores when courting females that
respond strongly to him. It seems to be the
nature of these males that they appear to be
reluctant to waste their precious sperm on
females that are not fully receptive. Female
newts will only become responsive to males
that sustain their complex courtship at a high
intensity. Once they have become responsive,

▶ (following page) A mating pair of golden
orb spiders (Nephila sp.). Sexual
dimorphism in many spiders takes the
form of an enormous difference in size
between male and female. Small size
increases the male's chances of living
unnoticed in some far corner of the
female's web until she is ready to mate.
On the other hand, it increases his risk of
being eaten by the intensely predatory
female when he approaches her, and
males of many species have evolved
elaborate ways of diverting her attention
during copulation.

COURTSHIP FEEDING

▲ A male bush cricket (*Orophus tessellata*) transfers his spermatophore to his mate (above).

In several species, the act of males giving food to females before, during or after mating is known as courtship feeding. While this behavior fulfills a number of functions, its main role is to bring benefit to the female, the male or both partners. For the male, giving a "nuptial gift" to the female may be a necessary prelude to mating with her; males without gifts are simply rejected as mates. In some instances, the food provided by the male is incorporated into the female's eggs, so that both male and female benefit because she produces more, or more heavily yolked eggs. If females impose the condition that prospective mates must provide a gift, this will put males to a test of their vigor, especially if food is hazardous to find. In the scorpion fly (*Hylobittacus apicalis*), the male has to find a dead arthropod to present to the female and he sometimes obtains one by stealing one from a spider's web.

During mating, male tree crickets feed females in two ways. One way is through the male's highly nutritious spermatophores, which the female eats after they have been emptied of sperm. The male also secretes a delicious fluid from glands on his back, which the female drinks. This food keeps the female interested in the male and distracts her from eating the spermatophore before it has been emptied.

In some birds, the rate at which food is provided by the male during courtship is a good predictor of his performance as a provider of food for the chicks. In the marsh tit (*Parus palustris*), females that are well fed by the male hatch their eggs earlier and have higher reproductive success than less fortunate females. In the silver gull (*Larus novaehollandiae*), females paired with males whose courtship feeding is poor will, in the following year, seek a different mate.

In some animals, it is clear that courtship feeding is purely symbolic and has no nutritive function. In some hanging flies, the male presents the female with an empty ball of silk. This behavior is similar to one that occurs in other insects, in which the silk is wrapped around the body of an insect.

Rudie H. Kuiter/Oxford Scientific Films

the male starts to deposit spermatophores and then females discriminate in favor of certain males, and are more likely to pick up the spermatophores of those males that have larger crests and thus appear more virile.

In fishes in which the male cares for and defends the eggs, females commonly prefer larger, stronger males that are better able to fight off egg predators. Sometimes, however, as in the stickleback, the female's choice of a mate is also influenced by the quality of his nest. In the flathead minnow (*Pinephela promelas*), males become more conscientious parents the more eggs they have in their nest, devoting more time to them and becoming more aggressive in nest-defense. As a result, females prefer males that already have eggs in their nest—such males are more likely to look after their eggs well. This has led to the evolution of a remarkable pattern of behavior, in which males steal eggs from the nests of other males, even though they have not fathered them, simply to make their nest more attractive to potential mates.

One of the most unusual forms of courtship is that of the bowerbirds of New Guinea and northern Australia, which build a large mound or canopy of twigs on the ground. This is not a nest—which is built by the female elsewhere—but is a display area, and the male decorates his bower with a carefully selected variety of colored or highly reflectant objects. In some species, males attack the bowers of their rivals, either by destroying them or stealing the bright objects to decorate their own bowers. Males of the satin bowerbird (*Ptilonorhynchus violaceus*) select for their bowers flowers that are blue and purple and never use orange, red or pink flowers. Blue and purple flowers are rare in the bower birds' habitat, while the other colors are common. It appears that males are forced to collect and decorate their bowers with rare colors because those are the shades that females prefer. Such a preference on the part of females will enable them to discriminate more reliably among males because only the stronger, more vigorous males are able to both defend their bowers against rivals and search for rare flowers at great distances.

The satin bowerbird provides an example of typical female behavior in that the males must undergo what amounts to a "test" of their strength, vigor or stamina. This aspect of courtship is also seen in the context of a particular form of male behavior, courtship feeding, which fulfills a number of biological functions (see section on Courtship Feeding).

One way by which a female can identify and mate preferentially with a strong, vigorous male is to base her choice on certain attributes of males that indicate their ability to compete successfully with other males. In a number of birds, there is variation in particular plumage patterns so that stronger, more dominant males develop these patterns to a greater degree. Examples of such patterns, called "badges of status", include the black bib on the throat of the male house sparrow (*Passer domesticus*) and the black stripe on the breast of the male great tit (*Parus major*). More dominant house sparrows have larger bibs, more dominant great tits have broader stripes. In both species, females prefer as mates those males that have more fully developed badges.

While many animals devote considerable amounts of time and energy to courtship, the act of mating itself is often very brief. The typical form of mating is that the male

ejaculates his sperm into the body of the female, where it is often kept in a special storage organ, or, in species in which fertilization occurs outside the body, onto her eggs. The seahorses (genus *Hippocampus*) are a striking exception; during mating the female delivers eggs to him through a penis-like organ and the male cares for the eggs, carrying them around in a special pouch on his body.

Among mammals, reptiles and arthropods, penises in males take a wide variety of shapes and sizes and, in many species, they are equipped with elaborate ridges, hooks or spines. These may serve one or more of three possible functions. First, they may act as a "lock and key" device, ensuring that a male can only mate with a female of the same species, which

◀ (*facing page*) A male short-snouted seahorse (*Hippocampus breviceps*) giving birth to his young. Taking parental role-reversal almost to its ultimate extreme, the female seahorse lays her eggs in a special incubator pouch in the male's belly, leaving him in sole charge of all subsequent rearing functions.

▼ Restricted to Australia and New Guinea, the bowerbirds have evolved a remarkable extension of the standard "spectacular male" gambit otherwise so common among birds. Instead of relying on fine plumage, male bowerbirds build elaborate and lavishly decorated structures on the ground by which to entice females. Here a male satin bowerbird (*Ptilonorhynchus violaceus*) rearranges his decorations on the stage of his bower.

▲ A pair of common blue damsonflies (*Enallagma cyathigerum*) mating in France. Dragonflies and damsonflies are unique among insects in that the male's copulatory organs are at the forward end of his abdomen.

structure on the end. When he mates with a female, the male uses this to extract sperm left in the female's storage organ by previous males before ejaculating his own. Some invertebrates have enormously long penises. The long, whip-like penis of snails emerges from an aperture on the side of the head and has to pass down a long convoluted series of ducts to reach the partner's sperm receptacle. Snails are hermaphrodites, that is, they are both male and female at the same time, and mating is a mutualistic exercise with both partners giving sperm to each other. Barnacles have two penises, each 40 times as long as the body. Being sessile animals attached permanently to rocks, they cannot approach a partner to mate and have to use their long penises to seek mates from a distance. Spiders practice internal fertilization, but the male does not have a penis. Instead, he uses a special organ, called a pedipalp. During mating, sperm is first expelled as a droplet onto the web before being taken up by the pedipalp. The male then inserts his pedipalp into the female's genital opening and pumps the sperm into her.

A number of groups of animals, including arthropods, cephalopods and salamanders, have evolved a form of mating in which

has a genital opening of a shape that receives only the penis of her own species. Secondly, spines and other structures may hold the penis firmly in place during mating, preventing separation of the pair should they be attacked by a rival male or otherwise disturbed. Thirdly, copulation may serve to stimulate the female, the protuberances on the penis setting up muscular contractions in the female's genital tract that enhance the uptake of sperm into her body. In many lizards and snakes, males have two penises, called "hemipenes", arranged side by side; these may be used alternately, a male mating first from one side, then the other. The male of the American damselfly (*Calopteryx maculata*) has a penis with a scoop-shaped

P. Losse/Planet Earth Pictures

Ken Lucas/Planet Earth Pictures

fertilization occurs inside the female's body, although the male has no penis. Instead, sperm are transferred in packets, called spermatophores, that must be passed from the male to the female. In the cephalopod mollusks (squid and octopuses), the male has a special arm, called the hectocotylus, that passes a worm-like spermatophore to the female. During mating, this detaches from the male and, under its own muscular power, moves around in the female's mantle cavity until it finds its way to her genital opening. Scorpions and salamanders deposit spermatophores on the ground and then either pull the female over it, or entice her across it by means of elaborate displays. When the female's genital opening contacts the spermatophore, the sperm pass automatically into her; the spermatophores of some scorpions incorporate a spring device which, when released by contact, propels the sperm forcibly upwards into the female's body. In several insects the male puts not only sperm but also nutritive substances into each spermatophore (see section on Courtship Feeding). The female detaches the nutritive part from the sperm-filled part and eats it while the sperm enter her. The spermato-phores of mormon crickets (*Anabrus simplex*) contain especially large quantities of nutrient and a single spermatophore may amount to as much as 40 percent of a male's weight.

In many animals, the act of mating marks the end of courtship; the partners separate and go their separate ways. In some creatures, however, courtship continues for some time after mating has been accomplished. In an antelope, the Uganda kob (*Adenota kob*), the male persistently nuzzles the female's genital region with his snout after mating. This stimulates her, causing a secretion of a hormone that causes contractions of her genital tract that carry the sperm up into her uterus.

In the American rough-skinned newt (*Taricha granulosa*), the male, having passed a spermatophore to a female, captures her and holds her tightly with all four of his limbs until she is no longer receptive. This prevents her mating with another male and is an example of a form of behavior called mate-guarding. Guarding of the female after mating also occurs in a variety of arthropods. Many male dragonflies and damselflies, for example, remain clasped to the female from the time of mating throughout the gestation period until she lays her eggs.

◀ Garden snails (*Helix aspersa*) mating, California. Like earthworms, snails are hermaphrodites—that is, each individual carries the organs of both sexes, and sperm is traded between both partners during copulation.

Herwarth Voigtmann/Planet Earth Pictures

THE TIMING OF MATING

As described before, an important function of courtship in many animals is to synchronize the behavior of males and females to exactly the right moment so that mating will be as successful as possible. However, there are other factors that determine the timing of mating. For example, most animals breed and mate only at certain times of year. For birds, insects and amphibians living in temperate climates, their habitual mating and breeding time is in the spring. Animals with very long gestation periods, such as sheep and red deer, mate in the autumn and give birth in the spring. In desert habitats, where seasons are generally not very regular, many animals breed opportunistically, often after periods of rain. The zebra finch, for example, breed at this time, when there is a rapid growth in the vegetation, which is sure to provide a lot of food in the form of seeds to sustain their breeding effort. Desert-living frogs, such as the spadefoot toad (*Scaphiopus couchii*), also respond very quickly to rain, emerging from their dry season hiding places, mating and laying their eggs in temporary pools. The tadpoles of such frogs are

◀ Mating cuttlefish, Maldive Islands. The male cuttlefish attracts the female with the aid of complex color changes, and by waving the colorful fourth tentacle on his left side, which is modified to form a copulatory organ called the hectocotylus. Tentacles intertwined, the male transfers bundles of spermatophores to his mate's genital opening.

▼ A pair of spotted grass frogs (*Lymnodynastes tasmaniensis*) in amplexus. One of the most common frogs of southeastern Australia, the female of this species lays up to 1,100 eggs in a foam nest, to be fertilized *en masse* by the males as they are laid.

C.A. Henley/Auscape

▲ North African scorpion males fighting. Desert scorpions live in underground burrows and hunt only at night.

capable of remarkably rapid growth and development, which enable them to leave the water as young frogs before the pond dries out again in the next season.

The features of the environment that play an important role in the timing of breeding are known as "proximate" and "ultimate" factors and are typically linked to cyclic and sporadic changes. Firstly, proximate factors are those changes that act as stimuli, directly influencing the physiology and behavior of animals, causing them to undergo the many hormonal, anatomic and other changes that bring them into breeding condition. Of these, the most important changes are day-length and temperature, for species that breed regularly at a particular time of year; and rainfall and food supply, for species, like the zebra finch, that breed opportunistically. With respect to day-length, some animals, such as red deer and sheep, are called short-day species because their reproductive development is triggered by a shortening of the day-length in the autumn. Other animals, among them mice and starlings, are long-day species and breed in spring in a biological response to increasing day-length.

Secondly, the ultimate factors controlling the timing of breeding are those that have determined, on an evolutionary timescale, the periods when it is most advantageous for animals to breed. For temperate species, breeding in the spring ensures that breeding animals have a plentiful supply of food to develop their eggs and, that in the early summer, there is an abundance of food on which the young can feed, giving them a reasonable chance of surviving the hardships of their first winter.

While the great majority of animals respond to changes in the environment, some species do not and their reproductive activity must be controlled by other mechanisms. For example, for mammals that spend their winter hibernating deep underground, like ground squirrels, there is no way that they can detect the changes in day-length and temperature that signal the onset of spring. To compensate for this, it appears that they possess an accurate annual "clock" that acts like an alarm, causing them to wake up in early spring, without direct reference to life above ground.

The breeding activity of many shore-dwelling animals is governed by the monthly rhythm of the tides. The grunion fish (*Leuresthes tennuis*) lives off the coast of California and spawns off the crest of high spring tides. At this time, males and females swarm in large numbers up the

Horizon/BVPL

population, some females may have laid too many eggs and are not able to feed all their chicks adequately, while others may lay too few and could have reared more than they actually do. In several species of birds, the females exploit surpluses of eggs by "dumping" them in other unguarded nests.

Many birds of prey and egrets have evolved a particular mechanism that adjusts brood size in relation to prevailing environmental conditions. A number of eggs are laid at intervals of two or more days and the female begins to incubate them as soon as the first one is laid. This means that the eggs hatch at intervals, unlike those of most birds which hatch at the same time because incubation does not begin until the last egg has been laid. As a result of asynchronous hatching, one chick is older and more fully developed than the rest of the brood. If it receives only a little food from its parents, it kills its younger siblings; if it receives a lot of food, the young are not in such intense competition with one another and the older chick does not attack and kill the younger ones. This mechanism ensures that the parents always produce at least one chick that is adequately fed and that, from year to year, they rear a number of chicks that display a stamina that is related to the quality of the environment.

(*following pages*) A wandering albatross pair in courtship display, South Georgia. Albatrosses live for several decades, mate for life, and breed slowly, producing at best only one young every two years. They maintain their pair bonds with ritualized displays.
Jean-Paul Ferrero/Auscape

▼Baby rabbits (*Oryctolagus cuniculus*) in the nest. The young of birds and mammals vary widely in their state of development at birth or hatching, depending on the species.

beach to mate and the females bury their fertilized eggs in the sand. Here, the eggs develop and remain untouched by water until the next high spring tide, about fifteen days later. They are then washed out to sea, where they hatch.

Many insects, notably gnats and mosquitos, gather in swarms to mate, as a result of many individuals emerging at the same time. Perhaps the most remarkable example of breeding synchrony is that of cicadas, different species of which reach sexual maturity and form mating swarms on an extremely long cycle of thirteen or seventeen years.

For some species, there will be occasions when favorable environmental conditions trigger the start of breeding but then deteriorate, so that breeding cannot be successfully sustained. Under such circumstances, a number of female mammals, such as mice, may abort their developing embryos or else reabsorb some or all of them into their bodies. In many birds, the number of eggs laid by a female can vary from year to year and is a response to conditions at the time of laying; these may or may not be good predictors of conditions later in the breeding season, when the chicks have to be fed. Thus, within a

Michael Leach/NHPA

Harold Palo/NHPA

PARENTAL BEHAVIOR

There is enormous variation among animals in the extent to which the young are nourished, protected and generally cared for by one or both of their parents. In animals that do care for their young there is, furthermore, variation between species in terms of whether it is the female, the male, or both parents that assume parental duties. A critical factor in determining how much and what kind of care the young require if they are to reach independence is the stage of development that they have reached when they are born. Among the birds and mammals, for example, there are species, described as "precocial", in which the young are born at an advanced stage of development. A young antelope or a pheasant chick is able to

see and move about almost immediately after it has emerged from its mother's womb or from the egg. In these species, there is relatively little parental care and the young soon assume independence from their parents, though most antelopes do conscientiously defend their calves against predators. In "altricial" species, by contrast, the young are born in a more helpless, undeveloped state. The young of rats and mice, and of most tree-nesting birds, are born blind, naked and with poorly developed limbs. Wholly dependent on their parents for warmth, food and protection, they require intensive parental care for a long time.

A second important factor in parental care is working out how the task can be achieved in the species' particular environment. Birds of

▲ Great egrets (*Egretta alba*) are among those birds that begin incubation at the time their first egg is laid, with the result that young in the nest hatch several days apart and thus differ in size and development. If food is scarce the smallest will soon die, and food fetched by the parents is then shared among fewer siblings, increasing the chance that at least one will survive to carry on the species.

◄ (*facing page*) Plains zebra (*Equus burchelli*) with newborn foal. In contrast to rabbits, young zebras can see and stand within minutes of birth, and can keep up with adults in full gallop within a few days.

▲ Parental care is by no means limited to birds and mammals, and even many insects are solicitous parents. Males of the American giant water bug (*Abedus* sp.), for example, carry their eggs on their backs until they hatch.

prey, for example, live in environments where food is typically scarce and to gather supplies requires considerable skill and effort. As the young are quite incapable of finding and catching food for themselves (it may take many weeks or months to develop their own hunting skills), they are, consequently, dependent on provisions from their parents. Seed-eating birds, by contrast, have access to a food that is often abundant. The young of hens and pheasants are able to feed themselves quite adequately a few days after hatching, once they have received some initial guidance from their mothers about where the food is.

The division of parental care between parents depends very largely on some fundamental differences between the sexes. Because females typically produce healthy eggs, they have made a much larger investment in each of their offspring before fertilization occurs, while males contribute only genetic material to the fertilized eggs. This inbalance between the sexes is greatly accentuated in birds, in which the eggs are especially large by virtue of their huge yolk content, and in mammals, in which the young remain in the female's womb throughout their early development. These factors, and others, thus

Ken Lucas/Planet Earth Pictures

Johnny Johnson/Bruce Coleman Limited

tadpoles on their backs, taking them from one pool to another. A feature common to frogs and sticklebacks, and many other fishes, is that the eggs are fertilized outside the female's body. In species with external fertilization, the female must produce the eggs before the male can fertilize them. As a result he is left "holding the babies". In internal fertilization, however, it is clearly the female that must care for the fertilized eggs on her own.

For birds, there are several categories of parental care that, to varying degrees, are performed by one or both parents. These include incubation of the eggs and feeding and protecting the young from attacks by predators. In some birds, such as the herring gull (*Larus argentatus*), both parents carry out all these functions more or less equally. Male and female take it in turns to be at the nest, while the partner flies away to feeding grounds some distance from the colony.

Herring gulls are subject to attack by many predators, including hedgehogs, rats, foxes and larger seabirds, though such predators are usually driven away by the combined efforts of many gulls which, in a dense colony, can

predispose females to be the sole or major provider of parental care. There are numerous examples of animals in which the male plays the major role in parental care, which shows that other factors are at work in determining which sex cares for the young.

In sticklebacks and in the European midwife toad (*Alytes obstetricans*), the male is the sole provider of parental care. Male midwife toads take strings of fertilized eggs from one or more females and carry them around for several days, wrapped around their hind legs, before taking them to pools where they hatch into tadpoles. Males of many poison-arrow frogs carry

▶ (*following pages*) Meerkats (*Suricata suricata*) are South African relatives of the mongoose. They are strongly inquisitive and social animals that live in permanent colonies in open country.
Barrie Wilkins/Bruce Coleman Limited

▼ Like many large carnivores, young grizzly bears (*Ursus arctos*) remain dependent on their mother for some considerable time after birth.

PARENTAL CARE IN FROGS

During their lives, amphibians are confined to damp or wet habitats because of the nature of their skin, which is delicate and permeable to water. This is especially true for eggs and larvae, which can only develop if they are thoroughly wet. Some frogs, like the European common frog (*Rana temporaria*), simply deposit their eggs, in huge masses, in ponds during the spring and then leave them to develop on their own. Their eggs, however, are food for many other creatures, including newts, fishes and insect larvae, and, generally, very few survive to become adult frogs. Common frogs counter this problem to some extent by preferring to lay their eggs in ephemeral pools that dry up in the summer, and are therefore unreliable habitats for predators. There is, however, an inherent risk in this strategy—that the larvae will die if the pond dries up too soon.

To combat the problem, many frogs have evolved forms of parental care which have helped more of their young to make it to adulthood. Of course, this may mean that fewer eggs are produced, but as discussed earlier, they will be of a better quality. The male gladiator frog (*Hyla rozenbergi*), for example, digs small pools beside a stream, and from this vantage point calls to attract females.

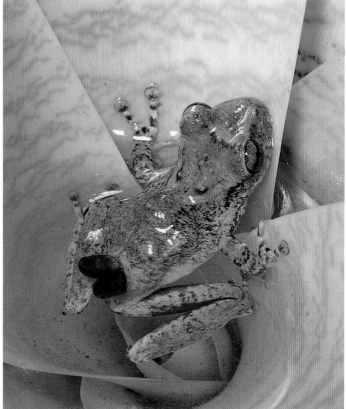

Michael Fogden/Oxford Scientific Films

▲ A female marsupial frog releases her tadpoles.

Leo Meier/Weldon Trannies

▲ Many frogs, like this green tree frog (*Litoria bicolor*) of tropical Australia, invest little or no care in their young; others display a huge range of complex parental behaviors involving either or both sexes.

Several frogs may also lay their eggs on vegetation hanging over a pond or stream. Here, safe from aquatic predators, the eggs are free to develop into tadpoles and then fall into the water. Other frog species will deposit their eggs in a mass of foam, secreted by the female and whipped up by the male. This provides a moist environment in which the developing eggs can be nurtured.

In the midwife toad (*Alytes obstetricans*), the male carries strings of eggs which are wrapped around his hind legs, while male poison-arrow frogs carry tadpoles on their backs. In other species, however, it is the female that cares for the young. The female South American marsupial frog (*Flectonotus pygmaeus*), for example, has a pouch on her back into which the fertilized eggs are inserted during a complicated mating procedure. When they have developed into tadpoles, the female drops them into water-filled hollows in bromeliads. In the surinam toad (*Pipa pipa*), the eggs are absorbed into individual pockets in the spongy skin on the female's back and remain there until they emerge as fully formed froglets. Most remarkable of all is the Australian gastric-brooding frog (*Rheobatrachus silus*), in which the female swallows the fertilized eggs. Safe in her stomach, they develop as fully formed froglets, and then are spat out of her mouth. Throughout their development, the normal tendency of the female to eat and digest food has to be suppressed.

collectively present predators with formidable opposition. A more serious threat comes from other herring gulls. Within a gull colony, adjacent nests are only 1–2 meters (about 3–6 feet) apart and, should a nest be left unattended, even for a few minutes, a neighbor will eat any eggs or chicks that it can grab.

In other birds, different aspects of parental care are carried out by different parents. In the yellow-billed hornbill (*Tockus flavirostris*), the parents typically nest in a tree-hole. The female settles down in the hole and walls herself in with mud brought to her by the male. This sets hard and provides a fortress between her and the outside world, with only a small hole left through which the male passes food. The female remains here for several weeks, carrying out all the incubation of the eggs and feeding of the chicks, until the young are so large that there is no longer room for them and her. She then breaks out of the nest and walls it up again, until the young are ready to leave. Both parents now bring food to the chicks.

In some mammals, notably monkeys and apes, the young are carried around by their parents, clinging to their bodies. In marsupials, the young are born at a very early stage in their development, and are carried around in a pouch on the female's stomach that encloses her nipples. Safe in its pouch, a baby kangaroo can feed while being transported by its mother. Marmosets (*Callithrix jacchus*) are small primates, related to monkeys, that always give birth to twins and, because the young are born at an advanced stage of development, they are too large for the mother to carry around together at once. As a type of compensatory measure, they live in extended families in which the older independent young stay with their parents and also carry and look after the young infants. In fact, in marmoset families, the mother herself carries the young less often than the other family members.

Parental care in some animals finds physical expression in the form of a burrow, den or nest. While nest building in many ground-nesting birds amounts to little more than surrounding a perfunctory scrape in the ground with some hastily collected grass and debris, other birds make beautifully constructed and elaborate nests. The weaver birds' nests, for example, are generally complex structures, meticulously woven out of grass and suspended from the branches of trees where few predators can reach them. Many have a tunnel-like entrance positioned in such a way that it is very difficult, even for the more agile nest-predators like snakes, to get into the nest. The male European wren (*Troglodytes troglodytes*) builds several nests in his breeding territory, each a

Francois Gohier/Ardea London

◀ (*previous page*) A South American spider monkey (*Ateles geoffroyi*), mother and young. Many arboreal mammals, such as monkeys, carry their young with them until they reach independence.

meticulously constructed, cave-like structure. When courting a female, he shows her all the nests that he has built and calls on her to select one of them in which to lay her eggs. The other nests are generally left unused.

Perhaps the most spectacular nests are those of social insects such as bees, wasps, ants and termites. For example the castle-like nests of termites can be several meters high. The nests are not solely built for the purpose of breeding, but provide a safe and controlled environment in which many individuals in a colony of insects live for their entire life.

Generally, the number of eggs that a bird can rear is limited to the maximum number that they can fit beneath them. However, this is not the case for a group of Australasian birds called megapodes (meaning "very large feet"), such as the mallee fowl (*Leipoa ocellata*). Megapodes lay

Jen and Des Bartlett/Bruce Coleman Limited

▲ Several female ostriches (*Struthio camelus*) may contribute eggs to the large clutches incubated mainly by the male although, as here, he is sometimes assisted by the primary female. After the chicks have hatched, they congregate in creches of 100 or more under the care of several adults, not necessarily their parents.

▶ Some snakes lay eggs, but most members of the viper family, including this sidewinder adder (*Bitis peringueyi*) escorting its young over the Namib Desert in South Africa, give birth to living young.

their eggs in large mounds filled with plant material that forms a rotting compost heap. This generates much of the heat necessary for the eggs to develop, but some also comes from the sun. A single female can lay as many as 33 eggs in a mound, though 19 is the average number. Because each egg is very large, even an average clutch has a total weight equivalent to that of the female, and it takes her several weeks to lay a full clutch. Although mound-nesting frees the parents from having to incubate the eggs, the male still has a great deal to do. For five and a half months, he visits his mound every day and checks the temperature inside it. He controls the temperature in the nest by adding or removing sand, using his large feet to shovel it, and so compensates for

David Hughes/Bruce Coleman Limited

Patrick Fagot/NHPA

▲ A family of red kangaroos (*Macropus rufus*). A baby kangaroo is born in a tiny, almost embryonic state; unaided, it then crawls through the mother's fur to locate the teat in her pouch.

▶ (*facing page*) In the African elephant the bond between mother and young is exceptionally close. The infant will not be weaned for several years, and it remains dependent on its mother for up to eight or even ten years.

variations in the amount of heat reaching the developing eggs.

Crocodiles and alligators also lay their eggs in large nests, and the female stays nearby to defend them from predators. She then carries the hatchlings in her jaws to the relative safety of water. A complication of this form of parental care is that the temperature during the development of the eggs affects the sex of the offspring. In the American alligator (*Alligator mississippiensis*), eggs incubated at a temperature of less than 30°C (86°F) between days 7 and 21 all hatch into females; while eggs incubated above 34°C (93°F) hatch into males. By contrast, in turtles and tortoises, warm temperatures produce more daughters, while cool temperatures more sons.

In some animals, most notably among birds, offspring also receive care from older individuals other than their parents. These individuals are called "helpers" and, in many instances, they are genetically related to the young birds for which they provide care. European moorhens (*Gallinula chloropus*), for example, typically produce more than one brood in a year, and the young of the first brood actually help their parents to feed and protect the younger chicks in the second and, sometimes, in a third brood.

In other cases, care is provided by non-related individuals, as in the "creche" behavior of ostriches and penguins. In these species, several adults gather together, each with their

own chicks, to form a single flock. While some adults go off to find food, others remain with the creche, defending it against predators. Helping is a feature of breeding behavior in a number of species, such as the Florida scrub jay (*Aphelocoma coerulescens*) and the acorn woodpecker of California (*Melanerpes formicivorus*), which form co-operative breeding groups that are largely stable in composition over several years. Only certain adults breed, while the others bring food to the chicks and protect them from predators.

There are, in fact, a number of factors involved in the evolution of co-operative breeding. First, it commonly occurs in environments that provide only limited opportunities for successful breeding, in terms of food supply or nest sites. Thus, for birds in which their own breeding prospects are poor, being a helper is a constructive option. In fact, belonging to a co-operative breeding group is in the long-term interests of helpers. Second, it provides them with experience of caring for young which, ultimately, makes them more successful as parents. Furthermore, helpers acquire higher and higher status within groups as older birds die so that, eventually, they have a good chance of assuming the role of breeding birds. Finally, helpers are commonly genetically related to the young in their group so that, indirectly, they are contributing to the spread of genes that they and their young are likely to have in common.

Chapter 4

HOMES AND HABITATS

Michael Hansell

Animal species constantly adapt to the volatility of their physical and biological worlds. In order to survive, animals must adapt to, master, and in some cases manipulate their environment.

THE TRAP MAKERS

Animals have devised ingenious ways of satisfying their basic needs. The trap makers, for example, have found that the best way to survive is to stay put and allow their food to come to them. Over time, they have become clever architects, engineering very creative ways of surprising their prey. Some even go to the added trouble of venturing out to lure their victims into their traps.

THE HOME BUILDERS

The home builders, on the other hand, survive by keeping the world out and living within the confines of a protected environment. Some species, such as beavers, go to great lengths to establish their private world. Once established in their realm, they are totally self-sufficient.

THE HABITAT MANIPULATORS

Perhaps the most ingenious of all animals are the habitat manipulators that masterfully adapt to an ever-changing environment. Whatever the conditions, they will find a way of coping. In times of plenty they gather their stocks, which are then brought out in times of famine. Places that are normally hot can become, with a little bit of engineering, agreeably cool.

HOMES AND HABITATS

Michael Hansell

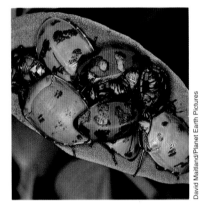

▲ A group of Australian harlequin bugs (*Tectocoris diophthalmus*) in winter hibernation.

Within their private realms, animals have devised ingenious ways of surviving their hazardous worlds. A vital survival stategy is mastery of the habitat, a necessary precursor to obtaining food.

The world about us is a restless place, perpetually changing in a variety of ways, some of which are predictable and some of which are not. Over the hundreds of millions of years that natural selection has operated, many different species of animals have become able to survive on our planet, and adapt to the volatility of its physical (season, daylight, rainfall) and biological (competitors, mates, predators, and food environments) challenges.

To do this, animals of many kinds have had to devise some very specialized and remarkable behavior. This chapter looks at such behavior in the trap makers, the home builders and the habitat manipulators.

For growth, reproduction, and indeed life itself, animals need food. If that food happens to be another animal then before it can be eaten, it must first be brought within arm's length and caught. Of course, arm's length does not extend very far out into the world, but many animals get over this problem by being mobile and going in search of their prey. However, the more an animal travels, the higher its fuel costs. It is less expensive to stay put. This can in fact be a profitable way of life, provided that your food comes to you. The trap makers, for example, have made stationary hunting a cost-effective way of life by using two ingenious devices. The first is to build a trap which essentially extends their reach beyond arm's length; the second is to persuade the prey to come to the trap.

For the home builders, the problem is one of keeping a hostile world at arm's length. The most basic solution to this problem is to place some kind of physical barrier between you and the world beyond. Inside the protective wall, the world then becomes a calmer place. The physical extremes of the world outside are blunted and the threats from other animals are reduced. There is, of course, a price to pay for this. Firstly, the cost of the building work itself in energy and materials, which are often secretions from the architect's own body. Secondly, the animal must adapt to the loss of mobility that results from living within an additional layer of physical protection.

In a world of change, it is the habitat manipulators that are best able to make for themselves an island of stability. Environments in which plenty alternates with famine can become habitable by laying up a stock of food reserves. Also, environments which are at times

▶ A dromedary (*Camelus dromedarius*) in the Judean desert. Some animals make no traps, build no homes, nor manipulate their environments.

146

oppressively hot and dry, then within hours become cool and humid, are made agreeable places. This may be achieved by creating an artificial world within the confines of a self-regulated fortress, which is fixed and enduring. But, amazingly, there is a totally opposite absolutely mobile solution and that is to move with the changing world, always keeping in the climate you like. This, in its most extreme form, may provide a climate almost as constant.

THE TRAP MAKERS

Caddis larval nets

The larvae of caddis flies (Trichoptera) are very much like the caterpillars of butterflies and moths (Lepidoptera); they are in fact closely related orders. Caddis larvae also resemble caterpillars in that they have a soft segmented body and a pair of spinnerets in the mouth which extrude a double strand of silk. We know ourselves the excellent quality of silk—its fine, light and strong fibers have many uses. Some species of caddis larvae use it to make nets to capture prey or filter particles washed down by the current in streams.

Exactly what is being carried down by a water current will depend in part on its speed. The more rapid the flow, the larger and heavier the particles that will be suspended in it. The faster the flow also the greater the force that will be exerted on the net, and so the greater the risk of it being torn apart. So, in faster flowing streams, the resistance offered by the net must be reduced by making it with a relatively large mesh size, but at the same time

MAKING TOOLS TO CATCH PREY: CAN ONLY CLEVER ANIMALS DO IT?

▲ A chimpanzee (*Pan calvus*) uses a stick to probe an otherwise inaccessible hole. Studies have shown that chimps are adept at making tools such as this. But tool making is not confined to the primates.

Jean Paul Ferrero/Auscape

Humans are rather special. Our intelligence and technical mastery far exceed that shown by the wisest gorilla or smartest chimp. One longstanding explanation (but not the only one) for the evolution of human intelligence is that the gradual development of upright posture in our early human ancestors released the hand for skillful manipulation. Intelligent individuals benefited from this, leading to the evolution of greater skill and knowledge.

The utilization of tools became identified as a landmark in human evolution, as it implied an insight into their use before they were manipulated. Many believed that only humans were capable of using tools.

However, the first field studies on apes in the 1960s showed that chimpanzees used and indeed made tools. For example, they could shape a fine grass stem and push it into a termite mound, where termite soldiers in defense of their colony would grab it with their jaws. The chimps then carefully withdrew the stem and ate the termites. A recent study shows that chimps in West Africa actually manipulate stone tools to act as sticks for catching ants.

Well, if we are not the only tool users, then perhaps other tool users are somehow special. The Galapagos woodpecker finch (*Geospiza pallida*) breaks off a cactus spine and with it extracts insect prey concealed in bark crevices; the northwestern crow (*Corvus caurinus*) does much the same with a small stick. But a moment's reflection on the manipulative skill of birds should assure us that the creation of a decorated avenue by a satin bowerbird is much more interesting and biologically important than a finch fiddling about with a cactus spine. We could try to bend the rules, as has been argued, by saying that a bower is a sort of tool, designed to maximize the efficiency of the process of courtship. But what then do we call the wonderfully elegant nests constructed by hundreds of species of small birds?

The special status of tool using, therefore, becomes untenable when we look at the increasing number of known invertebrate examples: the ants (*Aphaenogaster rudis*) that use bits of debris as sponges to mop up plant or animal juices; the solitary wasp (*Ammophila* sp.) that seals the entrance of its nest burrow by bashing the ground with a stone held in its jaw; or the predatory bug (*Salyavata variegata*) that dangles the carcass of a termite it has just sucked dry, in front of another termite. The termite worker, programmed to keep the nest free from the corpses of its colleagues, tries to pick up the husk, is caught and fed upon. Its remains are used to lure another termite.

So tool use is not a helpful concept, although it still remains a topic of some interest in the study of monkeys and apes in the context of human evolution. But we should always beware of selectively using evidence from the animal kingdom in the quest for our own uniqueness.

Heather Angel

as small as possible, so as to prevent valuable food items from being swept straight through it. The nets of the genus *Hydropsyche* are typical.

The net of *Hydropsyche*

Caddis larvae of this genus live at the bottom of streams and suspend their nets in the gaps between stones through which water is being swept. The nets have a beautiful regularity which, as is so often true in nature, is achieved by a very simple process. This is done by the larva which repeatedly extends its body and sweeps its head through a figure eight. While doing this, it extrudes a thread of silk from its mouth which is at first sticky but quickly hardens. The effect of this behavior is to build up a net attached at the edges to the rocks and by criss-crossing itself makes a capture surface of about 150 meshes with a mesh size of 200 to 300 microns (thousandths of a millimeter). Having completed its net, the agile predator—for that is what it is—sits in a silken tube under a stone, ready to pounce at any unfortunate creature, such as a small crustacean, which is swept into the net.

The indoor filter of *Macronema*

The workmanship of *Hydropsyche* is impressive because, to our eyes, it has not only regularity but delicacy. However, in truth it is a mere string bag compared with the silk strainer devised by another caddis of the same family, *Macronema transversum*. At first glance, what we observe of the *Macronema* construction is impressive enough. It is a little house made of

many hundreds of tiny regular-sized sand grains, stuck together with silk, and projecting up from the house is a sand grain funnel, curved at the top to face into the direction of water flow. It resembles the ventilation funnels that used to ornament the sides of ocean-going liners and its purpose is much the same.

On ocean liners the funnels capture the sea breezes to drive fresh air deep into the lower level of the ship. The *Macronema* construction is designed to do the same to the flowing water for the caddis larva: not simply to bring fresh oxygen-laden water, but also the fine particles upon which the larva feeds. This is a device designed for slow-moving water, in which only small particles will be suspended and the device by which they are trapped is again a net.

This net divides the sand mosaic chamber into two, with unfiltered water entering down the funnel on one side, and filtered water leaving by a shorter exhalant current on the other. The larva itself sits in a side passage from which it can lean out and glean captured particles from the upstream surface of the net. Some incoming fresh water is diverted through the side passage, providing the larva with a flow of fresh water over its gills.

The particles on which the larva feeds include diatoms and algae of only about 10 microns long, so a mesh size like that of *Hydropsyche* would simply let them through. In fact, the net is made up of thicker threads about 25 microns apart crossed by thinner ones which are only 3 microns apart, to create a net with an estimated 260,000 meshes.

▲ Caddis larvae live in streams, and are notable for constructing elaborate shelters for themselves from bits of debris, gluing it to their bodies to form a sort of tube. These are *Brachycentrus subnubilis*, living in a fast-flowing river in England.

The spider's orb web

The stereotype picture of a spider's trap is the orb web—a radiating array of silk threads which is interlaced with a spiral capture thread. The role of the radii is to allow the web to keep its shape until a flying insect collides with it. This kind of silk thread has a strength comparable to steel and is prestressed to give the web some rigidity, while at the same time allowing it a degree of elasticity with which to cope with local breezes. This, however, is not an ideal thread for the capture of flying prey, which might simply bounce back on impact.

What is needed, therefore, is an additional silk that can absorb the impact of a rapidly moving object and leave it motionless and stuck to the web. This is the role of the spiral thread. Amazingly, two completely different

▲ A garden spider (*Argrope aurantia*) carefully wraps its insect prey in a silken shroud for later consumption.

▶ (*facing page*) One disadvantage of a large efficient web is that it is prone to capture useless items as well as insect prey: here an orb-building spider (*Meta segmentata*) waits at the center of a web cluttered with the parachute seeds of the common ragwort.

types of capture thread are found: some species of orb web spider use one type of web and some the other. One particular type of thread contains droplets of sticky secretion, while the other has "puffs" of fine threads spaced along it within which the projecting edges and hairs of insects become entangled.

In the genus *Araneus*, the spiral capture thread is a pair of core fibers initially evenly coated with a viscous layer which quickly coalesces into a string of sticky beads. It is these droplets that do the catching, giving the spider time to rush across the web, and to bite and wrap the doomed dinner.

The silk core of the capture thread has the important role of absorbing the initial impact of the moving insect, but it appears that, even in this core, the sticky droplets play an ingenious

role. This is because the surface tension of the viscous coat of the thread draws slack core thread into the droplets, tensing the capture spiral but allowing it elongation.

At the molecular level, a very similar capability for extension without breaking is added. A highly regular crystalline molecular structure of the amino acid chains of the silk is interspersed in regions where the chains are in a random tangle. In these non-crystalline areas the bonds between the chains are weak, so that on the impact of an insect, they break. This allows the chains to straighten, while at the same time absorbing the victim's kinetic energy and bringing it to a halt. The two levels of extension, both at the molecular and at the level of the whole thread, allow the capture spiral to be extended two or three times its original length before breaking. This indeed is a formidable piece of capture technology.

In the face of the threat posed by spiders' webs, natural selection has favored flying insects that can avoid capture. In particular, some daytime insects are skillful at seeing the threads and taking evasive action. Orb web spiders that live in well-lit habitats, where reflection of light from the threads will be greater, tend to place their webs near background vegetation which disrupts the regular pattern of the threads. Even so, the power of flies to detect the trap may be high since they can sometimes be seen avoiding intact parts of a web to fly through holes.

In an apparent bid to combat the webs' detectability, some orb web-spinning species attach a thread to the center of the orb and tighten it to create a cone-shaped surface. This may give an insect as it flies towards the cone the impression that the web has a hole in the middle of it. When it reaches the web, however, the spider releases the tension, collapsing the web and entangling the fly.

The moth-catching specialists

Of course, the thicker the silk thread, the more detectable it will be. However, the larger the prey, the stronger the thread will need to be. So to specialize on larger prey, some spider species are forced into sites close to disruptive vegetation or dimly lit places. But some insects, namely butterflies and moths, have another ingenious anti-web defense. They have body scales which readily peel off, leaving an imprint on the sticky droplets of the web but allowing the insect to escape. For the spider, a solution to this problem is to evolve bigger sticky droplets which can overwhelm the defensive effect of the body scales. But bigger droplets will make the web even more visible, provided of course that the webs catch insects which fly in the light.

Moths are generally big, fat, fast and covered in scales—not easy to catch. But, as far as spiders are concerned they have a particular weakness—they fly at night. This has allowed spiders that are moth specialists to create a range of scale-defeating webs which are spun only at night and taken down before dawn.

Some of these specialist web designs are an elaboration of the basic orb web, while others show a completely opposite trend resulting in reduced or minimal web structures. One form of elaboration is a ladder web. The New Guinea ladder web spider, for example, builds an orb with the segment below the hub immensely stretched out, and with the sticky capture threads forming its rungs. If a moth hits this web, it will struggle to escape, rolling down the ladder's length and shedding its scales. But the principle of prey capture is that, before the moth falls off the bottom of the web and escapes, all its scales are shed and it hangs, immobilized, plucked and ready for execution.

By one of those wonderful symmetries of convergent evolution, a South American spider, *Scoloderus* sp., has independently evolved a ladder web from an ancestral orb. But here the hub is near the bottom and the rungs are stretched across a segment above it.

The moth specialist *Pasilobus* sp., also a native of New Guinea, is an example of how spiders can overcome moth defenses by a great simplification of the orb web design, using the principle that a few large drops of glue can overwhelm a moth's protective veneer of loose scales. The trap here consists of a horizontal segment of orb made up of only three radii, from which are loosely hung a small number of capture threads with large sticky droplets. When a capture thread is struck, it shears at its outer end, leaving the moth tethered and whirling, awaiting collection by the spider.

Reduction in the extent of the web, of course, suggests a reduced capture range for the spider. So, although extreme reduction of the web would make construction cheap, it is hard to see how it could be cost effective. This problem seems to have been completely overcome by one of the greatest moth-eating specialists of all, *Mastophora* sp.

Its web consists of a few threads, from which it hangs and holds a single thread with a large sticky ball at the end, waiting for moths to come to it. Along they come, winging their way upwind—all males and nearly all of only one moth species. They are attracted by a secretion produced by the spider that mimics the sex attractant of unmated female moths of their species. Alas it is not sexual fulfillment, but capture and death that await them. For the spider it is a monotonous but nutritious diet.

The lure of the bowerbird

Male satin bowerbirds (*Ptilonorhynchus violaceus*) are another species that try to lure others to them. Again they are only interested in one species and one sex—female satin bowerbirds—but the purpose this time is not prey capture but reproduction. Part of a male's ability to lure females depends upon his agile voice, and upon the dark bluish purple iridescence of his plumage, but a crucial part of the whole effect he creates upon the female resides in a special arrangement of twigs and ornaments he has created—the bower.

Among the 6,000 or so bird species, the development of male plumage adornment or elaborate song to attract females is rather common. The building of specialized structures to impress females is, however,

Michael Tweedie/NHPA

only found in one small family of birds, the bowerbirds (Ptilonorhynchidae), only 13 of which make a distinct construction of twigs with associated decorations.

The bowers they construct are of two fairly distinct types, *avenue* and *maypole*. The satin bowerbird is a typical avenue builder, while the range of construction demonstrated by maypole builders is nicely illustrated by the four species of *Amblyornis* bowerbirds.

The bowerbirds are closely related to the paradise birds (Paradisaeidae), celebrated for the extreme development of the male plumage. Yet in the aptly named brown gardener, a masterful bower builder, the male is no different in appearance from the female. So how did this transfer of the male display from plumage to bower come about?

The first element in the evolutionary process may simply have been the removal of leaves from branches in an area where male birds came to display. Such behavior is shown by certain paradise birds which remove the leaves in order that their colorful feathers are more clearly seen in their forest environment. It seems that the arrangement of the leaves removed from the trees then became, for the females, part of the display itself. Similar behavior can be seen in the toothbilled bowerbird, which does not construct a bower but clears an area of ground upon which it lays freshly picked leaves with their pale undersides facing upwards. From such a simple display, female preference for the most elaborately constructed displays has led to the building of distinctive bowers.

▼ Resting among the leaf litter on the forest floor, this male English lappet moth (*Gastropacha quercifolia*) demonstrates the effectiveness of camouflage.

females and there is a lot more to it than just upright sticks. To start with, the avenue between the sticks is aligned along near enough a north–south axis, and in front of one entrance to the avenue is a platform on which a variety of ornaments are placed. The avenue itself is quite free of ornaments and any placed there by interfering humans are removed.

The ornaments comprise a wonderful variety of objects gleaned from round about: blue flowers and parrot feathers, yellow leaves and flowers, gray fungi or fragments of wasp nest, brown snail shells or cicada skins, and pieces of cast snake skin. But blue is particularly favored: blue bottle tops or paper wrappers, even in one reported case a still-living blue centipede presumably carried to the bower very much against its will!

Although the avenue floor is kept quite free of these ornaments, it may be decorated along its inner sides with a kind of paint. This is made with the pulp of certain fruit, including of course blue ones, and sometimes with ash from bits of burned wood mixed with saliva. This paint may even be applied with the aid of a piece of soft bark held in the beak.

There may well be quite a number of bowers with attendant males within the commuting distance of one female. This gives her an opportunity to go round and compare bowers. We now know that females do indeed make use of this opportunity, visiting an average of three or four bowers and showing a tendency to mate with males who have superior constructions. Quality, it turns out, is judged with quite a sophisticated eye; females prefer a male whose bower shows a solid construction to the walls of the avenue, and which has a large number of ornaments such as snail shells and blue parrot feathers.

But does all this structural detail really tell a female that the male concerned is of high quality? A candid camera account of the behavior of males when not displaying to females reveals that it probably does.

Male satin bowerbirds are in fact terrible thieves, frequently raiding the bowers of their neighbors and carrying off prestigious decorations such as blue feathers. This not only benefits the thief but simultaneously diminishes the display of the victim—a double profit. Naturally, more dominant birds are more effective than lower ranking ones. Not only do they steal ornaments, but they also take the opportunity to do a bit of smashing up of the bower itself. In one group of satin bowerbirds studied, the average number of times that a bower was damaged by neighbors in one breeding season was 8, and one miserable male had his bower broken up 31 times!

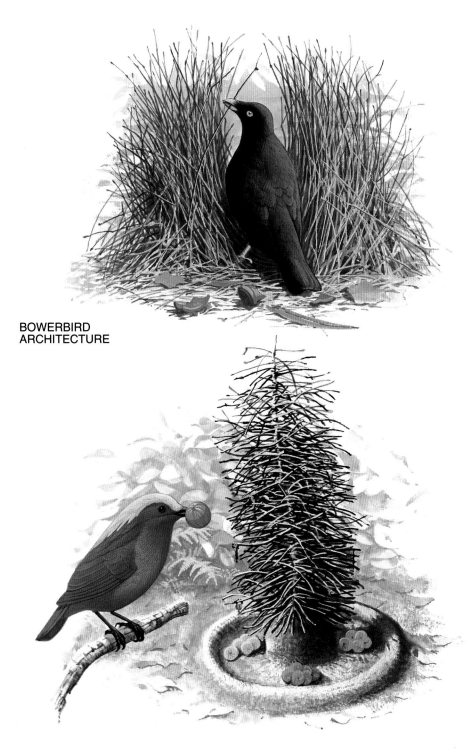

BOWERBIRD ARCHITECTURE

▲ The bowers built by bowerbirds vary widely in shape and structure between species, but two basic architectures can be distinguished, typified by the satin bowerbird (above) and the gardener bowerbird (below).

▶ (facing page) The bagworm moth (Eumeta hardenbergi) builds an elaborate nursery for its offspring. On hatching from this stick-and-webbing structure, each tiny larva spins a drifting skein of silk until it is long enough for the breeze to capture it.

The satin bowerbird

Male satin bowerbirds are a noted inhabitant of the forested coastal areas of eastern Australia because of the great tolerance they show human presence, and because of their vocal mimicry and their tendency to display at the same site year after year.

They are typical of avenue builders, creating a corridor between two walls of fine sticks which arch up on either side nearly touching at the top. If this were all there was to the bower, it would be unremarkable compared with the workmanship apparent in many birds' nests. But this is not a nest; it is designed to charm

THE HOME BUILDERS

Amoeba cases of sand and silica

A typical view of an amoeba is a protean mass of cytoplasm flowing across the bottom of some watery habitat. However, many species of amoebae also carry around a house which protects the main bulk of the cytoplasm while the flowing pseudopods carry it along.

In *Difflugia coronata*, the house is made of sand grains built to a very particular design. Its shape is essentially spherical with a round aperture at one end, but it also has some fancy additions. The entrance, for example, is surrounded by a collar of tiny sand grains crimped into a neat ruff, while the end opposite the entrance is adorned with five or six large spikes each made of a graded pile of sand particles. It is hard to imagine how a single-celled animal can actually create this complex structure, and even observations of *Difflugia* during case construction have provided little more information.

Amoebae reproduce by dividing a cell into two when it reaches the appropriate size. In *Difflugia*, the organism grows in the normal way, engulfing food particles as it travels around and carrying its case with it. But it also engulfs sand grains as well, which accumulate inside the cell until several hundred have been amassed. The organism then puts out a large pseudopod into which all the collected grains flow. They migrate to the surface of the cell and suddenly are arranged to create a new house complete with pleated collar and protective spikes with all the different sizes of particles allotted to their correct places. The cell then divides and the two organisms, each with its separate case, go their separate ways.

Other species of case-bearing amoebae create an even more regular architecture by cleverly manufacturing their own building bricks. In *Euglypha rotunda*, they make silica plates of two slightly different kinds, which consist of about 120 shell plates and 8 to 14 aperture plates. Before the cell divides, this number of new plates is manufactured and stored inside the existing cell, so that at cell division they can be arranged on the surface. The shell plates form an elongated balloon while the aperture plates encircle the opening.

In *Sphendoeria lenta*, the spherical case is composed of about 60 beautiful circular discs, while the aperture is made of a mass of small oval aperture plates forming a short protective sleeve. Less impressive, by comparison, is the somewhat flattened sphere of *Nebela vitrea* whose case, though neat, is made up of a mixture of round, oval and elongated plates. A moment of uncharitable reflection should

Anthony Bannister/NHPA

help to explain how it produces such a structure. Is it just bad at making tiles? No, it steals tiles from other case-building species. How does it manage to steal them? It preys upon smaller tile makers and adds those tiles to a collection which will form a new case when it divides again.

Caterpillar silk for cocoons and bags

We have already sung the praises of silk in the making of traps and houses. Caterpillars, the larvae of butterflies and moths (Lepidoptera), are like spiders in that they are also major manufacturers of silk. It is not surprising, then, that they are also skillful home builders.

For the silkworm (*Bombyx mori*), the closed capsule that the caterpillar creates from its own body secretion is a protection for the pupa against predators and its climate which, in its domesticated environment, it need no longer fear. For us it is one long strand of lustrous yarn. Similar silken containers are created by bagworms, which are members of a family of moths that construct portable houses which they carry around all their larval lives before finally closing them and pupating.

In the bagworm (*Thyridopteryx ephemeraeformis*) the bag is little more than a silken sleeve with a hole at one end through which the larva can stretch out its head and legs. It is, in fact, a bit more than that, as the fabric consists of several layers of silk. It is very strong and, therefore, very difficult for any predatory bird to damage.

But silk, as we have already seen with the caddis larvae, is also a good material for sticking things together—a quality which has not escaped the attention of caterpillars.

I collected a bagworm case of very elegant design in Thailand. It consisted of a tube triangular in section and was created by attaching short, straight sticks of wood tangentially to the silk-lined tube in which the animal lived. The width of the tube and the size of the sticks were progressively larger from its posterior to its anterior end, showing that the bag was regularly enlarged as the caterpillar grew within it. Also, each added triangle was displaced slightly from the position of the previous one, to create a three-sided spiral architecture that made it resistant to any peck but that of the strongest birds.

The majority of caterpillars are not protected by bags, but many do nevertheless have very well-developed physical protection against attacks by predators. This is the possession of long hairs or spines. Of course, when the caterpillar pupates this protective skin, it is shed to reveal the polished and more vulnerable surface of the chrysalis. This seems

like a waste of good hairs, just at a time when they could provide protection during the dangerous period of metamorphosis. Might it not be possible for the caterpillar to incorporate these valuable protective hairs into the silken fabric of the cocoon?

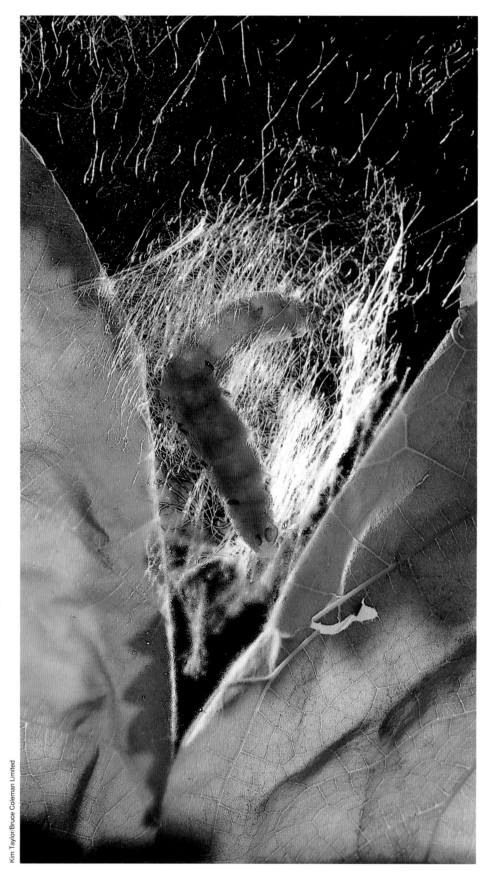

◀ (*facing page*) The pupa of an Australian crow butterfly (*Euploea core*). Here the caterpillar builds a secure home in which it transforms from larva to adult.

▼ The silk moth caterpillar spins a single filament around itself, to form a cocoon.in which it can pupate and metamorphose.

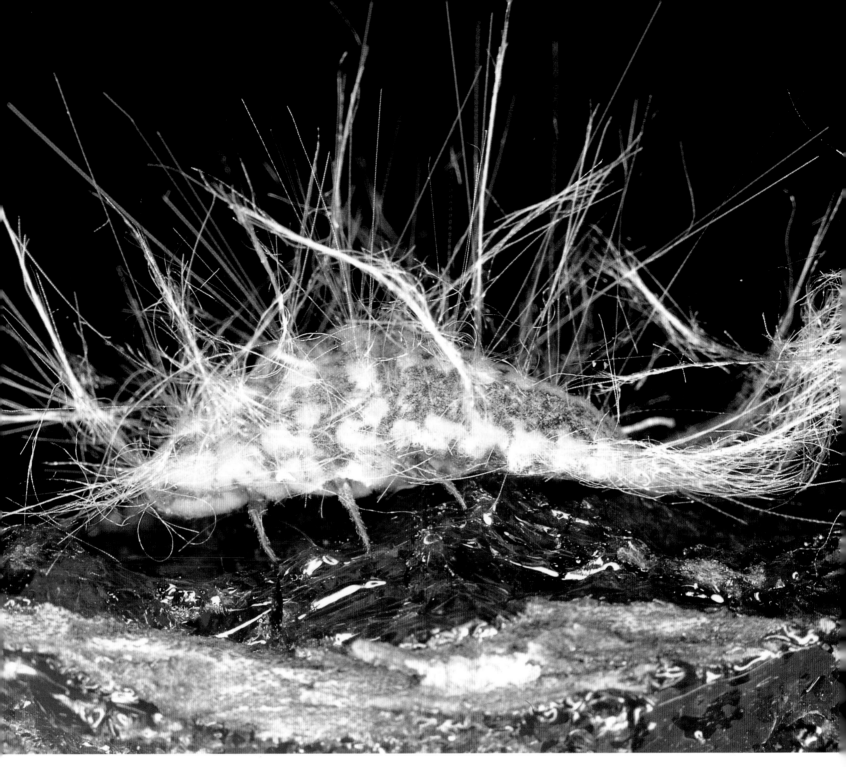

▲ An adult female margarodid bug (*Monophlebulus pilosior*) covered with wax hairs.

As has already become evident in this book, almost any such elegant solution seems already to have been devised and exploited during evolution; this idea is no exception. A Malaysian species of hairy caterpillar belonging to the tigermoth family (Arctiidae) pulls out its body hairs and sticks them together with silk, to create a domed cage inside which it suspends itself in a silken hammock before it reaches pupation

More remarkable still is the effort of *Aethria carnicauda* which is a species of the New World tropics. This hairy caterpillar, when it is about to pupate, climbs onto a grass stem and, by plucking its hairs out one by one, attaches them to the stem below itself to form a beautiful flower-like whorl. The larva shows great skill in doing this, doubling back on itself to grasp a single hair, plucking it out by the roots and positioning it so that its base is fastened to the side of the plant stem with the fine tip projecting outwards.

Having completed the first whorl, the caterpillar moves about 10 centimeters (4 inches) up the stem and constructs another whorl of hairs above itself. This routine is then repeated until there is a barrier of two or three collars of projecting hairs both above and below the caterpillar to frustrate marauders such as ants. Finally, the caterpillar begins to spin its silken cocoon, into which it incorporates all remaining body hairs to create a sturdy bag with a protective tuft projecting from each end. It is a remarkable display of skill in a complex procedure which is executed only once in the animal's lifetime.

DUNG PELLETS MAKE USEFUL BUILDING BRICKS

Making a house out of dung may seem like an inherently unhealthy idea; indeed it probably is. On the other hand, feces have an obvious economic advantage as a building material in that there is no additional cost to manufacture them! Moreover, they are produced in regular sized units.

The larva of the tropical beetle (*Cassida rubiginosa*) browses on foliage which also happens to be the hunting ground of predatory ants. As a special defense system, the beetle has a shield of dung held over its back which, when danger threatens, can be moved to block an attack from any quarter—head, side or back. The structural foundation of the shield is larval skins cast at previous molts which, instead of being abandoned, are held on two long tail spines. The shield is then enlarged and thickened with additional blobs of feces. To ensure that the shield grows in a balanced manner, the larva is able to position and direct each squirt of fecal material as the anus is positioned on the end of a telescopic turret.

Some rotifers, which are microscopic, filter-feeding aquatic organisms, make cases out of spherical dung pellets. Originally, these may have been produced to ensure that the animal did not recapture fine particles of excretal material in its feeding mechanism, but in the process they developed a new function of a useful building material.

The moth caterpillar (*Heterotropha tortriciformis*) also makes use of dung pellets in a similar way. Most caterpillars are leaf eaters and have rather dry, almost cubical feces, quite suitable for building but requiring rather a lot of work to fit them together to make a house. *H. tortriciformis* has altered the manufacturing process in a way which greatly simplifies construction. It produces fecal rods, usually of four pellets fused together. With these it builds and enlarges a space-frame structure covered with a curtain of silk to create a tube affording protection from the world. Using this technique, the caterpillar can create the framework of its dwelling out of only 30 to 40 rods.

Tim Shepherd/Oxford Scientific Films

▲ The larva of the tortoise beetle (*Cassida* sp.) carries on its back a protective shield constructed of its own feces.

Wasp nests and the architecture of paper

What did we do before we had plastic? Well, we certainly put a lot more things in paper bags. Strong, light and manufactured from abundant natural sources, paper was and still is a versatile material. Wasps make their houses out of it and had done so for a very long time before we came up with the idea. A fossil wasp nest has been dated as at least 60 million years old and the tradition probably goes back long beyond that.

The architecture of paper is hanging architecture. Supported at the top, a sheet of paper can bear heavy weight hanging from it, but, if it were supported from below with weights placed at the top, a simple paper structure would crumple. Wasp nests must defer to this principle; they hang from branches, undersides of leaves or roofs of caves. But, although made of paper and manufactured in sheets, their architecture is sophisticated. These paper homes have different parts and functions, and the architecture allows for the enlargement of the houses as the colonies within them grow.

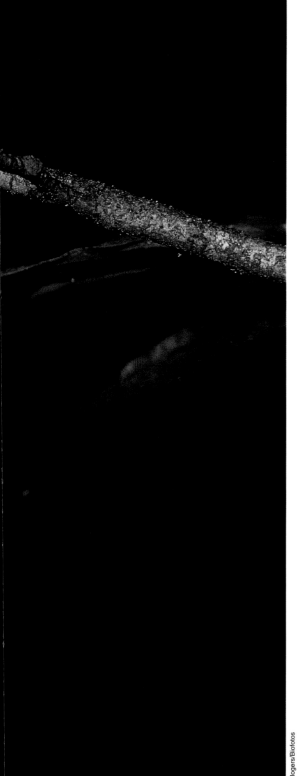

An ingenious design shown by certain members of the genus consists of vertically oriented cells clustered to form a horizontal disk-shaped comb, hanging from a thin stalk or petiole. This comb is covered in a secretion to repel ants that might prey upon the brood. A modification of this design has an extension to the outer wall of the cells at the edge of the comb. It creates a cavity below the cells to provide some protection and security to resting adult wasps.

In yet another *Mischocyttarus* species, the comb consists of vertical string cells, the first attached by a short stalk to a branch, and each successive one attached at one point to the lip at the bottom of the cell above. But cells are not even always oriented vertically. In one species, a vertical comb held on several short pedicels consists of two sets of horizontal cells placed back to back.

Such a diversity of comb designs in one genus of wasps suggests that rather simple changes in construction rules during the evolution process have resulted in quite new species-typical architectural forms. In social wasps that have much larger colony sizes, there may be a need for several brood combs, but again the versatility of paper has ensured that more than one solution to this problem is possible.

▶ *(following pages)* Wingless adult female aphids and nymphs on a lupin leaf. These tiny, plant-sucking insects are notable for the complexity of their life-cycles: one variation common to many species is parthenogenetic (sexless) and sexual reproduction in alternate generations. Aphids often infest a plant in such numbers as to kill or weaken it, and many are serious agricultural and garden pests. *Mark Mattock/Planet Earth Pictures*

▼ ◀ Many bees and wasps are social insects, which collaborate in building elaborate nests like that of the Brazilian forest wasp (*Apoica* sp., left), in which to rear their young, each larva housed in its own cell. These insects long ago stumbled on the mathematical truth that a hexagonal shape allows packing the maximum number of cells in the least area, shown by the nest of yellow-jacket wasps (*Vespa* sp., below).

The essential role of the wasp nest is to provide a secure place for rearing its young. In social wasps, the young are helpless, limbless grubs entirely dependent upon an army of adults to feed them. Each grub or larva has its own little paper compartment in which to grow—a cell—and lives with other cells that are grouped together in various ways to form a comb. The versatility of paper in wasp nest design can be seen in the manufacture of the comb alone, even within a single genus like *Mischocyttarus*.

Scott Camazine/Oxford Scientific Films

Brian Rogers/Biofotos

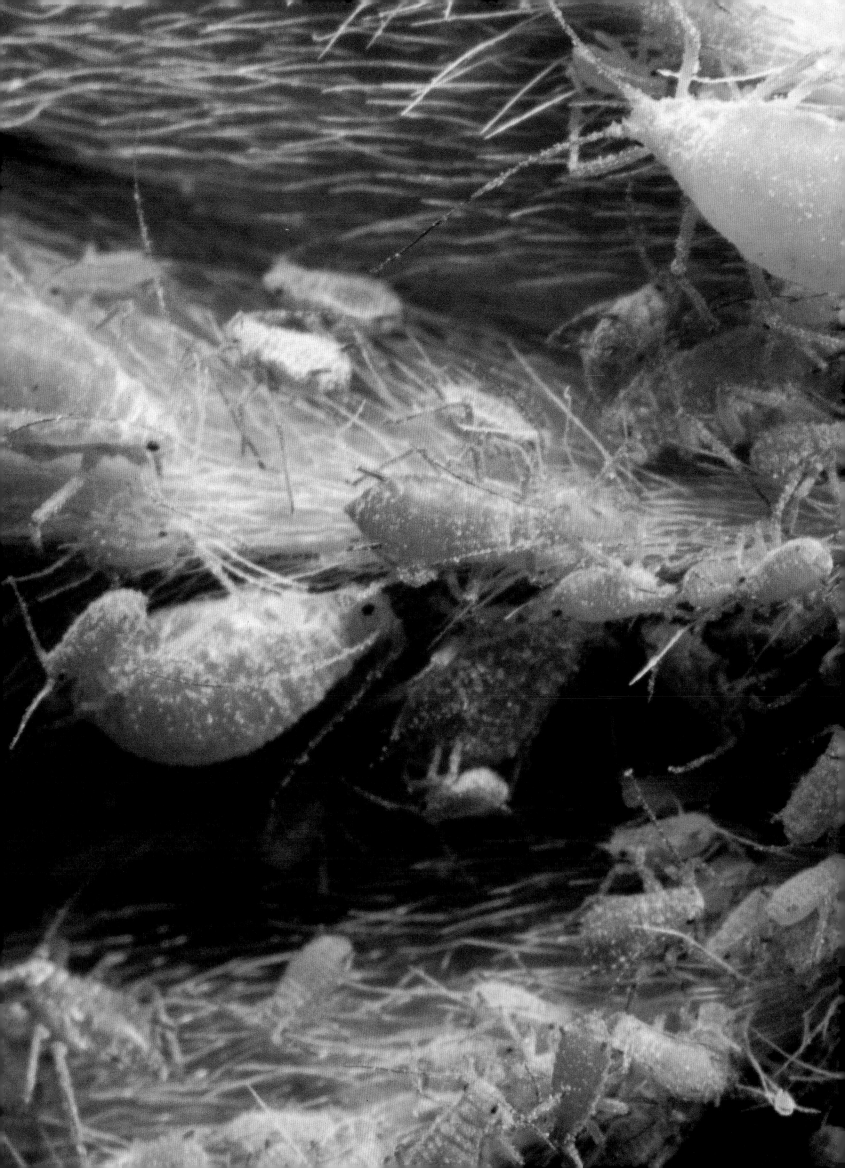

SPIRALLY EXPANDING NESTS

Heather Angel/Biofotos

▲ A whirlpool ramshorn snail (*Planorbis vortex*) displays the elegant spiral solution to the problem of combining constant protection with constant growth.

A snail shell is a wonderful design. Its unique structure allows for continuous enlargement of the snail's dwelling space without it ever having to leave, and all the time remains a compact shape to accommodate the size of the owner.

Wonderful also is that a colony of hundreds of thousands of wasps, working collectively with paper architecture, can produce the same solution for the enlargement of brood combs contained within a nest envelope. *Polybioides raphigastra* and some other species have arrived at a snail shell solution which involves the enlargement of the comb as a downwardly spiraling ramp,

enclosed in an enlarged spiral envelope. It is also remarkable that some species of stingless bee (*Trigona meliponini,* for example) produce a spirally extending wax comb of very similar design.

The wasp *Agelaia areata,* and some other species, have, however, evolved a different spiral principle. This starts with a vertical comb suspended below a branch that starts to curve upwards, and wraps itself round the branch like a bandage with a sandwich of space between each comb layer. Outwardly radiating cells open into this spiral space, which affords the whole nest protection by a spirally extending envelope.

A minority of species, like *Agelaia testacea*, suspend several combs vertically, each from separate petioles. A more common solution is that seen in yellowjackets (*Vespula* sp.) where there is a stack of horizontal combs of downwardly directed cells. Each comb is hung from the one above it by means of an array of petioles, which are of the same design as that which attached the initial comb to the branch.

Paper is basically pieces of mashed up plant material bound together by some kind of matrix. In the case of wasps, the matrix is a salivary secretion although, surprisingly, we have little idea of its composition or even from which glands it is secreted. It may even be a different substance in different species and it certainly varies greatly in importance between species. Some papers have almost none, while in others the plant fragments are obscured by a continuous glaze of secretion.

The nature of plant fragments is easier to determine either by keeping a close watch on the wasps or by having a careful look at the pieces of vegetation themselves. Yellowjackets (*Vespula* sp.) and paper wasps (*Polistes* sp.) can be seen chewing at weathered wooden fence posts and the woody fibers they collect are clearly visible in their nest paper. These long, strong fibers make rather fine quality paper—light and strong. Some other species of social wasp have fibrous papers, but the fibers are not obtained from exposed wood but harvested from the hairs which cover the leaves of certain plants. One particular family of plants, the Malpighiaceae, which have double-ended hairs (attached by a short stalk in the middle) seem to be particularly popular, being found in the nests of species of *Apoica*, *Protopolybia* and a species of *Mischocyttarus*.

But we are oversimplifying by saying that wasp nests are made of paper. Over and above salivary secretion and vegetation fragments, there is a third material—silk. It is now becoming clear that for many species, silk has a significant structural role. This can be seen for example in the hornet species (*Vespa*).

The first comb of a hornet nest is a cluster of vertical cells hanging from a petiole and enclosed in a multi-layered envelope. The whole structure is of paper manufactured from woody plant fibers and saliva. However, as the first batch of larvae reach maturity in the comb, each spins a silken cocoon around itself which lines the cell and closes it with a pure silken cap. As a consequence the wall of the cell immediately becomes much stronger and, as all neighboring larvae become mature, so does the whole comb. As a result, when a further comb comes to be suspended below it, the first comb is better able to bear the weight. But the combs are attached to one another and to the initial support by means of the petiole. How can these be made strong enough to support the growing weight of the new combs? They can, of course, be enlarged or made more numerous by the addition of more paper material, but inspection reveals that the new material includes patches of silk fabric. These are pieces of the silk caps of cells from which adults have now emerged. Silk is clearly such a valuable building material for hornets that it can be recycled within the nest.

Anthony Bannister/NHPA

The nests of hornets are dynamic structures requiring the continuous recycling of material to permit colony expansion. The problem is the envelope; it creates a finite space which is soon filled by the existing comb. If another comb is to be added, the cavity must be enlarged. The workers do this by dismantling the inner layers of envelope and using the recycled paper, together with newly collected material, to create new outer layers and then a new comb in the enlarged interior space.

▲ Armed with formidable stings, wasps and hornets are especially aggressive in defense of their colonial nests, as indicated by these South African wasps (*Rophalidia* sp.) raising their wings in agitation at the photographer's presence.

The weavers are aptly named, building elaborate woven nests of grass. Here a male grosbeak weaver (*Amblyospiza albifrons*) puts the finishing touches to his nest in Tanzania. The nest needs to be finished to a high standard of workmanship, because among weavers courtship is conducted after nest-construction, not before; the female will accept him as a mate solely on the basis of the quality of his nest.

The ingenious nest design of some *Polibia* species does nevertheless allow nest enlargement without recycling of the envelope. This is made possible by converting the outer wall of the bottom of the nest envelope into the surface. The surface is then enclosed in a further envelope, which naturally creates another surface to which an additional comb may later be attached. Since the weight of each comb in this design is borne by the envelope, the upper parts of the nest envelope need to be reinforced as additional combs are added. This is simply achieved by the plastering of extra material to its outer surface.

Birds as basket weavers

The overwhelming majority of birds use plant material to make all or most of the nest. These materials are often threaded through or twisted into one another to some degree to prevent the nest from falling apart when it has, for example, a family of chicks bouncing around in it. But these structures do not necessarily qualify as woven baskets. A woven fabric shows a regular alternation of strands of weft over and under parallel threads of warp oriented at right angles. Not much bird weaving attains this level of regularity. The essential features of woven bird nests are that firstly, they are made with long strips of material and secondly, that the nest is

Tom Leach/Oxford Scientific Films

Jack A. Bailey/Ardea London

held together and in position only by virtue of the way these strips are carefully and intricately interlocked.

In the weaverfinch family, Ploceidae, a number of different stitches are shown. These include the over-and-under weave or simple loops and, for tasks such as holding the hanging nest onto the tip of a branch, various knotting techniques from a half hitch and alternately reversed winding to proper overhand and slip knots.

These techniques are only possible with strands of vegetation which are long, thin and parallel-sided so that they slip through easily, as well as being flexible and tough enough not to snap under the strain of looping and knotting. The plants which meet these demanding specifications are in fact common in many habitats. They are monocotyledenous plants like palm trees and grasses and are characterized by long leaves with parallel veins running their whole length. So, a small bite into the side of a green leaf allows a long strip to be torn away along its length.

In the African village weaverbird, the nest is built by the male, which starts with the job of attaching leaf strips to the end of a twig. Typically this attachment covers two arms in the angle of a forked twig, which the bird then straddles to complete the ring of material.

▼ A long-tailed tit (*Aegithalos caudatus*) at its nest. Many birds' nests are little more than platforms of sticks, but members of this family (Aegithalidae) are notable for their nest-building skills, constructing elaborate domed nests, lined with feathers and carefully felted on the outside with plant down and lichens.

► *(facing page)* Some birds, like this African paradise flycatcher (*Terpsiphone viridis*), conspicuously decorate the outside of their nests with lichen, caterpillar cocoons and similar items, but it is not known why.

▼ The habit of tree-nesting places greater demands on the parents in the way of construction skills, but often offers considerable protection from predators, so much so that even some seabirds, such as this white-capped noddy (*Anous minutus*), have adopted the tree-nesting habit.

Standing more securely in this ring, the bird can now work forward adding strips to complete the nest chamber; then still standing in the same position, but leaning progressively backward, it creates a roofed entrance lobby. This architecture and technique are similar throughout the weaverfinches, but some do add a short or long entrance tube projecting down from the lobby. This seems designed to make it difficult for snakes to gain entry. In *Malimbus cassini* this tube is especially long and its fabric approaches the precise pattern of human cloth-making and basketry.

Clearly this is a very particular form of nest building, which depends on only one type of material and specialized building techniques. It has, however, evolved independently on at least two occasions. It is found not only in the Old World weaverfinches (Ploceidae) but also in the New World oropendolas and caciques (Icteridae). Their nest design consists of a deep hanging bag suspended by its top lip, while spiral loops, hitches and knots are again used as the construction technique.

Stolen sticky stuff: the utility material for small birds

Predator pressure on helpless eggs and chicks has had obvious effects on birds' nests. Nests hanging at the extreme tips of branches are a clear response to the threat of arboreal predators like snakes and monkeys. But, even for weaverbirds, securing a nest in such a position is not easy. As natural selection so frequently demonstrates, there is more than one solution to the problem. Many small birds have found it in the use of sticky spider silk. Hummingbirds like the rufous-breasted hermit (*Glaucis hirsuta*) can even lash a nest to a leaf.

Making the nest less visible is another adaptive response to predatory pressure. This poses a problem for nest builders since the best nest-building material may look a bit out of place, stuck up in a tree. Many small birds attach a special layer on the outside of the nest cup to help it blend in with the background, typically pieces of lichen which may already cover the tree's branches. The problem is how to secure the lichen. Whether the bird is a tropical flycatcher or temperate finch, the solution is still silk.

We know almost nothing about how the birds go about collecting the silk; whether they choose spider or even caterpillar silk, or if the silk of some spiders is preferred to others. Spider silk is available broadly in two forms, as web or as egg cocoons. The chaffinch (*Fringilla coelebs*) uses both to attach lichen onto the mossy nest cup. When collected, web material is broken up into small fragments, but cocoons with their tough fabric may be preserved even after incorporation into the nest.

A few species of birds use the cocoons themselves as the outer decoration, covering the cup in silvery white spider cocoons. This is true, for example, of the paradise flycatcher (*Terpsiphone incii*). It is difficult to imagine how the nest might be camouflaged. Possibly with the light reflected from the cocoons, the nest dissolves into the background.

Sticky spider silk also offers birds a material which can be used to prevent the whole nest cup from falling apart. This is well illustrated by fantails like the willie wagtail (*Riphidura leucophrys*), where the outer layer of the grass cup is covered with a skin of spider silk.

Silk is therefore a very handy material for small birds, where its strength and the quantity that is available can match the standards needed for nest building. It might nevertheless seem a rather specialized building material option. It is therefore surprising to find that, in spite of our great ignorance of the biology of silk use in birds, more than twenty families of small birds make use of silk for building in contrast to only two that show true weaving.

Horizon/Werner Langer

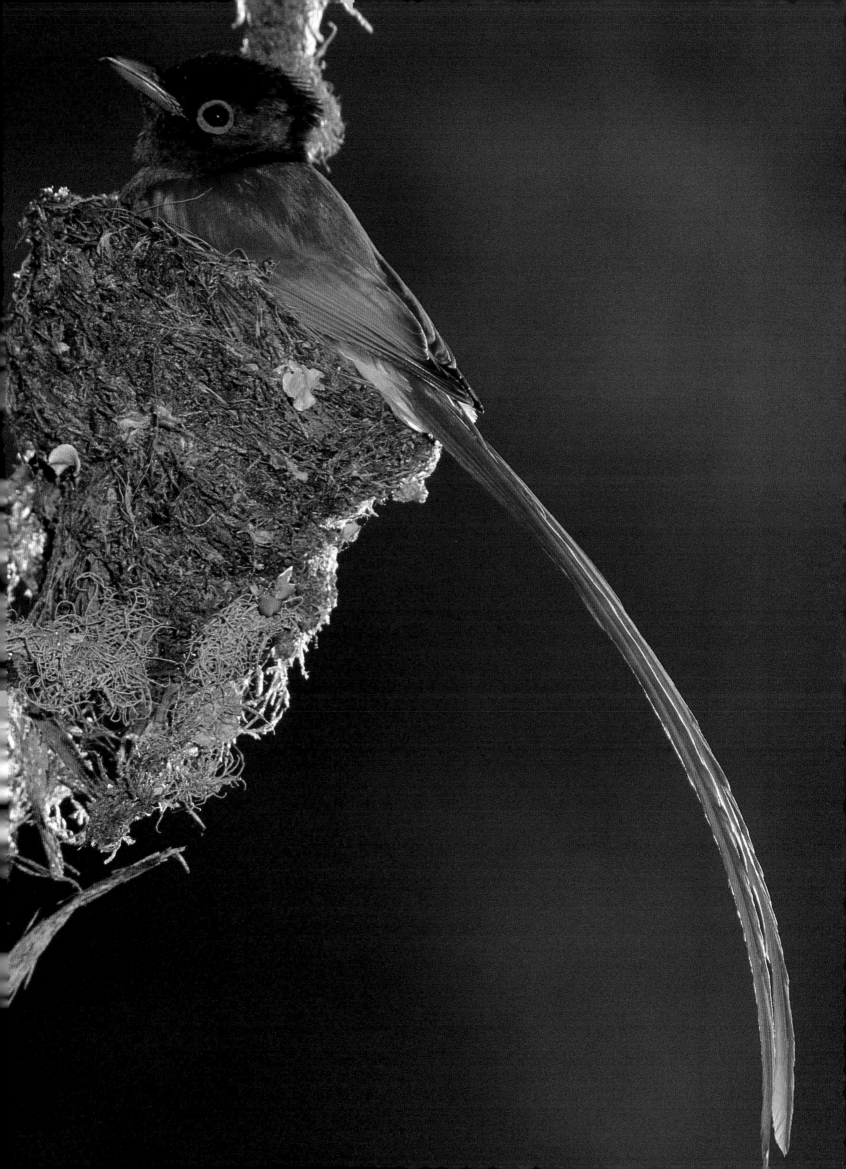

HOW OLD ARE ANIMAL HOUSES?

Human houses frequently reflect a great deal of effort and expense. Consequently they are maintained and kept going rather than abandoned and rebuilt. In Britain, houses that are 200 years old are quite common while village churches typically date back 500 years or more. Of course not all the material is original—roof timbers and stonework have been replaced—nor does the structure look the same; pieces have been added, others demolished. But the site has been in continuous occupation for a very long time and parts of the original can still be seen. Are any animal homes like that?

The simple answer is that we have very little idea, but some fragments of evidence suggest that certain animal homes could be as old as those of humans. For example, an African termite mound of the species *Macrotermes goliath* was found to contain human archaeological remains dated at 700 years old.

Another tantalizing example concerns the dens of badgers (*Meles meles*) and red foxes (*Vulpes vulpes*). A glance at the index of a British Isles road map reveals 25 village names beginning with *badger* or *brock* (an archaic name for the badger) and 14 villages starting with *fox*. These include the villages of Brockholes, Foxholes, Foxhole and Foxearth.

Badgers and foxes are certainly common British species, so perhaps no special significance should be attached to these village names. But it is possible that the places were so named, because of the enduring presence of badgers or foxes at a particular site, as a result of the burrows becoming a considerable accumulated investment of effort. A badger set excavated in England in 1977 suggests that this could be the case. A complete excavation of such a site by a team of professional archaeologists would give us the answer.

▲ An Australian dingo mother (*Canis familiaris dingo*) rests in her den with her pups. Such dens may be used over and over again for many years.

Jean Paul Ferrero/Ardea London

Horizon/Maslowski

◄ Though nesting in trees is often safer than nesting on the ground, it is not proof against all predators. Squirrels, in particular, are especially fond of supplementing their nut and pine-cone diet with any bird's eggs or young they may find.

THE HABITAT MANIPULATORS

Food storers

As storers, stealers and hoarders, the habitat manipulators ensure that their supply of food is kept relatively uniform throughout the year, and in doing so, gain some degree of control over their environment. To keep their supplies topped up, red foxes, for example, steal and hide birds' eggs from gulls and other animals in the springtime, so that they can dig them up and eat them months later. By then, the eggs might not be smelling too fresh but are a welcome snack in times of scarcity. Many carnivores cache small larders of prey.

While bits of meat or eggs may generally deteriorate too rapidly to be ideal for storage, for a wolf living in a cold habitat or a jackal in a dry one, cached meat or bones may still be edible months after the kill. However, some predators strive for a more ideal situation, and try to keep the meat stored live and in a manner which prevents it from running away.

European moles (*Talpa europaea*) are a good example. They make larders of earthworms or plaster them into the walls of the galleries near the nest chamber in preparation for the winter but, before doing so, they mutilate the first few segments of the worm, leaving it alive but unable to escape.

► (*following pages*) Adelie penguins at home. These polar birds are well adapted to their habitat of endlessly shifting icefloes in the Antarctic seas.
Clem Haagner/Ardea London

Pots of honey

By taking the nectar of flowers to make honey, bees create a large energy store which does not turn sour. This state is effected by salivary gland secretion, which inhibits microbial growth and is aided by the high sugar content of mature honey (about 80 percent) which is a natural preservative. This store has enabled honeybees to survive and prosper in places during long winters when flowers are not readily available. A guaranteed food supply for adult insects throughout the year has had a dramatic effect on the social life and economic organization of honeybees.

This is obvious when compared with the yellowjackets and hornets. In temperate regions, yellowjackets and hornets hibernate as solitary mated queens which emerge in the spring each year to found their own colony and rear a batch of workers. Throughout the summer, they enlarge the colony, raising more workers till the nest is a formidable garrison of several thousand adult insects. Before they die, at the end of summer, they raise a new crop of queens and males. The colony then collapses and the young queens now mated, disperse to hibernate.

The 15 to 20 kilograms (approximately 33 to 44 pounds) of honey that a colony of the

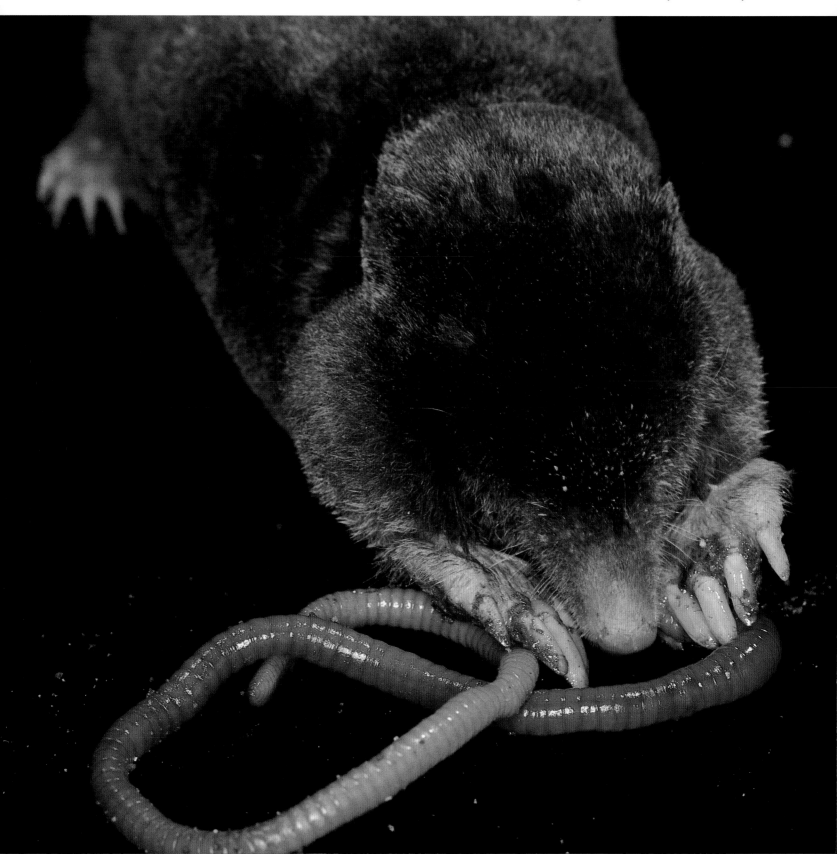

▼ A European mole subdues an earthworm, holding it down with its paws. Like chipmunks, moles lay up food stores against winter shortage, first mutilating each worm so that it remains alive but unable to escape.

HUMANS AND THE HONEYPOT

▲ A honeybee gathers nectar for transport back to the hive. Primitive man robbed beehives by stunning the bees with smoke, but this species is now almost fully domesticated.

Early bushman cave paintings show us that the human exploitation of bees for their honey started with the hunter-gatherers. In Africa, wild honeybees are still subdued with the aid of smoke and robbed, while in South America, Kayapo people burn wood shavings from a toxic vine to quell aggressive stingless bees or the recently introduced Africanized honeybees. In Thailand, nests of the small wild honeybee (*Apis florea*) are collected and the single comb sold complete.

The mixing together of honey and brood cells is, of course, not ideal for honey collection. This problem is overcome in the design of modern honeybee hives by the insertion of a queen excluder; a metal plate with holes just big enough to allow a worker to squeeze through to that part of the hive where honey-making is to be encouraged. The larger queen is excluded and lays her eggs on nursery combs in other parts of the hive.

In Central and South America, some stingless bee species are maintained on a semi-domesticated basis. The amount of honey they store is rather modest and its quality more watery than that of honeybees but, in a number of species, the globular honey-containing pots are built separate from the much smaller cells of the brood comb. Colonies like this may be kept outside houses in hollow logs with a small aperture in the middle for the bees to enter and leave. The brood combs are built near the entrance with the storage pots at either end of the space. As the ends of the log are removable, the honey-laden cells can be collected without disturbing the brood.

honeybee (*Apis mellifera*) stores through the summer ensures that not only the queen but also a large retinue of workers can feed and keep themselves warm all through the winter. A substantial workforce can then exploit the abundance of spring flowers, whose protein-rich pollen is used to raise more worker larvae. New colonies are then founded in the summer, not just by a lone queen, but with a band of several hundred workers to build the new nest.

Honey is not only stored by the seven or so species of honeybees, genus *Apis,* but by all the members of the bee family (Apidae) which includes the bumblebees and the stingless bees.

▼ Many species of both bees and wasps build elaborate nests, like that of this South American paper wasp, in which to raise their young, but bees also store honey for winter survival; wasps do not.

G.I.Bernard/NHPA

Anthony Bannister/NHPA

The stingless bees are confined to the tropics, but again it is honey that gives a colony the insurance of a continuous source of food energy in the face of fluctuations in rainfall or flowering. This allows colonies as large as 100,000 to be built up in some species. New colonies are founded by a queen and accompanied by a swarm of workers, which give vital protection against ant attacks in the vulnerable period of its establishment.

Silos of seeds
A seed is a comprehensive nutritional package coupled with a plant embryo. It therefore contains amino acids for protein formation as well as an energy store of starch or frequently of that most energy-rich fuel, oil. It is not

◄ Honeybees are not the only insects that hoard large stores of food. Many ants, like these harvester ants (*Messor* sp.), gather grass and other seeds from the surface for storage in underground granaries. In fact this habit is so widespread that many plants, especially in Australia, rely on harvester ants for seed dispersal, and many can germinate only after storage in such a granary.

surprising, therefore, that many animal species are specialist seed predators. Many seeds have also mastered the trick of surviving long periods until conditions are right for germination. This is dramatically illustrated by the explosion of growth and flowering of grasses and herbs that follows heavy rains in desert areas. So the message for animals that want a reliable food supply is store seeds.

Seed storage has, in fact, evolved several times independently in ants and no major arid area of the world is without a seed-harvesting species, while in some, desert ants are the dominant animal lifeform. In the Namibian desert of Africa, for example, it is estimated that more than 95 percent of the biomass of foraging animals is harvester ants.

Seeds are gathered one at a time by an industrious colony of thousands and tens of thousands of worker ants, and stored in underground granaries. In the highly specialized seed-storing genera like *Messor* and *Pheidole*, seeds may be dried in the sun above ground before storage, or even brought up from underground and dried again if a shower of rain penetrates the nest. Germination of stored seeds may also be inhibited by biting off the growing tip of the embryo. The effect is to be able to store the seeds in their most nutritious condition for as long as possible. This may be a very long time. Colonies of *Messor pergandei*, for example, have been observed to survive a rainless period of twelve years in parts of California.

▲ Ord's kangaroo-rats (*Dipodomys ordi*). So-called from their well-developed hind legs, kangaroo-rats inhabit the American southwest, feed largely on seeds, and spend much of their time in burrows.

Probably better known inhabitants of desert regions are rodents: pocket mice, kangaroo-rats and the like living in underground burrows; predominantly solitary but adapted to desert life in a number of specialized ways including, in several genera, the storage of seeds.

So the end of a short season of California desert rain also signals harvest time for the giant kangaroo-rat (*Dipodomys ingens*). Working at night, the kangaroo-rat forages for seeds and seed pods of plants such as pepper grass (*Lepidium nitidum*). These are stuffed into large cheek pouches so that a reasonable load can be gathered before the rat must return towards home. At this stage, however, the seeds are not

ready to be stored permanently but need some further drying. The kangaroo-rats therefore deposit their cheek pouch loads in superficial pit caches which are then covered over. As night after night the harvest is gathered in, the area around the burrow gradually becomes covered in small packets of hidden treasure. One kangaroo-rat was found to have created 875 of these temporary stores.

When the seeds in these surface stores have dried and there is no risk of their germination, they are uncovered and transported to large subterranean granaries within the burrow system. This provides the main food supply for the dry winter months. Exactly what is the

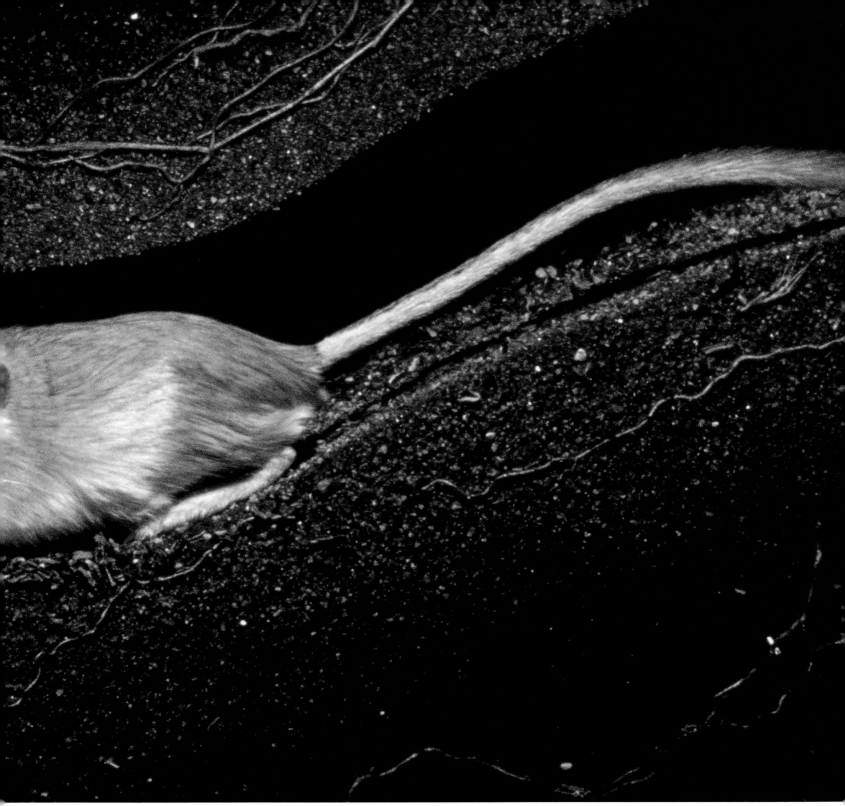

minimum required to achieve this is not known, but one giant kangaroo-rat burrow system was found to have nine storage chambers containing a total of more than 38 liters (65 pints) of pepper grass and filaree (*Erodium* sp.) seeds and seed pods.

Banner-tailed kangaroo-rats (*Dipodomys spectabilis*), also from the deserts of North America, hoard seeds on the same spectacular scale as their cousins *D. ingens*. They also show a remarkable ability to manage their seeds after they have been stored underground.

Each burrow system has several granaries, from superficial ones at about 30 centimeters (12 inches) below the surface to deep ones at 70 centimeters (approximately 28 inches) or so. These chambers vary in humidity, with the deepest ones being drier and the shallower ones more humid. The higher levels of humidity promote the growth of certain fungi on the grain which, you might expect, would make all but the deepest chambers unsatisfactory for seed storage. However, it turns out that banner-tailed kangaroo-rats prefer moldy seeds to ones with no fungal growth. Not too much; just slightly moldy.

Laboratory observations have shown that the rats themselves manipulate fungal growth to produce just the right level of moldiness that they prefer. During the experiment, when offered chambers of different humidities, the kangaroo-rats moved seeds which had no fungal growth into the most humid chamber, but when the desired level of moldiness was reached, the seeds were moved to drier chambers to halt further contamination. Probably this level of fungal growth provides some nutritional advantage whereas too much would undoubtedly make the seeds toxic.

day, to reach saturation before dawn; this results in the deposition of dew. The Australian mouse species *Pseudomys hermannbergensis* covers a large area around the entrance of its burrow with pebbles of a rather uniform size. It is suggested that the function of this is to provide surfaces on which dew can form. Better documented is the dew trap constructed by the Indian ant species *Diacamma rugosum*, which decorates the entrance of its subterranean nest with birds' feathers upon which dew forms at night. This is gathered by the ant workers and probably forms the only source of free water during the dry season.

Dam builders

There could hardly be a greater contrast between the hot dry habitat of a kangaroo-rat and the cold watery one of the beaver (*Castor fiber*), yet the problems of dealing with fluctuating food supply and changing climate are similar. Beavers are habitat manipulators that go to the extent of changing the whole landscape in which they live in order to gain almost total control over it.

The beaver is a member of the largest order of mammals, the rodents, that typically dwell in

▲ A European woodmouse (*Apodemus sylvaticus*) with its winter store of nuts, seeds and berries.

Colin Milkins/Oxford Scientific Films

Water gatherers

Food storers have taken a substantial step towards the creation of an artificial world. Deep inside the nest of the ant or the burrow of a kangaroo-rat, food may be constantly available, regardless of whether the surface of the desert above is carpeted with green or blowing away as dust on the wind. The burrow itself also provides escape from the temperature extremes above. Kangaroo-rats only emerge in the cool of the night and *Messor* shows peaks of seed collecting in early morning and late afternoon to avoid the hottest hours of daylight and thus conserve energy.

But arid habitats are unkind in another important respect—simply that they are arid. Control over the water supply would give desert animals an even more secure world in which to live. Rodents, of course, may show special adaptations to economize on the loss of such water as they manage to obtain—foraging at night and producing concentrated urine. But they could also benefit by boosting water income, if that were possible.

In some dry habitats, the sharp drop in temperature at night causes air, which has a very low relative humidity in the heat of the

Biofotos/Brian Rogers

burrows. The beaver, although not particularly noted for it, is in fact, a capable burrower. Where a high bank of soft soil can be found beside open water, beavers dig a burrow into it and excavate sleeping chambers. A burrow is not, however, the complete home but part of a bank lodge. This contains, in addition to the burrow, an underwater entrance to a feeding chamber which is partly roofed by a massive accumulation of branches and stout timbers. This pile of wood appears, at first glance, to have been thrown together in a rather haphazard manner; but closer inspection reveals that part of the roof is a solid structure. A section of it is composed of only loosely packed branches, permitting fresh air to permeate the feeding chamber.

If no suitable bank is available, beavers will make their lodge entirely out of branches from trees they have cut down and dismembered. Again the lodge contains an underwater entrance and a loosely packed ventilation channel. Within this lodge beavers experience temperatures that are much more constant the year round than in the world outside and they are also inaccessible to land predators. Yet it is not especially for the building of lodges that

beavers are known, but for creating dams to gain control of a constant food supply.

Beavers are vegetarian and in the winter survive by stripping the bark from branches stored in the water under the ice. A family of beavers will need a lot of branches for this purpose, which necessitates a large lagoon to contain them. If such a body of water does not exist, the beavers create it by putting a dam across a stream or small river. As the water level rises, the dam may reach tens of meters long and absorb the trunks and branches of many trees. To resist the enormous lateral pressure of the dammed water, the slope of the dam is shallower on the lower side and buttressed with carefully placed logs. During the summer, the beavers chop down trees with their powerful incisor teeth and drag the branches to the lagoon, which they may extend with the construction of canals to reduce the labor of transporting loads.

One community of beavers can inundate a large piece of former forest and substantially alter the growth of deciduous trees round about it. Their grip on the habitat can be so tenacious that foresters may have to resort to explosives to get rid of them.

▶ (*following pages*) Though they live in northern regions characterized by long severe winters, beavers do not hibernate. They rely for winter food on the bark of felled saplings stored underwater, sheltering from predators in substantial lodges of sticks and branches in which the central living chamber is above water-level but the only entrance is submerged. To guarantee this regime, they frequently build carefully engineered dams to impound water and control its level.

▼ Basking in the sunshine, a South American turtle (*Podocnemis* sp.) hitches a ride on the head of a spectacled caiman (*Caiman crocodilus*).

181

THE CONSTRUCTION OF A BEAVER DAM AND LODGE

An underwater entrance leads to a tunnel ending in living quarters roofed with timber and branches.

The lodge is built before the dam, its level carefully assessed so as not to be flooded when subsequent dam construction raises the water level.

Dam construction shows an instinctive awareness of the pressures exerted by impounded water.

Heavier logs run lengthwise braced with smaller branches crosswise. The gentler slope is on the downstream side.

▶ Over millennia, the social structure of termite colonies is so rigid that the queen is little more than a gigantic egg-laying machine. Forever imprisoned in her royal chamber and tended constantly by her workers, she may produce eggs at the rate of several hundred per day.

▶ (*overleaf*) Termites invented the air-conditioner, and the various species construct their nests according to several basic principles commonly used in human devices of this kind. One architectural type uses temperature difference to maintain an air flow. The mound contains hollow spaces above the actual living quarters, where the temperature is greatest. Warm air rises from the nest into these hollow spaces, drawing cooler air from subterranean spaces below the nest to take its place. The air cools as it rises, and is then guided downwards below ground level through channels close to the lateral surfaces of the mound, ultimately flowing into the coolest areas below ground to renew the cycle.

Creating a world apart

Proportionally, the size of even a large beaver dam is modest compared to the size of a large termite mound. Six meters (20 feet) high and 3 to 4 meters (10 to 13 feet) across at the base, a *Macrotermes* mound may contain as many as 2 million adult insects, each only a few millimeters long. Its massive structure contains an environment created by the termites which has attained a level of independence from the world outside which rivals even our own.

Macrotermes termites eat grass, leaf litter and even wood fragments, but these are poor in available nitrogen. At the same time they are largely lignin, which contains nitrogen, but with indigestible protein also bound to it. The feces do not, however, go to waste because deep in the darkness of a *Macrotermes* mound are gardens which need fertilizer. These are gardens of fungus which can unlock the lignin-bound nitrogen, upon which the termites feed. With this fungus-growing skill, *Macrotermes* are the major invertebrate decomposers of tropical Africa, and are responsible for the decomposition of one-third of all primary production in some areas.

The fungus-growing termites therefore do not store food but use a method of food processing which squeezes the maximum benefit out of a low-quality food source and introduces a time delay between its collection and consumption. The effect of both these is to enhance food availability through the year.

The termite mound is not only a garden, but also a fortress since its mud walls insulate the insects from both the climatic extremes and the predation dangers of the outside world. But the active fungus and busy termites within the mound consume oxygen, create carbon dioxide and generate heat which could threaten the life of the termites themselves. What is needed, and what *Macrotermes* have engineered, is an air-conditioning system. Or, to be more accurate they have created two different systems, one open and one closed. Both are built on a massive scale.

Macrotermes subhyalinus illustrates the open system. Its mound has a variable number of wide openings on the surface; those at the mound edge are placed on short turrets, while those at the center are on taller towers. In some cases, there is a central chimney projecting 2 or 3 meters (7 or 10 feet) above the top of the mound itself. These lead into a system of broad channels that dive down to a depth of up to 5 meters (around 16 feet) below ground level. These massive ventilation ducts, for that is what they are, do not enter directly into the living space of the termites, or at least only by small apertures, but their close contact as they penetrate through or past the nurseries allows

Anthony Bannister/NHPA

VENTILATION IN A TERMITE MOUND

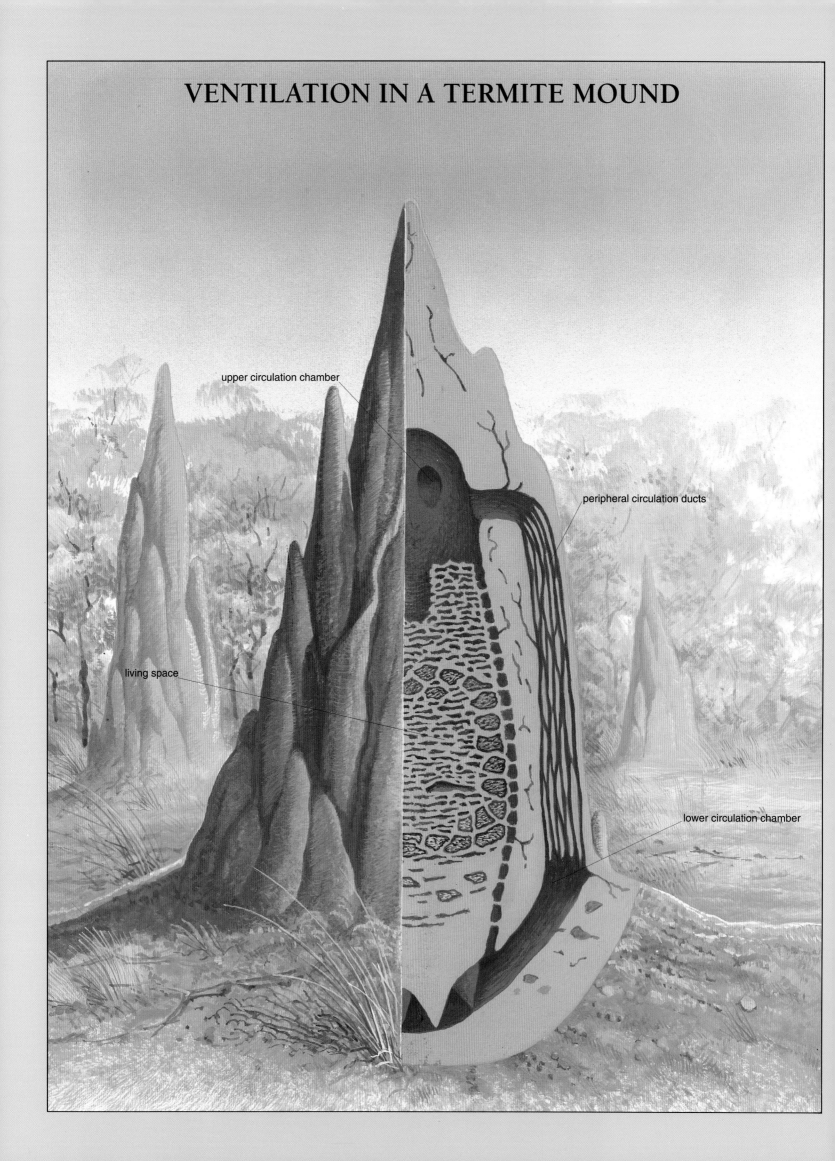

upper circulation chamber

peripheral circulation ducts

living space

lower circulation chamber

gas exchange, temperature and humidity control to be effected.

But what drives the ventilation system? A simple physical phenomenon called the "Venturi effect"—the same principle in fact that gives lift to aircraft wings. The greater wind speed passing over the uppermost apertures on the mound compared to the lower ones creates a pressure difference which sucks air into the lower openings and down through the mound, before being sucked up again and out through the upper apertures.

The closed system is typified by *Macrotermes bellicosus*. Its mound is also permeated by large channels and spaces above the nest, enveloping its cells and gardens and entering a basement from which shafts penetrate deep underground. But, in contrast to *M. subhyalinus,* there is no point where it emerges through the outer shell of the mound.

So what drives this system and how is the air conditioned? The motor in this case is temperature difference. The highest temperature, about 30°C (86°F), is found in the center of the nest itself. This causes the air to rise up into the spaces above. It begins to cool, while further rising hot air forces it into channels which come close to the surface of the mound itself. Here gas exchange can take place through the porous mud walls. This fresher air is now driven into the basement area where temperatures are about 5°C (41°F) lower than the nest above. This fresh cooler air is drawn up into the nest by rising air above, to repeat the cycle and maintain ventilation.

Surprisingly, these closed systems are quite variable in design and may not have such an obvious system of up and down ventilation channels. There are also distinct regional differences which are not obviously adaptations to differences in habitat. A dramatic illustration of this is a special design of basement only known from *Macrotermes bellicosus* mounds in a certain part of Nigeria. In mature mounds the nest itself sits above a cavernous basement 3.5 meters (11 feet) across and spacious enough to contain two reclining people, and with shafts that plunge from it several meters into the ground below. Supporting the weight of the nest is a massive central pillar and around it hangs a dramatic spiral arrangement of delicate mud gills or vanes up to 10 centimeters (4 inches) deep. A stage set of cut-out scenery, ring enveloping ring, of such scale and sophistication is hard to equate with the blind diminutive insects that designed and built it. These vanes seem to be an evaporative surface because they are coated with a fine layer of whitish mineral crystals. Exactly how it works is not clear but it is even harder to imagine that it does nothing.

Peter Davey/Bruce Coleman Limited

Chasing the world at large: the migrators

The idea that a hostile and unpredictable world can be tamed by the construction of barriers between the builder and its environment is a strong theme running through this chapter. Within the confines of these defenses, a microcosm of near-stability may be created where animals can spend most of their lives. It is a solution which is awe-inspiring in its architectural scale; however, it is also a solution that works solely within the boundaries of immobility. There is, however, an alternative perspective to this world—as the saying goes,

▲ A pride of lions (*Panthera leo*) enjoys a noonday siesta in the shade. Most social of all the cat family, lions have evolved a social structure that allows the co-operative style of hunting that most efficiently harvests the large migratory animals on which they mainly feed.

▼ A group of young hawksbill turtles (*Eretmochelys kempi*). Among the most solitary of all animals, marine turtles disperse rapidly to sea after hatching, and spend several years of almost ceaseless wandering over the open ocean before returning to breed.

Adrian Warren/Ardea London Limited

► (*facing page*) A herd of plains zebras (*Equus burchelli*) grazing. The zebra is a prominent member of an assemblage of large grass-eating mammals that follow the rains and fresh grass in an intricate pattern of separately staged migrations across the plains of East Africa.

▼ Common and familiar across most of the Northern Hemisphere, the migratory barn swallow (*Hirundo rustica*) is one of the long-distance champions among songbirds. Individuals breeding in Europe, for instance, may travel as far as South Africa to spend the winter. Here one snatches a drink in full flight.

"There is always somewhere which is just right for me, all I need to do is get there." The solution in this case is therefore not immobility but travel.

The Serengeti in East Africa is a region of seasonal rainfall within which large numbers of zebra (*Equus burchelli*), wildebeest (*Connochaetes taurinus*) and Thomson's gazelle (*Gazella thomsoni*) undertake an annual cycle of migration. The area is close to the equator with a dry season from July to November. During this period, large mammals are found in a habitat of open thorn woodland, where the best grazing can be found and the biting of the tsetse flies and mosquitoes is confined to areas close to water. In December, when the first storms heralding the wet season occur, great herds of animals stream southeast and onto the grassland plains some 200 kilometers (125 miles) away.

The zebra arrive first. Their rough cropping of the newly sprouted grass stems exposes the more digestible leaves to the wildebeest which follow. They, in turn, reveal the tender herbs to the Thomson's gazelle, which are the last to arrive. All three species then give birth to their young, which not only enjoy the benefits of fresh grass (that lasts till the end of the rains in May), but also the protection provided by huge concentrations of zebra and antelope which swamp the appetites of local carnivores. In June, as the plains grass dries up and is consumed, the return migration begins to the denser habitat of the thorn forest.

At different parts of the annual cycle animals may have different priorities. So migratory species may not only move to different types of habitat but may alter their way of life. The Eurasian curlew (*Numenius arquata*), with its long legs and slender curved beak, is a typical bird of mudflats in tidal estuaries. This habitat is among the most productive in the world and consequently rich in invertebrate prey throughout the year. In spite of that, it is a poor breeding location, giving little cover for chicks from aerial and ground predators. So, in search of nest sites, the curlew, in common with many other wader species, migrates inland, leaving the rich estuarine feeding grounds like an end of season holiday resort. The curlews head for the protective cover of rough moorland, where the dying fall of their sad voices serves to space out breeding pairs and tug the heartstrings of solitary hillwalkers.

The seasonal change in lifestyle is even more extreme in the handsome pomarine skua or jaeger (*Stercorarius longicauda*), which is a land bird when breeding, and an ocean bird when not. Outside the breeding season it is found where upwellings of oceanic currents produce rich feeding grounds for fish—off the coasts of West Africa, Ecuador and Peru and beyond eastern Australia are known sites. It feeds in part by catching fish for itself or by gathering where fishing vessels discard offal, but it also preys upon small ocean-going surface-feeding birds such as the phalarope.

When summer comes to the Arctic, pomarine skuas migrate far north into the tundra to breed, not near the sea but inland to prey upon small mammals, especially lemmings. During the breeding season they hunt like owls or hawks. One problem is that their webbed feet are not suited to snatching rodents. Instead they rely on their strong beaks, even digging into burrow systems after lemmings that have gone to ground.

Yet, even with such masterly changes of character, the pomarine skua is not fully in control of its destiny. Good lemming years tend to occur at the same time over a wideranging area, resulting in dramatic changes in numbers of breeding birds—for example, 150-fold difference in breeding density within a few years at one site in Alaska.

Nevertheless, some birds do seem able to select a site at whatever time of year which gives them the best that is on offer. This is particularly well illustrated by small, insect-eating species which breed in Europe during the Northern Hemisphere summer and travel south into Africa as winter approaches. It might be anticipated that they would head for the luxuriance and stability of the equatorial

Stephen Dalton/NHPA

tropical forests but instead they seek out those areas of boom and bust ecology—the grasslands of the southern fringes of the Sahara and the East African plains. The reason for this seems to be that the forests have a resident population of insectivores already exploiting resources to the full, whereas the grasslands after the rain became suddenly productive and superabundant in food.

The departure of these migrants from the fading European summer coincides with the end of the rainy season in the grasslands to the north of the equator. Many of the bird species spend the whole winter in this area despite the progressive desiccation of the landscape. Some, however, like the diminutive marsh warbler (*Acrocephalus palustris*), follow the rains of the tropical convergence zone over the equator to end their non-breeding season in the climate at southern Africa still enjoying rich grasslands and associated insect fauna. Well fortified, the birds then fly the 9,000–10,000 kilometers (5,600–6,200 miles) back to Europe for the breeding season in April/May.

This strategy of seasonal migration to stay in a favorable environment has therefore evolved in some species to an extent where quite small birds perform annual migrations of thousands of kilometers. This is seen probably in its most extreme form in the Arctic tern. *Sterna paradisaea* breeds, as its name suggests, at the northern fringes of North America, Europe and Asia, mostly within the Arctic Circle. A land of midnight sun therefore allows them around-the-clock foraging for fish and insect prey to feed themselves and raise their chicks. But, as the sun comes to set again and the days shorten, so the birds head south, not to spend the winter in the warmth of the tropics, but to follow the sun to the limits of the southern oceans to enjoy uninterrupted fishing near and within the Antarctic Circle, 16,000 kilometers (10,000 miles) from their breeding sites. It is possible that an Arctic tern could experience 24 hours of daylight for between six and eight months of the year. The kind of environmental constancy achieved here could rival that of a beaver or even a mound-building termite.

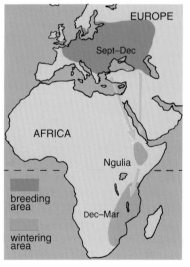

▲ Migration paths of the marsh warbler (*Acrocephalus palustris*). A migrant's winter quarters are often as distinct and circumscribed as its breeding distribution and, as is currently happening with many European migrants in particular, habitat destruction in the winter quarters can affect a migrant as drastically as damage to its breeding grounds.

189

Chapter 5

STRATEGIES FOR SURVIVAL

Michael H. Robinson

The animal world, it seems, is involved in a perpetual
relay race. The prize is survival and the winners pass
on their genes to the next generation. But how do they
get to the finish line?

FIRST LINE OF DEFENSE: PREVENTING ATTACK

In order to survive, animals need some line of defense against
other competitors in the race. Camouflage is a universal form
of defense and is found in every major group of animals.
Disguise provides another form of defense.

DEFENSE BY ADVERTISING: DETERRENCE

Another method of preventing attack is to deter predators by being
excessively obnoxious, distasteful or nasty.

DEFENSE AFTER DISCOVERY: COUNTERMEASURES

When an animal is discovered, disguise or camouflage fall by the
wayside and tactics like escape or repelling the predator take over.

ALLIANCES FOR PROGRESS

While the animal kingdom was never peaceful and never innocent,
malice and hatred have never been attributes of animals. Relationships
can create benefits for those involved.

FIGHTING DISEASE AND INJURY

In any race, survival and fitness are affected by injury and disease.
Here too, an animal must have a code of defense to ward off attack.

SURVIVING HOSTILE CLIMATES

Animals must cope with the vagaries of climate. At high temperatures
proteins coagulate, and below freezing point water turns to ice, so it is
within this range of conditions that animals must exist.

STRATEGIES FOR SURVIVAL

Michael H. Robinson

For any species, the most crucial facet of its existence is to live long enough to reproduce and pass on its genes to another generation. From this necessity has emerged an extraordinary array of behavioral patterns.

Alex Kerstitch/Planet Earth Pictures

▲ When disturbed, a fire-bellied toad (*Bombina orientalis*) warns of its toxic defenses by arching its back to display the bright red and black markings on its underparts.

The focus of this book is on the marvelous adaptations of animals. All adaptations are directly or indirectly involved in survival, and survival is what life is all about. But despite our romantic illusions to the contrary, the function of animal and plant existence is relatively simple. It is to reproduce. The biological "purpose" of all creatures is to live long enough to reach sexual maturity and pass on their genes to another generation. They convert resources into offspring.

This objective is the result of the way that evolution works. It affects biological processes, structures and behaviors. Natural selection works only through reproductive success; and only those characteristics that contribute to

Konrad Wothe/Oxford Scientific Films

survival to reproductive age are maintained by the selection processes of evolution.

Part of the huge investment that is involved in strategies for survival goes into social behavior and adaptations. But there is also another exciting area of survival devices. These are the strategies to deal with the world beyond one's own species. This is the world of foes and food, diseases and parasites, and of the menacing physical world of climate. To reach maturity animals need to eat, and avoid being eaten; they must reduce the risks of injury, parasitization and disease, and survive excessive heat, cold, moisture, dryness and harmful radiation. Very small animals even have to survive the buffeting of random molecular movement! Relations with other species are often complex, specialized and highly exciting. They can be either antagonistic, neutral or mutualistic.

One of the great complex of antagonisms is involved in predator–prey relationships. The amazing adaptations of predators for finding food have already been described in detail in Chapter Two. They are splendid in their variety, complexity, specialization and frequent perfection. Defensive adaptations essentially involve the complement of finding food, which is to avoid being fed upon. Both are crucial to an animal's survival.

Beyond that, it is interesting to contrast the biological arms races of predation and aggression. There is after all a very considerable difference between the two. Most biologists agree that the term aggression should be restricted to conflicts within a species. This means fighting over resources, territories, nest sites, mates and so on. Predation is simply one species feeding on another. Death is the objective of the predator, while survival is the

▼ Two red foxes (*Vulpes vulpes*) fighting in Canadian snow. It is unlikely that such a squabble will lead to serious injury. Among animals the general principle is, the more lethal the weapons, the more compelling the rituals controlling them when dealing with mates and rivals. When he has had enough, the loser will adopt a submissive posture recognized by the victor, and the fight will end.

objective of the prospective prey. But aggression is very different. It is not in the animal's interests to die for the resources it needs for propagation. The dead cannot breed. So in the course of evolution, animal aggression has been channeled into conventionalized combat, where rituals minimize lethality.

The warfare of our own species does not necessarily resemble animal aggression. Although it occurs within one species, it has not historically involved devices that prevent killing. In fact, in its tendency to bloody

An arms race implies a dynamism between attack and defense. When one studies the biological arms race, it is quite easy to become emotionally involved with both sides of the struggle. For instance, many people find cats attractive. They are the quintessential predators. Their lithe muscularity, extraordinary quickness, and finely honed senses invite comparison with the superbly engineered fighter aircraft of today. But we also tend to empathize with their prey. Playing "cat and mouse" is criticism not praise. For every predatory adaptation there is usually a defense.

Matthews Purdy/Survival Anglia

▲ Every sense alert, a female lion (*Panthera leo*) cautiously stalks her prey. She seeks surprise and a quick kill, not only for efficiency's sake, but also because predators can little afford the risk of injury. Her prey will fight back with everything it has, and a poor kill could mean a festering wound that slows her down for weeks while it heals. Today's dinner may be secure, but what about tomorrow's?

slaughter, it resembles predation in animals more than aggression. Military historians teeter on the edge of recognizing this fact. Here, for instance, are some comments on the wars of the sixteenth and seventeenth centuries: "from the brutalized perspective of the hapless peasant or townsman, the entire cycle of wars might best be understood as a savage people hunt, with themselves as quarry." Religious differences were seen as "most effective in undermining a sense of shared humanity and allowing men to behave as if enemies are actually of another species."

Defenses may be highly specialized because they involve co-adaptation and escalation.

The military arms race of the twentieth century has driven weapons technology, offensive and defensive, to amazing heights of intricacy. And so too, the evolutionary arms race has strong parallels with that of weapons. Evolution always carries the baggage of the past; it builds on existing patterns by modification. A graphic example of this in warfare is the evolution of fighter airplanes in World War II. The British Supermarine Spitfire, one of the participants in the famous Battle of

Britain, went through more than 20 modified versions during the war. Some of these were so different from their predecessors that if they had been animals they would have been described by taxonomists as separate species. But they retained enough elements of the "ancestral" form, the shape of the wings or undercarriage, to be recognizably related.

So it is also with animal defenses, that they do not normally wipe the slate clean and start from a totally new beginning. The baggage of past successes can frequently be seen in present structures, behaviors and systems. Escalation occurs as each "offensive" advance by the predator is met by a defensive adaptation by the prey. This escalation in the living world is often reflected in increased specialization, and often by what looks like increased perfection in camouflage, mimicry and so on.

In fact there was a time when some evolutionary biologists argued that some defensive devices were better than they needed to be. They argued that as leaf-mimics, insects were so lifelike that they exceeded the discriminatory powers of their predators, the birds. This kind of armchair logic has been confounded by the study of the perceptive acuity of predators.

One of the best places to study both sides of the biological arms race is in the rainforests of the tropics. In the rainforests there are overwhelmingly more species of animals and plants than anywhere else on Earth. As a consequence the struggles to survive are complex and intense, so that the specializations are many and varied. It is therefore easy to pick an overture of examples.

FIRST LINE OF DEFENSE:
PREVENTING ATTACK
When attempting categorization of complex phenomena, it always helps to group like with like. One way of looking at defensive systems is to divide them into those that work to prevent attack by predators, and those that work after an attack starts, to reduce a predator's chance of success. Attack-prevention can be simply called primary defense. Camouflage is an almost universal primary defense. It is found in every major group of animals on land, in every ocean and in the air. The operational principle is to fool the sense of the predator, so as not to be found, so as not to be detected. For most animals, the trick is to find a way not to be seen.

Military camouflage, which parallels natural camouflage (and may sometimes be inspired by

▲ Camouflage is one of the simplest and most effective means of defense, but it can also be used to fool potential prey. A formidable predator, this leaf-mimicking praying mantid (*Choerododis rhombicollis*) is lying in wait for some unwary insect to come within striking range.

biological studies), started off as concealment from the eyes of the enemy. Now it has extended to concealment from the electronic "eyes" of the enemy, to radar, sonar, infrared and other detectors. The biological arms race has led to detectors that work in the infrared, in the ultraviolet, and to sonar and electro-detection. It is almost certain that counter-measures have evolved; natural examples of nonvisual camouflage probably are waiting to be discovered.

Camouflage does not work without immobility and yet one characteristic of nearly

all animals is that they move. Even sessile animals, fixed in one place, have moving parts. Movement is one of the most effective attention getters. We wave to attract attention.

This aspect is so characteristic of animal life that it has become a clue to its detection. The first eyes to evolve were movement detectors and, as they have fought in the biological arms race, both predators and prey have evolved complex eyes to enhance movement detection. It is small wonder, then, that an animal's efforts at concealment involve dealing with movement.

CAMOUFLAGE FOR PREDATION

Camouflage is not always defensive. Predators may conceal themselves so that unsuspecting prey actually approach closely, secure and unafraid. This is the strategy of many sit-and-wait predators. Camouflage can also aid those that stalk in a dash-and-freeze style, like lions, leopards and tigers. As an aid to predation it is commonly called aggressive camouflage.

But in the case of smaller predators, the situation is not so easily defined, as they may be, at one and the same time, both predators and potential prey. In this case, their aggressive camouflage is not easy to distinguish from its defensive form. For example, does a yellow crab spider sitting on a yellow flower conceal itself as a predator from the bees and wasps, or is it camouflaged defensively against the birds that might eat it?

This question, at first sight, seems unanswerable, but recent research makes an informed answer possible. We know that flower-visiting insects are sensitive to the ultraviolet end of the color spectrum. They see colors that birds, mammals and we humans cannot see. However, with an ultraviolet adapted television camera, modern technology allows us to see things from a bee's-eye view. Under such close scrutiny we can, for example, look at a yellow spider on a flower. What we find is that the yellow spider does not match the yellow flower. It becomes instead a conspicuously dark blot, a Rorschach spider.

From this observation, it becomes clear that the camouflage is not directed at the prey but at the predators. Sitting on a flower exposes spiders; so they need to be camouflaged.

▼ Bright yellow to match its perch, a crab spider catches and devours a bee. Is the spider yellow to fool its insect prey, or to hide from birds that might eat it? Recent research has found the answer.

PRAIRIE DOG TOWN

Group members greet each other with "kissing" ceremonies.

Members of adjacent suburbs identify each other by sniffing.

A female builds her underground nest of grass.

Guards, alert for danger, whistle in alarm.

A ferret, the prairie dog's greatest enemy, snakes down a burrow in search of prey.

Prairie dogs live within a social unit, or "coterie". A number of coteries with interconnecting burrows form a prairie dog "town".

Lodgers, such as rattlesnakes and burrowing owls, often take over unused burrows and chambers.

◀ (*previous pages*) Before the arrival of Europeans, large areas of western North American grasslands were given over to the subterranean towns and cities built and inhabited by prairie dogs. Prairie dog colonies are divided into distinct wards, their boundaries defended by their inhabitants. "Kissing" ceremonies serve to exchange passwords. Burrows have several entrances, one generally mounded to lift its entrance higher than the others to promote air flow through the tunnel system. Turning bays provide some security from predators, such as the badger (far right).

▼ The common European mole (*Talpa europaea*) surfaces only to seek leaves and grass for its subterranean nest, or to dump surplus soil from its foraging tunnels.

The curtains of the night

The simplest form of concealment is to rely on darkness. Legions of animals are nocturnal because, in general, movement is safer by night than by day. Being nocturnal demands doing something to avoid detection by day. Living out of sight is one solution. Creeping into cracks and crevices also works but it needs a special body design. Some insects have such a flat body structure that they can edge into the narrowest cracks. Holes are another good place to hide. Insects often rest in one hole by day, until they can find another one. But the availability of these hideouts may be restricted. The world is not full of holes, but as the famous World War I cartoon soldier, Old Bill, said "if you can find a better hole, go to it."

However, many animals do not need to find holes because they can make them. Diggers are found wherever there are materials in which to dig, enemies from which to escape, and structures that can become shovels, drills and augers. Some digging devices are quite bizarre. Moles, for example, dig for food as well as shelter. They have stubby spade-like front legs and feet that act as extraordinary tools. But there is also a group of insects called the mole-crickets that dig with front legs that look so superficially like mole's legs that the whole insect immediately conjures up a vision of "Moley" from *Wind in the Willows*.

A less bizarre form of convergence is in the marsupial moles of Australia. Their adaptations for digging include parallels to true moles right down to their strong shoulder bones, tiny eyes and external ears. They construct burrows which are variously reinforced to prevent entry and pursuit. Burrowing spiders may also build silk "air-lock" doors or, as in the case of trapdoor spiders, beautifully hinged earth doors that totally conceal the entrance. (Of course burrows can be used to escape from heat, cold, desiccation, or to find food or protect the young.) If you don't dig a hole, you can build one. Marine tube worms can construct elaborate burrows out of a type of lime cement. These may be attached to rocks or even to seaweed fronds.

If you can't make a den site then you can carry one around. Caddis larvae, case-building caterpillars and hermit crabs are all classic examples of animals that either occupy or build mobile homes—a behavior that displays unique skill. In particular, case-building behavior can become very complex and some caddis larvae have the capacity to build extraordinary cases from twigs or stones. There are also species that build special "masonry" cases and are renowned for arranging stones in ordered precision, very much like neat stone walls. Experiments carried out on stone selection show that tiny-brained grubs are actually programmed to measure stones during complex manipulations. They can also be induced to repair their cases with pieces of lead, glass beads and a wide variety of materials not available in streams and ponds. Such caddis cases function like burrows in the sense that the animal retreats out of view. Since the cases are built with habitat-specific material they look like part of the backdrop of nature.

The houses of hermit crabs are less inconspicuous but nonetheless usually appear as part of the normal "scene". The crabs are capable of occupying a wide range of suitable containers found on the seabed, but commonly live in empty shells. Their house-choosing

Heather Angel/Biofotos

behavior has been intensively studied and is particularly complex. The crabs choose from what is available. Because of this, it is possible to induce hermit crabs to live in glass houses, artfully blown to resemble whelk shells. In public aquariums, this makes an exciting spectacle because the entire complex body of the crab is made visible. Through the glass, one can see all the complex breathing movements of dozens of joined appendages and the worms that may live as house guests with the crab. Borrowed homes, however, do not grow so hermit crabs have to house-hunt regularly as they outgrow their adopted shells.

Some sea anemones live exclusively on the shells of hermits in a symbiotic relationship. One such anemone, the cloak anemone (*Adamsia palliata*) surrounds the "doorway" of the adopted shell and provides a "porch". By extending its size, the anemone helps to extend the hermit crab's use of the shell.

Home-building can also extend into condominium construction with some social insects making mighty structures. Many termites, almost naked roach relatives, build huge earthen mounds or great aerial nests attached to tree branches. The nasute termites, for example, squirt gum at their enemies and build covered walkways wherever they go so they are dwellers in darkness both at home and abroad. Wasps invented paper, millions of years before humans, and bees use wax to build their nurseries in tunnels and hollows. And there are also many bizarre examples of mobile homes in the ocean. When threatened, some fishes retreat inside the digestive tract of a sea cucumber. This is a "burrow" with a difference. Living within the tentacles of sea anemones and jellyfish is not concealing but certainly protective, but more of that later.

In defense, if you can't stay out of sight then you should try not to be seen! This is camouflage. In its simplest form it is color matching. Green on green, brown on brown, helps concealment, confounds the eye. The first military camouflage is said to have arisen when British troops, conspicuous in their summer whites on the dry brown frontiers of India, dyed them brown by dipping the cotton in tea! When personal combat became a long-distance affair, formerly conspicuous uniforms, meant to terrify, were replaced with the dull inconspicuousness of camouflage. Khaki and field gray replaced scarlet. Interestingly enough, uniforms were consistently one color through all of World War I and World War II. Today's patterned, blotched and spotted, and fashionable "camouflage colors" had to wait for a new technology in fabric production, but animals did it long before troops.

Stephen Dalton/NHPA

HERMIT CRAB

▲ Adult caddisflies (*Tricoptera* sp.) somewhat resemble moths, but their larvae are completely aquatic creatures that build cases or tubes of twigs, tiny pebbles or other debris in which to live. At the end of the larval stage they seal the case and pupate within, in due course biting their way free and swimming to the surface as adults.

◄ Combining the strengths of molluskan and crustacean architecture: the soft-bodied hermit crab lives in abandoned seashells, which it carries around on its back at all times.

Camouflage

Simple camouflage relies upon the animal's color, programmed roughly by evolution, to make an appropriate match to the colors in its habitat. If the habitat changes, defenses must then change accordingly. Such changes are usually more-or-less in pace with each other. But as humans are changing habitats more rapidly than nature's normal rate of change, this can lead to problems.

One striking example of human-induced habitat change occurred during the Industrial Revolution in Europe, when coal-burning factories spewed enormous quantities of black soot into the atmosphere. During this period, gray tree trunks on which the gray peppered moth (*Biston betularia*) rested by day began to turn black. The gray moth was no longer camouflaged on the soot-blackened trees. This could have spelt disaster for the species but it was saved by the existence of a rare black mutant moth that appeared among the gray forms. When the industrial change came, the black form of the moth survived on the blackened trees, while the gray moths were conspicuous and were eaten. Gradually the melanistic black moths became the dominant form. In this case, evolution met the challenge. This interesting story might have passed unnoticed but for the amateur entomologist's passion for rarity. English moth collectors gathered the rare black forms with the same avidity that stamp collectors longed for "Penny Black" stamps. To date, we do not know whether other species have changed or disappeared because of industrial change.

One of the problems with camouflage is that the animal needs a background to blend into,

but some animals have the predicament of not being able to rest close to a background. Web-building spiders, for example, have to live "up in the air" at the center of their webs. What can they do to conceal themselves? One solution is to build a background into the web. At least one group of spiders belonging to the genus *Cyclosa* builds perpendicular stripes of dead prey husks and plant debris into the web, producing a mass of dingy brown suspended in the silk. The spider makes a gap in this brown stripe that matches the length and color of its body. It sits in the gap and is marvelously concealed among the surrounding trash. However, this behavior goes disastrously wrong if an experimenter throws small fragments of brightly colored paper into the web. The spider uses these and builds a brightly colored stripe instead of a brown one. Her contrasting brown body is then made very conspicuous.

Although there are uniformly colored animals, just like early camouflaged military uniforms, patterned camouflage is much more common. Concealment clearly depends on other things beside background matching. A minute's thought reveals that object recognition often depends on outlines or shapes. A green lizard on a green background, for example, may be betrayed by a telltale shape. But this can be concealed by outline-obliterating patterns. This is called "disruptive coloration" and is a very common feature of camouflage. In military terms it is "dazzle-patterning" and the eye is disrupted by the combination of lines and blotches. Outlines and shapes are emphasized by the highlight and shadow that result from the natural effects of sunlight. Every painter and photographer consciously emphasizes

◀ (*facing page*) Most chameleons, like this high-casqued chameleon (*Chamaeleo bitraeniatus*), inhabit Africa and Madagascar. They feed on insects, captured with lightning flicks of the long tongue, which can be extended nearly the same length as the body; sticky saliva secures the prey. Two large blood vessels and elastic ligaments extend from the base to the tip of the tongue, which is straightened and extended by a sudden surge of blood in an action something like blowing a party squeaker; muscular action recoils it back into the mouth.

◀ The rainforests of Central and South America are home to a large number of species of colorful frogs, like this red-eyed leaf-frog (*Agalychnis callidryas*).

OF SLOTHS AND MOTHS

Michael Fogden/Bruce Coleman Limited

Sloths are almost an ecosystem in themselves. They are a slow-moving, leaf-eating mammal, found in the New World tropics, and belonging to a once-widespread family that included the giant ground sloths (that were bigger than grizzly bears). They live in the humid rainforests and their camouflage is enhanced by the green algae that grow on their fur. However, this dense covering of fur is also home to a variety of insects, ranging from moths to beetles of many species. The three-toed sloth (*Bradypus* sp.) is the major host and up to 120 moths have been found on a single animal, running around in its fur.

The entire association is based on the coprophagous (that is, dung-feeding) habits of the sloth-moth caterpillars; and the digestive peculiarities of the sloth.

Since sloths eat nothing but leaves that are packed with normally indigestible cellulose (fiber), their strategy for digestion consists of keeping their food in the gut for long periods to allow bacteria to break down the cellulose.

▲ The shaggy fur of the arboreal, leaf-eating, slow-moving two-toed sloth (*Choloepus hoffmanni*) provides food and shelter for a veritable zoo of insect hitch-hikers, including several species of moth.

The long period of food retention also affects their defecation frequency. This explains why the sloth moths live on the sloth. The female moths stay on the sloth to be present when it descends from the tree in which it feeds, to defecate on the ground. At that stage the moth flies off the sloth and deposits its eggs on the highly nutritious remains of the sloth's leaf diet. Traveling on the sloth ensures that the moth is at the right place at the right time to ensure access to a food resource for its larvae. Male sloth moths probably use the sloth as a lekking ground (a display arena) on which to attract females.

It is believed that sloth moths may have originally been species with coprophagous larvae, that ranged the forest freely in quest of feces.

these effects, but evolution has developed defensive "countershading" that reduces their effect. Countershaded animals have dark backs and light undersides. Dark colors reduce highlights and light undersides reduce the shadow effect. Animals crouch to reduce shadows and many animals have outline-reducing hair fringes.

Animals can camouflage themselves effectively by using some elements of their surroundings to cover their body. Decorator crabs (*Stenorhynchus inachus*) attach bits of sponge and seaweed to their spiny surface and finally become covered with a "garden" of seabed organisms. Some insect larvae attach detritus to their bodies and become walking scrap-piles, while some beetles from the misty high mountains of New Guinea become covered in lichens, mosses and algae and blend into the vegetation of moss forests. Sloths have grooved hairs in which minute algae flourish. The sloth becomes a greenish garden among the trees, the nearest thing to green fur. In the wonderful tropical forest musical *Yanamamo* the sloth sings, slowly, "we are green, so as not to be seen." Sloths and slow lorises (*Nyctericebus coucang*) have solved the problem of moving while being camouflaged. They move very, very

slowly. Other animals dash and freeze like advancing soldiers or SWAT teams.

One problem about background matching camouflage is that the animal has to choose the appropriate background for its "perch". This may involve complex searching behavior and a lot of energy use. One of the complications in the process is that the nocturnal animal usually chooses its resting site before dawn, so that it has few clues about color. Being able to change colors eliminates this problem.

Color change is displayed in varying degrees in different animals. Chameleons may be the classic example of a color changing animal, but their fame far exceeds their abilities. They are surpassed by the likes of reef squid (*Sepioteuthis sepiodea*) and cuttlefish, which change their color almost instantly. The chameleon, on the other hand, changes color slowly and the leopard cannot change his spots at all! Not only can the cuttlefish change its color in an instant but, as it wriggles into the sand, it can also change its skin texture from smooth to granular. This group of mollusks, the cephalopods, have the color cells in their naked skins under rapid nervous control. Their surface is highly responsive. Cephalopods use their color-changing ability for concealment

▼ A giant cuttle (*Sepia apama*) in close-up. Cuttles, along with their relatives the squids, differ from octopuses most conspicuously in having ten, not eight, tentacles. Notable for the fluidity and speed with which they can effect the change, they alter the color of their skins to match their backgrounds or to signal mood and status to potential mates.

Horizon/Martin Coleman

and also for social display, to signal hospitality or reproductive arousal.

While having scales, furs or feathers on the outside limits background matching changes, there are some interesting developmental changes that reflect the need for camouflage in changing environments. Young emerald tree-pythons (*Chondropython viridis*) become yellow-striped as adults, resting in coiled hanks, like wool on a branch. Young gulls are splotched like commando uniforms and so are in perfect camouflage for the ground nest site. At maturity nearly all gulls are white, and this reduces their conspicuousness against the sky when fishing. Young tapirs, secluded in the forest by day, are spotted and striped, and look like Bambi with a wiggly nose. In Malaysia, the adults are black and white, while in other areas such as in the

▼ A marine spider crab (*Macropodia rostrata*) conceals its identity by means of the random hunks of seaweed it carries around on its body and legs.

Heather Angel/Biofotos

Kim Westerskov/Oxford Scientific Films

New World, they may appear black. As youth is a period of extreme vulnerability, camouflage can be a necessity, while at maturity the requirements of defense become secondary to those of sex, courtship and social dominance. There may also be seasonal changes in camouflage. Animals turning white in winter, for example, provided the royal families of Europe with the ermine edging of their robes.

Camouflage may also act on an animal's senses other than its vision. Since we are predominantly visual animals, we do not easily detect olfactory or acoustic camouflage devices, but they almost certainly exist. Think of a dog rolling in ordure to conceal its scent from potential prey or the spider transmitting the pheromone sex attractant of a male moth.

Disguise

Another way to overcome the real constraints of background-matching is disguise. This is often lumped together with camouflage, but it definitely works in a different way. The

camouflaged animal "hopes" not to be seen, while the disguised animal is seen but "pretends" to be something else—something that would not be edible to predators. Many people find this to be a difficult distinction, but a military analogy makes it simple. On the human battlefield, the camouflaged battle tank is concealed against its background. The camouflage only works if the weapon is not discernable as a separate object. The same tank tricked out to look like a haystack or a farm cart, is discernable but is confused with an innocuous object known to be harmless.

In nature, the objects mimicked in "animal disguises" are the common features of most habitats: sticks, leaves, flowers, feces, stones and so on. One of the great advantages of disguise is that it should work completely out of context. A stick is inedible to birds whether it is in the middle of a desert, on the seashore, floating in a stream or on the forest floor. Of course, looking like a plant part, a leaf, bird dropping or some other inedible object may require quite complex and specialized disguise.

Telltale features of the "normal" animal have to be concealed, and simultaneously the animal has to be convincingly like the model. Stick insects have to be the right color, long and stick-like, and cannot afford to betray themselves by having legs visible. The behaviors associated with disguise are often highly complex, involving body postures of almost unreal specialization. For a bird to imitate a stick or a reed involves a whole spectrum of changes that deviate from what we perceive as "normal" bird behavior.

Despite, or probably because of, the extraordinary discriminatory powers of predators, there are outstanding examples of near-perfect disguise. Stick and leaf insects are well known. One whole order of insects, the Phasmids, consists almost entirely of creatures with detailed disguises. Among this group some leaf and stick insects are not only extraordinary in structure, improbably flattened like leaves or long like sticks, but they also have remarkable behaviors to match. Most phasmid stick insects extend their long front legs, side-by-side in line

▲ Many animals have built-in camouflage: the varied bumps, lumps, spines and ragged fins on the body of this red scorpionfish (*Scorpaena cardinalis*) break up and hide its outline as it lurks on the sea floor, alert for prey.

207

▼ Appropriate behavior patterns enhance the camouflage of many insects. This young Australian stick-insect nymph (*Extatosoma tiraratum*) sways slowly back and forth as it walks, mimicking the gentle breeze-blown motion of the leaves around it.

with their long bodies. This conceals the characteristic insect legs, the head, and the long antennae. It also increases the apparent length of the "stick". Some species go even further and hold the other two pairs of legs in concealing positions. Other insects and spiders mimic flowers and even bird droppings.

Being disguised may impose restrictions on a way of life. This is particularly true of sex and family care. A leaf-mimicking insect does not look like a leaf if it is mating. Because mating spoils the deception, most disguised insects mate at night. Mantids, however, are an exception and they mate by day. The reason

is probably very simple. The males of these insects almost certainly need to keep their eyes on the female because she is a highly predatory creature. If the male approaches from behind he is safe, but approaching from in front puts him within range of the female's marvelously spiny front legs. These are her prey-capture

Jane Burton/Bruce Coleman Limited

weapons and are used to strike moving insects. As the male is the right size for a prey item, he is constantly at risk if he moves into her field of vision. Male mantids can still mate even when their heads have been chewed off. This is a nice evolutionary provision for coping with the dangers involved. One extraordinary species of leaf-like mantid from Central America copulates only in a narrow, 20 minute or so, time window at dawn. Mating by dawn's early light makes good use of a period when insect-eating birds are not hunting. At this time, their disguise can be temporarily abandoned in the interests of procreation.

Walking or swimming is not a characteristic of leaves or twigs and certainly not of feces or thorns. If disguised animals have to move by day, it is essential that they should, as far as possible, move in a "vegetable-like" way, or at the very least, inconspicuously. Stick and leaf insects rock from side to side as they walk, rather like swaying vegetation. Young European nightjars (*Caprimulgus europaeus*) hatch on the ground and, looking like dead leaves, may also rock. This has been called wind-mimicry. Bitterns (*Botaurus stellaris*) stand in reed beds with their necks outstretched and bills pointing skywards. In this attenuated posture they blend with the long, thin reeds and are said to intensify the disguise by swaying from side to side like the reeds themselves.

Vine snakes edge forward slowly with a fore and aft "hesitation waltz" movement and Amazonian leaf fish propel themselves with transparent fins, stiff as leaves. These fish not only appear simply to drift smoothly along, disconcertingly in the absence of any current, but often swim on their sides. They look just like current-borne leaves. The pipefishes and sea horses that are disguised as seaweed fronds also appear to drift along through the water, propelled not by sinuous fish-like locomotion but by inconspicuously undulating dorsal fins. All of these disguises make the animals that wear them seem inedible.

Disguise works not only in defense but also in offense, just as in camouflage. Some predators use disguise to conceal themselves from their prey. Again, as with camouflage, it isn't always easy to determine whether the predator is defending itself against its own predators or using disguise to lure or reassure potential prey. The jury is out in most cases but situations where defense is really clear are the light-flashing mimicry of some fireflies, and the chemical mimicry of the bolas spider. Do flower disguises in mantids attract pollinating insects which the mantid then catches and eats? While the evidence is apocryphal, stranger things have indeed happened!

of power": potential enemies assembled enough allies so that each side more-or-less equaled the other. A stalemate resulted, at least in theory. In the second half of our century, the existence of nuclear weapons has given rise to a theory of deterrence. These weapons are so appallingly destructive that war between nuclear powers would result in mutual annihilation. War is therefore deemed to be unthinkable. Whether or not this theory is true is arguable, but in nature, real deterrence certainly exists. Not only does it exist but it is advertised in bright shining colors. These warning signals are just the opposite of camouflage.

Camouflage uses the earth tones of inconspicuous greens, browns and grays while "warning coloration", or *aposematism* as it is called scientifically, uses the reds, yellows and contrasts of black and white. These are the very combinations that we humans use in eye-catching warning labels, advertising, and for lifejackets and safety clothing. Look at the yellow-jacketed roadworker, the orange lifejacket or dayglo advertising posters, and think of wasps, coral snakes and pufferfishes. The principle is the same—heightened visibility. What is easily seen, strikingly patterned, is easily remembered and learned quickly. The quicker the learning by the predator the fewer the defenders that die or are mutilated in the process.

▲ A red-and-blue poison-arrow frog (*Dendrobates pumilio*). The forest tribes of the Amazon use the virulent poison secreted by glands in the skin of these frogs to daub the points of their blow-gun darts.

Ken Lucas/Planet Earth Pictures

DEFENSE BY ADVERTISING: DETERRENCE

Another method of preventing attack is to deter predators by being excessively obnoxious, distasteful or nasty. The theory of deterrence in warfare was for centuries based on the "balance

▼ An extreme example of an intimidation display: when disturbed the pufferfish swallows water at a prodigious rate, pumping it into special sacs distributed throughout the body, until the aggressor finds itself confronted with a startling spiny globe instead of the conventional fishy shape it expected.

▶ (*facing page*) The conspicuous black and yellow coloration of these blister beetles (*Mylabris occulaia*) signals caution to any would-be attacker. These insects squirt a jet of intensely irritating fluid when disturbed.

DEFENSE BY INTIMIDATION

What kinds of animals are able to wear warning colors? These range from skunks (*Mephitis mephitis*) to poison arrow frogs (*Dendrobates* spp.); from seasnakes (*Pelamus platurus*) to monarch butterflies (*Danaus plexippus*); from blister beetles (*Meloe* spp.) to sea-slugs. Coral snakes look like sticks of candy, and are among the most decorated of animals. Their poison is extremely virulent and it must pay to advertise that fact. In general, animals that smell bad, taste bad, sting, bite, prickle, poison or irritate can afford to advertise their deterrent weapons.

There is an interesting example from Japanese cuisine. Pufferfishes are almost all conspicuously colored. They are often very poisonous and presumably predators learn to avoid them. But they are also the basis of a culinary specialty. Highly trained *fugu* chefs prepare them as food by techniques that largely detoxify the dish. Lips tingle but the effect is not lethal. But mistakes can be made and customers in *fugu* restaurants do die. Perhaps the danger adds to the zest of the meal. Be that as it may, the experience must certainly sharpen the chef's senses. It is highly significant that *fugu* chefs have to be licensed. In essence this is licensing discrimination, where the chefs and customers as predators are pushed towards sharper discernment.

But colored villains are not alone. Animals that really impress their nastiness on those that try to kill them can also support harmless imitators. Innocent creatures can "cash-in" on another's expensive armaments. All that is needed is the right appearance. This method of defense by cheating was first described by a naturalist named Henry Bates, who discovered it in butterflies. It is called, in his honor, Batesian mimicry. The butterfly that tastes bad is called the model, while its perfectly edible imitators are the mimics. One really nasty model can support several species of mimics. Model and mimic need not be closely related and can come from distant families. Lookalike butterflies in a mimicry complex may have almost exactly similar color patterns on their wings. Mimics can become virtually

▼ Bright colors usually convey warning, as in the caterpillar of the tiger swallowtail (*Papilio glaucus*). The warning here relates to the intricate network of spines which have a toxin that is intensely irritating.

SACRIFICES AND DEFLECTIONS

Alex Kerstitch/Planet Earth Pictures

In chess, a good means of escape is sometimes to sacrifice a pawn. It gives the player under threat a chance to escape, and the opportunity to fight again. In the world of animal defense, sacrifice can be similar in its effect. Under pressure, certain animals are actually equipped to lose a non-essential part of their body to preserve their essence. Certain lizards, for example, may shed their tail. This is an example of what might be called evolutionary pre-planning. The lizard's tail has a built-in fracture line, and such tail-shedding ensures that the predator is left with a wriggling prey remnant while the rest of the animal escapes, shortened but still functional and able to reproduce.

Many kinds of insects under attack can autotomize their legs—that is, deliberately cut them off, internally, close to the base. The word combines the roots "auto", meaning self, and "tomy", meaning to cut (as in appendectomy). Even more impressive is the attack autotomy of some terrestrial crabs from the tropics. The crab attacks its attacker with its big claw, nips it onto a soft part, then autotomizes it. The muscles of the shed claw maintain a powerful "bite" in contraction, and the crab escapes while the attacker is being painfully pinched. This defense can only work twice for each crab, or at least until the crab molts and grows another set of claws.

▲ A sea-hare (*Aplysia* sp.) releases its smoke screen of colored mucus. Harmless but grotesque in appearance, and with an almost world-wide distribution, these are shell-less relatives of the snails.

Another device that may preoccupy the predator while its prey escapes is the production of pigment clouds in water. Squids and cuttlefish "ink" when disturbed. The effect may appear similar to that of a wartime smokescreen, but Jacques Cousteau has suggested that the discrete cloud of ink may also form a kind of "pseudo" prey—not unlike the lizard's tail—to deflect the attack.

Deflecting the attack can also be achieved via the display of false targets on expendable parts of the body. For example, some butterflies have target marks on the back edge of their hind wings. Students can therefore determine when butterflies have been attacked by birds and escaped.

Some nymphalid butterflies even have false heads, complete with imitation antennae, on the hind wing. Since lethal attacks are often directed at heads, a false one is a first-class deflection device. Furthermore, the efficacy of this lure is enhanced by movements of the butterfly's wings that produce a twitching movement of the false antennae. Realism must pay off.

▶ (facing page) Light, long-toed and extremely agile, a South American basilisk or Jesus Christ lizard (*Basiliscus* sp.) can even cross water in sudden sprints from danger.

indistinguishable from the model. Such is the power of natural selection that it drives mimics to greater and greater detailed resemblance. A crude mimic may have some protection but smart or experienced predators will eat it. The more difficult it is to "tell the difference", the greater the protection conferred on the mimic. If one has been stung by a bee, if one knows the pain, one hesitates mightily before picking up a harmless bee- or wasp-mimicking fly.

There is a real parallel between this and the way predators are pushed to sharpen their discriminatory powers for survival. "He who breaks the clue eats"—it is this discrimination that drives the mimicry sometimes to near perfection. There is good experimental evidence to show that hunger drives predators to try out animals that they have previously found unpalatable. In the same way, starving people in World War II ate daffodil bulbs. The dynamics of the biological arms race presents each defense with a new attack.

DEFENSE AFTER DISCOVERY: COUNTERMEASURES

Once the predator is very close, discovery or attack may be imminent. The potential prey must then either sit tight, hoping to be overlooked, or try something else. Close-quarter tactics can include repelling the predator or trying to escape. Simply taking flight may work and many animals zigzag as they swim, run or fly in escape, which confuses the predator. Jumping is also a great escape strategy and many grasshoppers and crickets only use the full power of their enlarged hind legs for their momentous escape leap. Click beetles leap in the air like jumping beans, using a complex mechanical joint between segments of their thorax to power their sudden escape. Releasing a kind of cuticular trigger catch is rather like releasing a spring. Their method of defense combines noisy surprise and a much faster movement.

Startle works, in the same way as the shout in martial arts. Many animals take flight explosively, often with loud bursts of sound as they break cover. Agoutis leap out of concealment with a loud bark. Fright may cause momentary confusion. Animals that live above ground can use gravity as an escape device. The so-called flying frogs and snakes of Malaysia glide long distances when disturbed. The frogs glide on webbed toe "wings" and the snakes flatten their lateral skin to produce very long "wings", like paper darts. This gliding can put hundreds of meters between potential prey and the would-be predator. Many insects just drop, when disturbed. Spiders do even better, they can drop belayed on a silk line.

Diving into water may be a good escape when an animal is pursued by a land-living predator. Some birds do this, as do frogs and some lizards. At least one tropical lizard, the basilisk, of Central and South America, runs across the surface of the water. No mammal can follow that act. Its Spanish name translates to Jesus Christ lizard. Walking, which is more like running, on water necessitates great momentum and frilled toes.

A most interesting form of aerial escape parallels a World War II bomber tactic. When Allied bombers electronically detected German fighters that were locked onto them by radar, they went into violent evasive maneuvers. These included dropping precipitously in power dives, and jinking convulsively from side to side. The parallel can be made with bats, which may be seen as sonar equipped "nightfighters", and some moths that are like "bombers" with listening devices to detect the bats. Not only do some moths drop precipitously from their flight path when they hear the bat's ultrasonic detector cries, but they also make noises that may confuse the bat. These noises are functionally parallel to the radar-jamming devices used by aircraft in warfare. The bat–moth interaction is a good example of the escalating biological arms race. Recent observations indicate that the bats may have stepped-up their echo-location to deal with moths that have developed "ears".

One remarkable escape device used by many insects, some frogs and birds, depends on color confusion. As the animal takes off, by leaping or flying, it reveals previously hidden colors. The green frog or insect may transform into a flash of scarlet or orange, drop to the ground and seem to disappear. The mechanism is relatively simple. In insects and birds the bright wing colors are concealed by their folded outer surfaces when the animal is at rest. The colors flash while the animal is in flight and are immediately concealed again on landing. Tropical leaf frogs have brightly colored bellies, and the sides and inner surfaces of their legs may be dazzlingly hued. When they leap, all the color is revealed. When they land, all is somber again. The great ethologist Konrad Lorenz reported that his tame jackdaws (*Corvus monedula*) were utterly confused by the flash colors of the grasshoppers that leaped away from them as they foraged in the grass. Springboks also flash black and white patterns as they leap away from lions. But these are not quite so startling as the flash colors of frogs.

Any disorientation of an attacking predator is regarded as good tactics, and buying time for escape is done in a wide range of elegant ways. Sometimes apparent attack is the best means of

defense. Moving towards the predator instead of away may buy time for escape. Zigzagging also helps and was a tactic used extensively in World War II by convoys of ships seeking to disorientate pursuing submarines. In the same way, European hares zigzag in escape as do the antelopes of the great African plains. Unpredictability after attack has been called protean behavior, so that animals that unpredictably use a melange of escape behaviors are so classified. Praying mantids which have been studied in detail seem unpredictable in their display, may drop from vegetation or freeze in response to attacks. This may be considered true protean behavior.

Real counterattack may buy time for a retreat. Retaliation, for example, may come in the form of biting and stinging, which sharply surprises the predator. The experience of unhanding a stinging wasp is widespread. Bluffing is another tactic that works, even in human combat. Animal bluffing frequently involves looking bigger. Praying mantids and katydids erect their wings, reveal bright frightening colors and sometimes hiss. Pufferfishes inflate themselves to several times their original size and some lizards drop their ribs to expand their sidewards profile. In the New World, opossums hiss like steam valves when attacked, and rattlesnakes rattle. All this is good, and sometimes effective, bluff. Think of a defensive domestic cat, with its ears back, body arched to twice its height and that explosive spitting noise. Even big dogs retreat.

Dennis Green/Bruce Coleman Limited

▶ A peacock pufferfish (*Canthigaster solandri*), an inhabitant of coral reefs. The flesh of this and many other members of the family Tetraontidae is poisonous.

Max Gibbs/Oxford Scientific Films

Two kinds of intimidation display involve revealing behavior. When disturbed, some caterpillars inflate part of their body into a snakehead: "painted" vertebrate eyes appear on the head and it begins to twitch from side to side in a very brusque movement. No snake as small as a caterpillar is really dangerous, but the defense seems to work. Predators may be so endangered by poisonous snakes that the miniaturization is ignored.

Another very widespread scaring device uses the sudden appearance of large vertebrate-type eyes on an otherwise concealed surface. Automerid moths are the past masters of such eyespot displays. The false eyes are located on the upper surface of their hind wings and these marks are covered by the inconspicuous forewings when the moth is in its triangular resting posture. A peck from a bird immediately transforms the situation. In response, the moth snaps its forewings open, and simultaneously curls its abdomen under its body. The "eyes" suddenly appear and are erected to face the attacking bird. Experiments show that this display scares off some birds. However, the really interesting thing is that evolution has "painted" a very accurate eye pattern on the moth's wing. This pattern may be equipped with a three-dimensional effect through shading and even a built-in pupillary highlight. Why are these eyes effective deterrents? One suggestion is that they trigger a built-in response to owls, of which many small birds are scared. All this is in the service of defense. Staying alive is worth it.

In secondary defense, chemical weapons may be employed. Of course skunks are a classic case. To be "skunked" is a memorable experience and even dogs, with their apparent delight in malodors, are reduced to whining discomfort! The evacuation of bowels may also have been selected as a defense in some specialized cases. Foul feces from snakes and lizards discourage attack, but are relatively unsophisticated weapons compared to insect defenses. Stinkbugs have glands entirely devoted to a repellent function, while bombardier beetles literally let off steam and make loud explosions. They break down hydrogen peroxide to water and oxygen in chambers located under the rear of their wing

▲ Many forms of intimidation display involve icons that resemble the vertebrate eye: a female peacock butterfly (*Inachis io*, above) reveals such defensive patterns on its hind wings.

▼ A caterpillar of the eyed silkmoth (*Putomeris* sp.) warns of its heavily defended status with poisonous spines and garish warning colors.

cases. The reaction is exothermic and the liquid reaches 100°C (212° F), temperatures hot enough to form steam. Some stick insects spray offensive liquids quite literally into the faces of their enemies. The orifices out of which this liquid is squirted can be swiveled around, under muscular control, and aimed quite accurately. At least one predator, a mouse opossum, has learned to deal with the chemical weapon: it seizes the insect and rapidly pushes it head first into the sand, where the glands discharge into the ground.

Some insects produce hydrogen cyanide in defense, as a particularly lethal response.

DEFENSIVE BEHAVIOR OF THE SKUNK

A skunk is confronted by an aggressor.

It raises its tail in warning.

Further provoked, the skunk turns its back on its aggressor.

The skunk finally ejects a foul-smelling spray into the face of its aggressor.

Nasute termites are so-called because they have nose-like projections on their heads. If they were our size they would look like the nightmarish characters from a Bosch painting. The "nose" is a gum-spraying device that is used to defend the colony or the colony's covered trails. Any attack results in a Western-style "circle the wagons" response. Nasutes form a ring against the attacker, noses facing outwards. The lethal force of stinging in colony defense by bees has been highlighted by the effects of the hyperaggressive "Africanized" bees as they have spread northwards from Brazil. Humans, horses and cattle have actually been killed when they inadvertently stumbled into a nest. Australia has its own killer, the funnel-web spider, that uses its poison defensively against intruding mammals.

Rolling into a ball when attacked works for spiny or armored animals, including everything from hedgehogs and armadillos to pillbugs. Some armored animals can clamp down onto a surface and then resist displacement. This works well for limpets, until some predator drills through their shell. Sitting tight is a defense used by some beetles which clamp down, and then cement their feet to the leaf on which they are resting. Trying to pry off a glued-down beetle probably frustrates most predators. Perhaps the most bizarre insect defense is found in the beetle larva that accumulates fecal pellets on the tip of its abdomen. In time it builds up a huge fecal shield, or mace, that it can wield against predatory ants acting from all around the compass points.

▲ An ambling skunk in search of prey is confronted by a larger animal such as a bear. It first raises its tail in warning and stamps its feet. Provoked further, it turns its back on its aggressor, watching it over its shoulder. If the aggressor does not leave, but continues its harassment, the skunk finally stands on its forepaws and ejects a foul-smelling spray from its anal glands, usually with considerable accuracy, into the face of its attacker.

PLANTS AND ANIMALS IN CO-OPERATION

A remarkable relationship that involves productive association and hygiene is that of diverse and ubiquitous ants. Acacia ants (*Pseudomyrmex* spp.) live inside several species of bull's horn acacia, including *Acacia sphaerocephala*. The acacia plants produce greatly enlarged hollow thorns—the bull's horns—in which the ants live, along with extrafloral nectaries and special proteinaceous organs called Beltian bodies.

The ants feed on the nectar and the Beltian bodies, and make holes in the side of the hollow thorns which provide their

Surprisingly, Australia, which has the richest acacia flora in the world, has no ant-occupied species. This has led to the theory that the primary function of the association between ant and plant is to fight off vertebrate browsers. There is no large and effective group of browsing mammals in Australia and hence, it is argued, the absence of myrmecophily (literally, ant-love). While this theory has not been proved, there is little doubt that the ants could be an effective browser deterrent. Colonies in a single bush may reach a population of over 10,000 workers.

Stephen J. Krasemann/NHPA

▲ In one of the most extraordinary of all plant–animal relationships, ants of certain genera, such as *Crematogaster* and *Pseudomyrmex*, live in hollow thorns and globular galls grown by several species of the shrub *Acacia* in Africa.

dwellings. The plant also benefits from the relationship since the ants patrol its leaves and remove insects that would otherwise feed upon its sap or leaves. In addition, they attack and maul seedlings within a 40-centimeter (16-inch) radius of the acacia and bite off branches of plants that intrude onto its "air-space." The result of this co-operative effort is that the plant produces more biomass in the presence of its standing army than it does when deprived of its defenders.

The ants are quickly alerted by the odor of mammals, including cows and humans, and their sting is immediately painful.

The acacia–ant relationship is but one of several hundred examples of myrmecophily from around the world, and it echoes the housing and defensive alliances between fixed marine stingers, such as corals and sea anemones, and mobile animals. In this case the plant provides both food and shelter while the animal provides defense and help with hygiene.

ALLIANCES FOR PROGRESS

Not all relationships between species are adversarial. Eat or be eaten, attack and defend are certainly universals throughout the living world. It never was a peaceable kingdom; and it never was innocent. But at the same time malice and hatred are not attributes of animal relationships. In fact, there are many interspecific relationships in which one or both participants benefit, or in which the slightest of disadvantages is minimized.

At our disposal is a huge array of special terms which are used to describe the spectrum of such interactions. However, the terminology remains bedeviled by differences in usage. So, it is best to avoid the complications of terms like mutualisms, symbioses, commensalisms and so on. Examples speak louder than terms.

Interspecific relationships are part of the strategies for survival, that is beyond doubt.

They create benefits for those involved including defense, transportation, food acquisition, shelter, resources for reproduction, hygiene augmentation and so on. Often the benefits conferred by one partner are shared involuntarily and certainly unwittingly by the other. While there is mutual benefit, sometimes one partner suffers at the expense of the other. If the suffering is significant, and if it reduces reproductive fitness, then one partner is called a parasite on the other.

Interspecies relationships may occur between animals, between animals and plants, and between plants. As in the case of defense, some of the most interesting relationships occur in the tropics.

Ants in particular have become the dominant species in the invertebrate world of the tropics. E. O. Wilson has said that they are as dominant in the invertebrate world as

▼ A clown anemonefish shelters amid the tentacles of its sea-anemone host in the Red Sea.

humans are among vertebrates. The biomass of ants in the Amazon rainforest exceeds that of all vertebrates combined by four to one. Given the extraordinary adaptive plasticity of ants, it is small wonder that they are involved in a wide range of inter-relationships throughout the world. The army ants of the New World are remarkable, with each colony consisting of up to 700,000 individuals.

They build no permanent nests, only bivouacs on the march, in hollow trees, holes and other sheltered locations. The raiding behavior follows a four to six week cycle, during half of which the workers return to the same bivouac each day. For the rest of the time, called the nomadic phase, they camp afresh each night. The ants maraud across the forest floor subsisting on small animals, mainly insects that they catch in the leaf litter. This is an awesome march of predation but not quite as spectacular as Hollywood has made it. Army ants do not overcome mammals, except occasionally when they catch the very tiniest specimens.

However, they do consume enormous quantities of insects and are the basis of a complex of inter-relationships that is an ecosystem in itself. As the swarm advances across the forest floor the resemblance to a battlefield is heightened. Swarms of flies hover around the advancing front parasitizing insects

that escape from the ants by jumping or flying upwards. They depend on the ants to provide food for their larvae. Above the flies, at perches higher in the undergrowth, are the ant birds feeding on other escapees. These ant birds may be so highly specialized that they are obligate ant followers unable to make a living any other way. The ants flush insects out of the litter and the birds eat them. This evokes images of beaters and shooters on a tiger hunt.

An even closer intimacy is involved in the animals that actually march in the ant column. They are true camp-followers, some of which are unbelievably specialized. There is a beetle that rides on the ant workers; a silverfish (primitive insect) that rides on the ants, licks off their bodily secretions and shares their food; a mite that rides on the inside edge of the worker ant's jaws, and another species that occurs only on the ant's foot. Millipedes march in the column and act as scavengers. Other social insects have nestmates. Even predatory colonial spiders may have caterpillars living in their communal webs munching on the skeletal remains of the spider's prey.

Coral reefs abound with intimate inter-relationships between species. The presence of so many attached sedentary coral and other animals equipped with complex defenses, spines, sting cells and poison, is in effect, an

222

Philip K Sharpe/Oxford Scientific Films

In addition to mutual domesticity there is defense by alliance. Hermit crabs may be associated with sea anemones, and other crabs may carry stinging sea anemones in their claws to thrust in the face of attackers, just as city dwellers carry tear gas sprays. In other coral reef relationships mobility may be conferred on the immobile and enhanced mobility on those with limited mobility. While some of these relationships may have started "accidentally", they have evolved into obligate partnerships of considerable complexity.

Barnacles settle on a wide variety of surfaces. Most pre-human sites for barnacles stayed put but we humans have filled the seas with moving ships and floating debris. So a behavior that resulted in life stuck to a rock can now lead to life stuck to a very large ocean liner. So far no specialized adaptations to using boats for phoresis have been discovered but barnacles have traveled the world stuck to ships. Some Australian species, for instance, are now found in south Wales as a result. But barnacles did become specialized for attachment to some species of whales and are thereby carried into plankton-rich surface waters where they could not otherwise subsist. This is a far cry from the reef situation but it illustrates the chance origins of alliances.

While the relationships are often one-sided, and frequently verge on the parasitic, they can be splendid in their complexity. In the end there is no question that there are more symbioses in the sea than anywhere else. This is probably because the groups involved have been around for a long, long time. They have, in proportion to land animals, far fewer rooted plants to live amongst and far more rooted animals. This may explain the profusion of adaptations to alliances. Surprisingly, there are proportionally many fewer such adaptations in fresh water, despite the richness of such systems as the Amazon.

Some other examples of relationships involving the transportation of relatively immobile animals by wide-ranging species have already been mentioned (moths by sloths, and mites by ants). The passenger phenomenon is widespread, and is probably best called "hitch-hiking" because the transporter is seldom rewarded. One example that the airlines would appreciate is the use of beetles as transporters of pseudoscorpion passengers. Pseudoscorpions are smallish arachnids, wingless and harmless except to their prey. Hundreds of them have been found riding under the wing covers of large tropical beetles. The harlequin beetle is a common carrier in the New World. The pseudoscorpions are transported from feeding ground to feeding ground by their coleopteran

"urban" landscape of animate homes in which other creatures can dwell. Whether they dwell inside the digestive cavity of sea anemones and sea cucumbers; in the shell-houses of hermit crabs; in the burrows of snails, worms and fishes; or the tentacles of sea anemones or jellyfish, there is adventitious protection.

Parasitic fishes live inside the intestinal canal of sea cucumbers and have bodies that are adapted for that home. The anus, for example, is positioned unusually close to its head so that it can excrete outside the cucumber's body. Other examples of inquilinism include crabs that live in worm burrows alongside the worms; some nereid bristle worms live-in alongside hermit crabs in their houses; and there are porcellinid crabs that live within mussel shells. It certainly seems that prime sites for attached organisms provide homes for many.

Of course, a really fundamental symbiosis is the relationship between unicellular algae and the corals themselves. The plants live inside the coral cells, a relationship that must be the ultimate in intimacy. The relationship enhances the coral's ability to survive by providing it with nutrients while at the same time limiting its distribution to clear water and to the depth at which sunlight can penetrate to fuel the photosynthesis of the algae.

▲ Specialists in removing ticks from the hide of large mammals, a group of red-billed oxpeckers (*Buphagus erythrorhynchus*) rides a young giraffe in the Masai Mara Reserve, Kenya.

Jonathon Scott/Planet Earth Pictures

Aids to hygiene may be tolerated in nests where scavenging is useful, or by individual animals that cannot remove skin parasites by their own endeavors.

Mutual grooming within a species is widespread and very intricately developed in primates including those human groups where social conventions do not inhibit natural behavior. Interspecific grooming is a beautiful thing to watch. In all continents, there are birds that have become specialized at feeding on ticks. They even pick ticks off mammals that can't reach them themselves. In Africa, a range of different birds forage on the skin of rhinos and wild cattle, enjoying a valuable food source. Up to a dozen tick birds may be active at one time on an adult zebra. African oxpeckers have sharp claws and can run all over their host, along its back, onto the face and even upside down on its belly. Some of the birds are so attached to their mobile feeding grounds that they even court and mate on the rhino's back. Ticks are presumably high nutrient food sources once they are filled with the host's blood. These arachnid "blood sausages", or "black puddings", are much easier to see and detach than the flattened, undistended, unfed ticks. The birds consequently get the best food. In addition to ticks, skin flakes and blowflies, the birds may also feed on wounds and thereby delay healing. They are not an unmixed blessing. Where tick birds are present, domestic cattle also benefit from their grooming.

In the sea, cleaner fishes perform a similar function. They stand by particular localities, above conspicuous rocks or coral heads, and are visited by their clients. The clients are larger fishes that have infestations of ectoparasites on their skin or gills. Presumably they visit the cleaning stations when they are irritated by the parasites. At the cleaning station the clients sometimes assume a special attitude, which may help to solicit grooming. However, the cleaner fish, as in all relationships, is susceptible to cheating. The legitimate cleaners are wrasses (Labridae) but may be mimicked by blennies (Blenidae), distant relatives, that resemble the true cleaners in color and behavior.

This is aggressive mimicry with a vengeance. The fish soliciting cleaning is approached by the cheater with the same zigzag dance as that of the legitimate cleaner; it is approached by an elongate, striped, more-or-less lookalike fish, but in the end it receives not a delousing but an attack on its flesh. The cheat takes chunks out of its victim with its fierce set of predatory teeth. A tiger in disguise! Fishes at cleaning stations frequented by cheats are distinctly edgy and ill at ease. No wonder.

jumbo jet. Whales are frequently hosts to barnacles, which may range over hundreds of kilometers attached to their host. Sucker fishes, remoras, hitch a ride on sharks and have special attachments on the dorsal surface of their head region. They are so adept at following large objects that they will even respond to scuba divers by attempting to hitch a ride.

The ultimate alliance: animal pollination of plants

In days gone by, when plants and animals were confined to living in the sea, their sex cells were united in the water and set the agenda for the nature of future reproduction. Male cells, defined by their mobility, swam to unite with female cells. Sexual reproduction, born in the water, started with the union of two cells and proceeded to multiplication. Plants, mobile in the plankton, became sessile and retained swimming cells for sexual union. When plants and animals conquered the land, they retained the reproductive behavior of swimming male cells. To begin with sperm swam in the inland waters where eggs were shed. As time went on the sperm of reptiles, birds and mammals swam in the moisture lining the female's reproductive tract. An internalized sea also cushioned the embryo in the eggs of reptiles and birds, and the womb of mammals.

The first land plants were confined to perpetually damp areas and their male cells swam in the film of moisture that surrounded them. These plants were not fully liberated from an aquatic life until the development of pollen and pollination which superseded the water-dependent swimming cells. The male organs of plants produced pollen cells that were light enough to be carried on the winds from plant to plant. With this change the questing directionality of the swimming male gamete was replaced by blind chance. Wind pollination is wasteful in the extreme. Millions of sperm perish for the few that succeed but hundreds of millions of pollen grains are lost in airborne profligacy. They fill the air so heavily that humans suffer from agonizing allergies.

The great breakthrough for plants came when they harnessed mobile animals as the ultimate carriers of their immotile sex cells. Animal pollination is the ultimate phoresy. The stages in its evolution are not easy to hypothesize but the end results fill our world with the color, beauty and fragrance of flowers. The flowers that we recognize and admire are overwhelmingly those that are pollinated by insects. "A rose by any other name" smells for bees and wasps, not for Juliet. When insects became the first creatures in flight, they were preadapted to become pollen carriers. As a result of this the co-evolution of flowers and insects has produced some of the most amazing adaptations in the entire living world.

Bees, moths and butterflies are exclusive flower visitors and pollinators on a grand scale. Their mouthparts have highly specialized nectar-sucking tongues and are perfectly adapted to reach the bait that flowers provide to attract them.

Nectar provides the carbohydrate fuel for flight muscles, while the bees use the protein-rich pollen grains for growing their young. Bees have even evolved tongues to match the flowers on which they specialize. The honeybees' (*Apis melifera*) general purpose medium-sized tongues match a median range of flower-tube length; while bumblebees (*Bombus* spp.) have much longer tongues and alone can pollinate the long-tubed clovers. Orchid bees, euglossids (*Euglossa* spp.), have extraordinarily long tongues adapted to the structures of orchids. In this case, male orchid bees collect fragrances from the flowers as well as nectar and store the fragrances in what might be called "perfume purses". They use the flower scents as attractants for the opposite sex. Humans adopted this practice millions of years after the bees.

Owen Newman/Oxford Scientific Films

Bees have plume-like hairs, an adaptation that ensures that their bodies collect pollen, which they brush into pollen baskets with hairbrushes on their legs. Feathery hairs work like feather dusters. Pollen baskets are on the legs of some bees, including honeybees and bumblebees, and are located beneath the abdomen in others. Wasps, which do not store pollen, generally have straight hairs which do not facilitate pollen collection like the feathery hairs of bees. If you want to distinguish a bee, look at its hairs at root level.

The bee's complex of anatomical devices tailored to exploiting flowers, including tongue, hairs, brushes and baskets, is matched by its color vision and behavioral complexity which has evolved into the functional equivalent of language. This gives it the ability to communicate to its nestmates the direction and distance of flowers that are good nectar sources. Returning workers do this by running in a

▲ A dog rose (*Rosa canina*) flower illuminated by ultraviolet light. For the convenience of insect visitors, veins and bands visible only under such light serve as arrows marking the path to the source of nectar. Some flowers even alter their ultraviolet patterns according to whether the nectaries are full or empty.

G.I. Bernard/Oxford Scientific Films

▲ The nocturnal hawkmoths are among the strongest and most vigorous of insect fliers, able to fly fast and far and to hover at flowers for lengthy periods while sucking the nectar on which they feed through a long proboscis. This is the elephant hawkmoth (*Deilephila elpenor*), a European species with a special fondness for honeysuckle.

▶ (*facing page*) The eastern pygmy-possum (*Cercartetus nanus*) of southeastern Australia feeds largely on nectar and pollen, especially of various species of banksias, and may play an important role in pollination.

stereotyped pattern on vertical surfaces of honeycomb. They act out a rough figure-of-eight, whilst waggling their abdomen on the up or down stroke. This waggle dance is very information specific, in fact the dance language of bees is a remarkable facet of pollination. Bees can also navigate by using the polarization of light, have time-sense and can see into the ultraviolet end of the spectrum.

Amazing insect adaptations for flower visiting are matched only by their counterparts, those of the flower. Darwin's great book, *On the Various Contrivances by Which British and Foreign Orchids are Fertilised by Insects*, is a masterly analysis of some of the most remarkable specializations found in the living world. There are orchids whose pollinia, the pollen-bearing male parts, actually detach themselves and grip onto the probing tongues of bees positioned in exactly the right place to brush against the female parts of the next flower the bees visit. This pseudomuscled "animation" of the pollinia is powered by water pressure, but functions efficiently. Some flowers are pollinated by bats whose furry faces transmit pollen from one durian flower to another.

In Australia hairy-faced climbing possums pollinate nocturnal blossoms, and in the New World hummingbirds are remarkably adapted to the flower–animal interface. They can hover, are uniquely able to fly backwards and have

probing bills reminiscent of the proboscises of insects. Hummingbird flowers advertise themselves in red, are seldom scented, and bloom by day. Nocturnal flowers, visited by moths and bats, are white and heavily scented. Insect-pollinated flowers are often significantly patterned in ultraviolet, which is in response to the ultraviolet vision of bees and wasps. Some flowers signal the direction of their nectaries with ultraviolet stripes, which act as guides like traffic lines down the center of a road. Other flowers may change their ultraviolet reflectance to indicate that nectar production is over.

Perhaps the most bizarre product of plant–animal co-evolution is the one that attracts carrion-feeding flies to flowers. These are improbable pollinators only in the sense that they are specialized for another food source. They fly well and are hairy, and therefore possess two essential attributes for a pollinator. Flowers respond to the sensory preferences of flies by producing, as attractants, odors of corruption. Fly-pollinated flowers, like rafflesia, the world's largest flower, stink of rotten meat. The giant victorial lily of the Amazon traps beetles inside its flowers to release them a day later, thoroughly covered in pollen, to visit other flowers at a different stage of development. Flowers that temporarily trap their pollinators are not uncommon—their devices are devious almost beyond belief.

▲ The golden langur (*Semnopithecus geei*) is a forest monkey inhabiting Bhutan and western Assam. Long-haired and long-tailed, it feeds on leaves and similar vegetation.

Martyn Colbeck/Oxford Scientific Films

FIGHTING DISEASE AND INJURY

The end point of life is converting resources into offspring. In the struggle for survival animals have to avoid predation or they do not live to reproduce. Because reproduction is an imperative it is not surprising that antipredator adaptations are seen everywhere, are often very complex indeed, and have long since fascinated naturalists. But there are other complex problems that animals face beyond those posed by predators. Methods of dealing with ectoparasites, for example, that have a high potential for causing reduced fitness, have clearly been subject to intense selection pressure. Mutual grooming and self-grooming behaviors are common to many animals and interspecific interaction for parasite removal may be highly specialized. Survival and fitness are also affected by injuries and disease. Injured and sick animals may die as a direct result of these causes, or indirectly because they cannot feed themselves or cannot avoid predation. Even if they avoid death they may simply be unable to compete for mates; then they face genetic death. Indirect evidence for the importance of avoiding injury is seen in the many aspects of animal combat and aggression that serve to reduce the risks of injury resulting from disputes.

When all that has been taken into account it is still important to realize that wounding, injuries, internal parasitization and disease do occur and that defenses against their effects are almost certainly just as crucial as defenses against predators. The physiological defenses of animals against disease and injury are the subject of constant revelation as human and veterinary medicine advances. The immune system is incredibly complex and substantially effective. In vertebrates, clotting, wound healing and bone repair are marvels of physiological mobilization. Many mammals show a capacity for wound healing that seems to be far beyond that of humans. But this is not confined to mammals. Recently, a researcher working with a species of tropical frog noticed that skin incisions healed remarkably. This observation led to the discovery of a new family of antibiotics, produced in the frog's skin.

The complexity of the physiological defenses that animals have evolved speaks to the importance of fighting disease and the consequences of injury. Unfortunately few biologists have considered the possibility that animals may have means of self-medication in addition to their physiological defenses. Since humans frequently need to supplement the inbuilt defenses of the body with medicines and external aids, it is clear that these defenses are not always adequate to the problems they face. We do know that there are simple, widely observed, behavioral supplements to bodily defences. Many vertebrates, for example, lick wounds. The saliva of some animals has been shown to have antibiotic effects. Are there other behavioral defenses? There are a number of tantalizing indications that there may be. An observation of an injured tiger chewing up clay and rolling on it, apparently to anoint the wound, is suggestive. Even more interesting are anecdotal accounts of possible self-medication by several different mammals.

Perhaps the most striking of these involves chimpanzees. Richard Wragham, studying chimpanzees at Gombe in Tanzania, noticed that some of them were searching for and then feeding on a particular species of the plant, *Aspilia,* which is related to dandelions and daisies. The chimpanzees sought out the plant in the early morning before feeding, and swallowed the leaves whole rather than chewing them in the usual way they dealt with food. This alerted him to the possibility that something special was taking place. After much frustration, he eventually found someone interested and able to analyze the *Aspilia* leaves. They turned out to contain an oily substance called Thiarubrine A. By coincidence this was under investigation elsewhere because it had been isolated from an unrelated North American plant used medicinally by Amerindians. The oil has since proved to be a powerful antibiotic, fungicide, vermicide, an effective antiviral compound and is potent against some tumor cells. In the face of these discoveries, the supposition that the chimpanzees may have been using the leaves medicinally sounds perfectly plausible. It also raises the intriguing possibility that animals could be used as "prospectors" for pharmaceuticals. Certainly they cannot be influenced by strong cultural perceptions about herbs.

Further suggestive evidence about self-medication has come from observations on elephants, rhinos, monkeys and bears. For instance, Asian rhinos in Nepal are known to actively seek out the leaves of a plant which on analysis turns out to contain a strong vermifuge. Observations on soil eating by rhesus monkeys show that this provides trace elements and mineral salts missing from their diet. If this is true, it suggests an ability to somehow detect deficiencies and identify corrective measures. This ability could be little different from detecting nutrients from other sources. However, there is the additional possibility that the animals are using the soil as a source of medicinal compounds. The line of distinction between nutritional requirements and medicinals is blurred. Experimental studies of laboratory rats have shown that they can choose diets that correct vitamin deficiencies, despite the fact that the vitamins cannot be detected by taste and odor. All this, while not hard evidence, strongly suggests that there may as yet be a largely undetected and unexplored complex of animal adaptations involved in their battles against disease. Hopefully future studies will show this more clearly.

SURVIVING HOSTILE CLIMATES

In their struggle for survival, animals face threats from competitors, predators, parasites, injuries and disease. Small wonder that reproduction is so conspicuously compensatory. It seems almost profligate for the codfish to make millions of eggs in its lifetime to replace one pair of fishes in the next generation, or for a mouse to make dozens of babies to achieve the same end. But this is reality. In addition to threats from within the living world, animals and plants have to cope with the manifold vagaries of climate.

The materials of life and its essential processes are limited by a very narrow range of operating conditions. Above 40°C (104°F) protein, the stuff of life, coagulates. Below freezing point water crystallizes into ice and quickly brings life processes to a halt. Many metabolic reactions have an optimum temperature confined to a few degrees. All life on Earth subsists in narrow limits. Life began in the sea and carries with it a legacy of processes dependent on water. Water requirements fall within similar confining bounds to those of temperature. Since all life is grass, in the sense that virtually all living things are ultimately dependent on the photosynthetic processes of plants, sunlight at certain levels is needed to sustain ecosystems. Tropical temperatures are suitable for many life processes, while life in the temperate regions is invaded by originally tropical forms. During this invasion, adaptations have arisen to meet the challenge of suboptimal physical conditions. In the same way, the transition from life in water, the original home, to life on land required a range of adaptations to conquer its less salubrious characteristics.

A prime example of a major and conspicuous adaptation to deal with inimical physical conditions is bird migration. As winter brings down the iron curtain on many aspects of life in the temperate regions, falling temperatures and shorter days reduce photosynthesis and primary productivity. This reduction directly affects the food supply for the entire system. The reduction in warmth and light also bears directly on the lives of animals of all shapes and sizes. Mammals may hibernate, greatly reduce their activity, or wander towards warmer and more productive regions. Migrations of herbivores are more conspicuous in the Northern Hemisphere where most of the temperate landmasses are distributed. Insects often overwinter in a dormant state but some butterflies, such as the monarch, migrate like birds to the tropics. In Mexico, overwintering monarch butterflies festoon the trees of their winter roosts, like millions of flowers.

▲ The Weddell seal (*Leptonychotes weddelli*) rarely sees land, its distribution almost entirely restricted to the belts of fast ice surrounding Antarctica. It can dive to depths of 600 meters (2,000 feet) and stay under for nearly an hour, surfacing to breathe at holes in the ice. It keeps the holes open by chewing the edges with its teeth.

But despite mammal and butterfly migration, the best known of all migrations is that of many species of birds. It is such a conspicuous phenomenon that it was noted at the dawn of written history. The birds overwhelmingly fly to and from the tropics, but there are also some remarkable exceptions. Shearwaters fly from pole to pole, from one season of nutrient upwelling plankton bloom and consequent fishing, to another. The mechanics of migration, celestial navigation and all, are remarkable. One of the wonders of the process is that birds raised in the north temperate region can find their way south. A less obvious and much less studied question concerns how birds hatched in temperate forests feed themselves in the markedly different tropical forests of their winter homes. Because of the enormous differences in species diversity the insect-eating bird, for instance, arriving in the tropics for the first time, is confronted by a vast array of insects:

unfamiliar, concealed, disguised, dangerous or otherwise well defended. If the bird has to learn how to cope with the diversity how does it survive long enough to do so? One possibility is that it joins mixed-species flocks and learns from them.

Animals must further contend with the rigors of extreme climatic conditions. Heat and drought may be just as inimical to life as the winter. Direct sunshine heats up all surfaces and the closer to the equator the more intense is the heating. Many animals therefore face problems of overheating. Some methods of coping with this are interesting. Clearly, moving into shade is one response.

The giant tortoises of the island of Aldabra, whose biomass per hectare equals that of the plains herbivores of East Africa, cluster in the shade of low bushes by day. However, during dry spells, they have to travel considerable distances to drinking water and may get caught in the sun as they lumber ponderously back to

Jean-Paul Ferrero/Ardea London

overheating. The Australian leaf-rolling spider makes a shelter from a dead leaf at the hub of the web. This is both a shelter and a reflectant sunshade. The golden-web spiders, *Nephila* species, whose huge webs are common throughout the tropics, have a "gymnastic" form of heat reduction. They can align themselves so that their bodies point with the least possible area exposed to the sun. rotating their long axis like the hour hand of a clock to changing angles of the sun. This behavior is quite remarkably effective in reducing exposure. It is the exact opposite of the sunbathing behavior found in animals, such as lizards, that need to warm up their bodies rather than cool them down.

Exposing massive surfaces to act as radiators works in animals where blood circulation may carry heat from the interior to the exterior. This becomes particularly important in large animals because of the relationship between volume and surface area. Elephants, for example have thermoregulation problems—an analogy to a car engine working at the equator is quite appropriate. Heat is produced by metabolism and supplemented by the ambient temperature. The motor itself has a very small surface area so the coolant water (blood in the animal) must be taken to a large surface—the radiator (a honeycomb of waterpassages) in cars does this and is nowadays fan assisted on demand. The elephant ears, honeycombed with blood vessels, do the same job—they can even be fan assisted as the elephant flaps its ears. Other mammals may use their ears as radiators; those of rabbits certainly go red in the heat. Blushing was originally a thermoregulatory device. Hair, feather and scale erection can expose the skin to radiate heat. Goose pimples are our atavistic vestige (a characteristic passed on from a distant, primitive ancestor) of thermoregulatory hair erection.

One of the ancient devices of human medicine for cooling down feverish patients is called tepid sponging. The naked patient is sponged with cool water and beads of moisture are left behind to evaporate. Evaporation causes cooling, as the inventors of the earliest form of air conditioning, the Indian *Punkah* realized: the large cloth that was pulled to and fro rhythmically was wetted with water. Evaporative cooling is also used by many animals. In mammals sweating is a common form. Australian marsupials and domestic cats lick their paws, and dogs cool themselves by evaporation from the highly vascular tongue. Tongues are used by butterflies and moths to effect cooling. When overheated, a sphinx moth (*Pholus achemon*) uncoils its long proboscis, extrudes droplets of water from it,

life-giving shade. Heat prostration is a major cause of mortality in their predator-free island paradise. Building burrows provides shelter but animals may be too small to build burrows deep enough to be cool. A Middle Eastern dryland isopod is too small to build such burrows in the desert but has become astoundingly social. Working together, these relatives of the woodlouse can dig deep. Each colony has a separate odor and they defend their heat refuges against strangers.

Other social responses to excessive heat include that of many bees and wasps whose workers fan with their wings at the nest entrance to create excurrent air movement. They may also wet down surfaces to create evaporative cooling. Invertebrates, being smaller, heat up faster. They have more surface area per volume to absorb heat. Web-building spiders that need to stay at the center of their webs by day to be at the nodal point for prey capture may face serious problems of

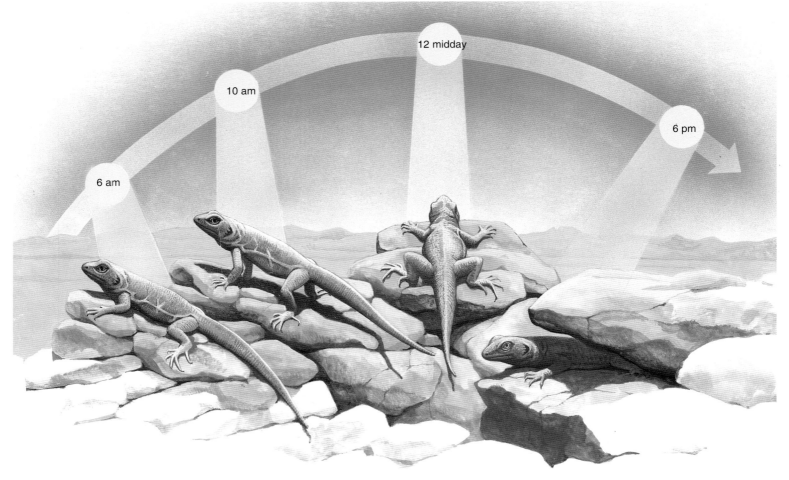

▲ The distinction between cold- and warm-bloodedness is blurred. Reptiles, for example, cannot raise their internal temperature by metabolic means as birds and mammals do, but they use a range of behavioral mechanisms to achieve substantially the same result. In the early morning, a lizard basks broadside to the rising sun, exposing as much skin surface as possible to its warmth. As the sun rises higher, the lizard gradually lifts its body clear of the rock to control heat absorption from the surface and allow cooling air to flow beneath. Later, it may also lift even its toes clear of the surface. Towards noon it moves to face into the sun to minimize the area exposed. Finally, it retires to the shade to suspend the warming process.

and immediate cooling results. Slightly more esoteric is using genitalia as cooling surfaces. Butterflies do this and African desert beetles, tenebrionids related to the mealworm beetle, extrude their moist genitalia when the temperature rises above 40°C (104°F). This provides an evaporative surface to cool down.

Warming up may be necessary for both cold- and warm-blooded animals and is not restricted to particular temperature regions. Many highland tropical areas for example, have marked cooling at night. In the case of insects in such environments, their flight muscles may not work well at temperatures below 30°C (86°F) and may be unable to fly off when disturbed at rest. To compensate, many produce eyespot or other startle displays to warm up their flight muscles.

Color variations in an animal may also compensate for climatic conditions. Animals that are black generally have the ability to warm up while white-shaded species would experience the opposite effect. Cold-blooded animals may turn on the dark coloration in the morning and then lighten for camouflage purposes as they warm up. This phenomenon applies to animals as diverse as iguanas and

grasshoppers. The Australian alpine grasshopper is black while sunning in the morning, and becomes light blue as the day progresses. All white animals may have trouble sunbathing and the white whistling swan has been observed holding one of its black feet over its back in cold conditions. This increases heat absorption.

Animals of small size must protect themselves from rain which can cool them disastrously or even drown them, and must learn to shield from many other climatic variables. A smattering of examples shows that animal adaptations for dealing with the elements have been able to match what evolution, in all its complexity, has thrown their way. The conclusion must be that the world of life is one of infinite variety, beauty, intricacy, and should evoke our sense of wonder. Now more than ever before in the history of life, we face the loss of millions of species due to the activity of one species alone—humankind. If we have a sense of wonder at the glory of life on Earth we must translate it into concern and then action. Tomorrow, with the next century around the corner, may be too late.

FOOD RESERVES

Hibernation and migration are not the only solutions animals find to the problem of food shortages, especially in winter. Animals can also store winter food during the summer, squirrels being the notable exemplars of this provident behavior. But their virtues are paralleled by pikas, small rabbit-like creatures that make hay, and even by birds such as acorn woodpeckers.

Insects may store food too. Honeybees store honey against the period when flowers are not in bloom, and depend on the same principle as human jam-making. If the sugar concentration is high neither bacteria nor molds will degrade it. (Honey that is too watery will ferment. This may have led to the discovery of mead—an early alcoholic drink.)

Ants are among the more specialized food hoarders and have evolved habits of storage in response to seasonal food supplies in dry regions rather than winter. Harvester ants may store great quantities of seeds in underground granaries—a behavior that anticipated human agricultural practices by millions of years. It is a successful tactic; in some Australian localities harvester ants constitute the overwhelming majority of all ant colonies.

Food storage, in response to unpredictable conditions, is found in an unusual form in honeypot ants whose specialized workers, called repletes, serve as living storage vessels for nectar. As they are fed nectar by foraging workers, the repletes' crops become enormously distended, their abdomens swelling like balloons. Honeypot ants are strangely distributed on a world scale, with a large concentration of species occurring in Australasia and in North America.

The social insect's response to food shortage has been parasitized by our species. Humans discovered the stored troves of honey, and bees have been known as producers of sweetness since early times. To find such a prize Africans followed honeyguides to the feast, while Australian Aborigines also know and feed upon honeypot ants. It took the mass production of sugar to turn a rare robber's pleasure into a health risk.

▼ A food cache is important to the common European dormouse (*Muscardinus avellanarius*) because it spends much of the winter in a dormant state that is not true hibernation, and it awakens every week or so to feed.

Jane Burton/Bruce Coleman Limited

NOTES ON CONTRIBUTORS

TIM GUILFORD

As recipient of a Royal Society University Research Fellowship in the Zoology Department at Oxford University, Tim Guilford is interested in the evolution of animal signals—especially prey defensive signals and the way predators process them. His research has included a close look at the evolution of defensive coloration in prey, and predator "search image" formation. He is also interested in the broader evolution of signal design, embarking on extensive field projects with Dr. Marian Dawkins. These projects are trying to establish how signal receiver psychology affects the evolution of signals. Dr. Guilford has published several studies on bird olfaction, mimicry, and the risks of crashing in flying birds.

TIMOTHY HALLIDAY

After extensive studies in the field of biology, Timothy Halliday received his Ph.D. at Oxford University in 1972. Five years later, he moved to the Open University, Milton Keynes, where he is currently a Professor of Biology. Some of his most important work includes study of the evolution of sexual behavior in animals, and the biology of amphibians including their life history, ecology and conservation. He is author of several publications, including *The Vanishing Birds* (1978) and *Sexual Strategy* (1980) and has written more than 50 papers for scientific journals. From 1982 to 1986, Professor Halliday was the European editor of the journal, *Animal Behavior*.

Henry Ausloos/NHPA

Stan Osolinski/Oxford Scientific Films

MICHAEL HANSELL

Born in Cromer, Norfolk (England), Michael Hansell first studied zoology at Trinity College, Dublin (Eire) after failing to become a vet. From there, he moved to Oxford (where he later received his Ph.D.) to research the case-building behavior of caddis fly larvae under subsequent Nobel Prize winner, Niko Tinbergen. In 1966 he took up an appointment as Lecturer in Zoology at the University of Khartoum (Sudan) to study mosquito behavior, and new habitats and cultures. In 1968, he moved to the Zoology Department at Glasgow University (Scotland), where he currently presides. His latest research focuses on the nest materials of social wasps, the use of spider silk in birds' nests, and the functional architecture of rodent burrows. Dr. Hansell is married with two children and delights in finding new areas of interest in the building behavior of animals.

TERENCE LINDSEY

Terence Lindsey was born in England, but raised and educated in Canada. After six consecutive Arctic winters, he realized he could no longer live in the cold and set off in search of any place where the birds would be interesting and the climate warm enough for the water to be liquid! In 1968, he decided to settle in Australia. Since then, he

has traveled widely throughout Australasia and the south-west Pacific, and has written several books on birds. He has also acted as editor, contributor, consultant, researcher and illustrator on many other publications. Active in several ornithological societies, he is an Associate of the Australian Museum, and a part-time teacher with the Department of Continuing Education, University of Sydney.

MICHAEL H. ROBINSON

Michael Robinson is the director of the National Zoological Park, Smithsonian Institution, Washington D.C. After graduation in 1966, he was appointed biologist at the Smithsonian Tropical Research Institute, Panama. Stationed there from 1965 to 1984, he carried out research in various aspects of tropical biology including predator–prey interactions, predatory behavior, anti-predatory adaptations, courtship and mating behavior, phenology, species diversity and complex symbioses, collecting his material from over 20 tropical countries. By 1984, he had been made deputy director of the Panama Institute and then was offered the directorship of the National Zoological Park. Dr. Robinson is author of more than 100 scientific and popular articles. He has also written a book on courtship and mating behavior in spiders and has edited a volume on human–animal relationships.

INDEX

ACKNOWLEDGMENTS

Every effort has been made to acknowledge copyright holders of all material published in this book, but in the event of any omission, please contact Weldon Owen.

Page 16: *Thornbill niches* is adapted from *Birds of Australia*, by Stanley Breeden and Peter Slater (1968), Angus & Robertson, Sydney. **Pages 20–21:** *The diversity of animal forms* is adapted from illustrations by Richard Orr and Michael Woods in *The Animal Family*, edited by Dr. Philip Whitfield (1990), Hamlyn, London; and from illustrations by Norman Weaver in *The Fresh & Salt Water Fishes of the World*, by Edward C. Migdalski and George S. Fichter (1975), Bay Books, Sydney. **Page 31:** *The construction of a mole tunnel* is adapted from *The Mole*, by Kenneth Mellanby (1971), Collins, London. **Page 34:** *A fish of the ocean depths* is adapted from an illustration by Norman Weaver in *The Fresh & Salt Water Fishes of the World*, p. 104. **Page 36:** *In the air* is adapted from illustrations by Richard Orr and Michael Woods in *The Animal Family*, pp. 35, 44–45; *The Animal Kingdom*, edited by Frederick Drimmer, G. G. Goodwin *et al* (1954), Garden City Books, New York; *Animal Camouflage*, by Adolf Portmann (translated from German by A. J. Pometrans), Ann Arbor, Michigan University Press; and from illustrations by Tony Pyrzakowski in *Birds of Prey* (1990), Merehurst, London. **Pages 48–49:** *The search and capture tactics of a typical bat* is adapted from *The Animal Kingdom*, pp. 112, 119, 121, 131; and from *Scientific American*, June 1990, p. 37. **Page 63:** *Recognizing prey* is adapted from *The Ecology of Antipredator Behavior*, by Raymond L. Ditmars (1969), Macmillan, New York. **Pages 66–67:** *A Lion hunt* is adapted from illustrations by Richard Orr and Michael Woods in *The Animal Family*, pp. 152–153; and from illustrations by Frank Knight in *Great Cats* (1991), Reader's Digest, Sydney, p. 32. **Page 74:** *The ways of the spider* is adapted from *Journal of Natural History*, Volume 6, Robinson & Robinson (1972), pp. 687–694; *External Construction by Animals*, edited by Nicholas E. Collias and Elsie C. Collias, (1976), Dowden, Hutchinson & Ross, Pennsylvania, pp. 171–172; and from *Spiders of the World*, by Ron and Ken Preston-Malham (1984), Bladford Press, UK, pp. 57, 108, 121. **Page 76:** *The life cycle of a mosquito* is adapted from *Insects in Perspective*, by Michael Atkins (1978), Macmillan, New York, p. 363. **Page 82:** *The archer fish* is adapted from *Animal Behavior*, by J. R. Lucas (1982); *Fresh & Salt Water Fishes of the World*, p. 247; and from *Encyclopedia of Underwater Life*, edited by Dr. Keith Banister and Dr. Andrew Campbell (1985), Allen & Unwin, p. 110.

Page 89: *The underground world of the naked mole rat* is adapted from *Food Hoarding in Animals*, by Stephen B. Vanderball (1990), University of Chicago, Chicago, pp. 257, 269. **Page 91:** *Hummingbirds* is adapted from photos by Walter Scheithauer in *Hummingbirds—The Flying Jewels*, (translated from German by G. Vevers) (1967), Arthur Baker, London. **Page 108:** *Penis structures* is adapted from an illustration by Richard Orr and Michael Woods in *The Animal Family*, p. 62; *Introduction to Herpetology*, by Colemann J. Coin (1971), Freeman, San Francisco; *Text Atlas of Cat Anatomy*, by James E. Crouch (1969), Lea & Febiger, Philadelphia; *Dissection of the Dog and Cat*, by Michael J. and Bonny Shively (1985), Iowa State University, Ames; and from *Laboratory Anatomy of the Cat*, by Ernest S. Booth and Robert B. Chiasson (1967), WMC Brown, Iowa. **Pages 114–115:** *The courtship of a stickleback* is adapted from *Biology of the Sticklebacks*, by Robin Jeremy Wootton (1976), London Academic Press, pp. 267–318; and from an illustration by Norman Weaver in *The Fresh & Salt Water Fishes of the World*, p. 196. **Page 154:** *Bowerbird architecture* is adapted from illustrations by J. M. Diamond in *Science*, 216, (1982), pp. 413–433. **Pages 182–183:** *The construction of a beaver dam and lodge* is adapted from illustrations in *Mammalia*, by P. B. Richard (1955), pp. 293–301; *External Construction by Animals*, edited by Collias and Collias (1976), Dowden, Hutchinson & Ross; and from *The Animal Family*, pp. 90–91. **Page 186:** *Ventilation of a termite mound* is adapted from illustrations by M. Luscher in *Scientific American*, 205, 1961, pp. 138–145; and from an article by N. M. Collins in *Insects Soliaux*, 26, 1979, pp. 240–246. **Page 189:** *Map of the migration paths of the marsh warbler* is adapted from *Bird Migration*, by T. Alderstam (1990), Cambridge University Press. **Pages 198–199:** *Prairie dog town* is adapted from an illustration by Richard Orr and Michael Woods in *The Animal Family*, pp. 92–93. **Page 201:** *Hermit crab* is adapted from *The Encyclopedia of Underwater Life*, p. 236. **Page 210:** *Defense by intimidation* is adapted from *Living World of Animals*, (1978), Reader's Digest in conjunction with World Wildlife Fund, Sydney, p. 303. **Page 219:** *Defensive behavior of the skunk* is adapted from *Our Amazing World of Nature, Its Marvels and Mysteries* (1969), Reader's Digest, Sydney, p. 104. **Page 232:** *Controlling temperature* is adapted from *Reptiles of the World*, by Raymond L. Ditmers (1966), Macmillan, New York, pp. 130–33.

The publishers would like to thank Margaret Olds, Kate Etherington and Veronica Hilton for their assistance in the production of this book.